STEWARDS OF THE MARKET

STEWARDS *of*
the MARKET

HOW THE FEDERAL
RESERVE MADE SENSE OF
THE FINANCIAL CRISIS

Mitchel Y. Abolafia

Harvard University Press

Cambridge, Massachusetts
London, England

2020

Library of Congress Cataloging-in-Publication Data
Names: Abolafia, Mitchel, author.
Title: Stewards of the market : how the Federal Reserve made sense of the
Financial Crisis / Mitchel Y. Abolafia.
Description: First. | Cambridge, Massachusetts : Harvard University Press,
2020. | Includes index. | Summary: "Mitchel Abolafia goes behind the
scenes with the Federal Reserve's powerful Open Market Committee as it
responded to the 2008–2009 financial crisis. Relying on verbatim
transcripts of closed meetings, Abolafia shows how assumptions about
self-correcting markets stymied the Fed and how its leaders came to
embrace new ideas"—Provided by publisher.
Identifiers: LCCN 2019044032 | ISBN 9780674980785 (cloth)
Subjects: LCSH: United States. Federal Open Market Committee. | Board of
Governors of the Federal Reserve System (U.S.) | United States—Economic
conditions—2001–2009. | United States—Economic policy—2001–2009. |
United States—Economic policy—2009–
Classification: LCC HC106.83 .A26 2020 | DDC 330.973/0931—dc23
LC record available at https://lccn.loc.gov/2019044032

To Amy

CONTENTS

Introduction

MAKING SENSE OF A CRISIS

Of course, the big developments since our last meeting were in
financial markets. . . . We seem to be repeatedly surprised with
the depth and duration of the deterioration in these markets;
and the financial fallout from developments in the subprime
markets, which I now perceive to be spreading beyond that
sector, is a source of appreciable angst.[1]

—FOMC TRANSCRIPT, AUGUST 7, 2007, 31

I was thinking that Edward R. Murrow said that anybody who
isn't confused really doesn't understand the situation [*laughter*].
I'm confused, and I don't understand the situation.

—FOMC TRANSCRIPT, DECEMBER 11, 2007, 60

We are in uncharted waters, but we are groping our way forward.

—FOMC TRANSCRIPT, DECEMBER 15–16, 2008, 198

Surprise. Confusion. Groping forward. These are the reactions of policymakers at the Federal Reserve in the midst of dealing with the financial
crisis of 2008. They are frank acknowledgments of the difficulty involved in
the interpretation of a breach in the fabric of accustomed expectations. They
reflect the vulnerable sentiments of colleagues addressing each other. These
colleagues share a responsibility, not only to understand the breach, but to
mitigate its consequences. The surprise, confusion, and groping toward an
interpretation can be described as "sensemaking," a term that refers to the
moment when people, in this case policymakers, ask the question, "What's
going on here?"[2] This moment occurred repeatedly over the course of the

financial crisis when Federal Reserve (the Fed) policymakers were confronted by unexpected and often ambiguous circumstances.

It is rare that we catch sight of policymakers in the midst of sensemaking. Such deliberations usually occur beyond the public gaze. An unusual opportunity is afforded by the existence of verbatim transcripts of policy meetings that include all seven of the governors of the Federal Reserve and the twelve presidents of its regional Reserve Banks.[3] These transcripts offer a remarkable source for examining the unfolding sensemaking of Fed policymakers.[4] The policymakers meet every six weeks to search out shifts in the economy and to adjust the supply of money and credit consistent with the Fed's mandated goals of price stability and maximizing employment. As such, the Federal Open Market Committee (FOMC) is designed for collective sensemaking. During a crisis, the urgency of that sensemaking is magnified. The existence of the transcripts allows us to map the changing content of sensemaking to see how the policymakers' understanding of events evolved and to examine their changing justifications for actions taken and not taken.

Sensemaking during the crisis did not occur in a vacuum. It was a social process. The policymakers not only received volumes of data and analysis from their staffs, they also met with business leaders, they read private-sector analyses of the situation, and, of course, they influenced each other.[5] At an institutional level, sensemaking was shaped by the conventions of macroeconomics and central banking in which policymakers were expert practitioners. These conventions included a professional tool kit of established cues, accepted theories, historical precedent, and competing logics that are available to every policymaker.[6] The competing logics reflect contentious political and economic debates over the role of the state in the marketplace. The Fed is at the center of these controversies not only because of its position at the intersection of the state, the market, and the academy, but because of its power to intervene in the economy and its responsibility to maintain stability in the system.[7] Sensemaking was shaped by these tools. Policymakers employed them over the course of their deliberations, negotiating over their meaning and, at times, redefining them to fit the situation. The use of this tool kit, depending on the circumstances, either enabled or inhibited learning, innovation, and improvisation by the group.[8]

In the ensuing analysis, my purpose is to understand the Fed's unfolding interpretation of the financial crisis.[9] Although speculative excess is the proximal cause of the financial crisis, only the state and its agents are accountable for its resolution. This makes the FOMC's sensemaking highly significant and the transcripts the best available record of that policy process.[10] Most academic observers of the FOMC's policy process prior to the crisis saw it as suboptimal because it was based on analytic discretion that varied from meeting to meeting rather than the application of a consistent model or rule.[11] Many studies argued that following a policy rule, such as an inflation target, would improve the Fed's performance.[12] As one critique of the Fed's policy process explained, "Without the guidance or discipline offered by an analytic model and formal targets for nonfinancial variables, the formulation of monetary policy often seemed to be a seat-of-the pants operation."[13] More recently, a former governor of the Fed, Alan Blinder, responded, "We do not know the model, and we do not know the objective function, so we cannot compute the optimal policy rule."[14] In this sense, analytic discretion (sensemaking) was the default option.

Current research suggests that Fed policy adhered more closely in recent years to a neo-Keynesian framework but not a formal model.[15] Although policymaking became increasingly "rule-like" as the FOMC focused on inflation in the decades prior to the financial crisis, the transcripts studied here continue to exhibit considerable discretion and deliberation in the policy process, examining a diverse set of cues that change from meeting to meeting and constructing competing narratives.[16] These deliberations became more conflictual as the crisis progressed. The sensemaking perspective offers a close analysis of the Fed's discretionary policy process, decoding the elements of its approach to understanding the policy environment. My analysis will show how the policymakers' way of knowing what is going on, their epistemology, is a synthesis of conventionalized economic facts, constructed narratives, and pragmatic experimentation. My analysis begins in August 2007, observing how the Fed understood and misunderstood the early signs of significant turmoil in financial markets, and proceeds through the unprecedented action taken by the Fed in the fall of 2008. Along the way we will gain insight into the forces shaping the sensemaking process—forces that reflect the Fed's role as "the most powerful economic institution in the country."[17]

Controlling the Money Supply

The mechanism for control of the money supply has changed over the course of US history. This change has generally been in the direction of increased government control over the market for money, but it has not been without conflict. There has always been a tension between the appropriate functions of the market and the state. Farmers, merchants, bankers, and political parties representing their interests have contested the appropriate means and degree of control by the state. The conflict over control of monetary policy can be divided into three stages: market-based control, bureaucratic control, and technocratic control. A short digression into history will orient our understanding of the Fed's response to the financial crisis.

Market-Based Control. The Constitution of the United States, when written in 1787, gave the federal government the power to "coin money and regulate the value thereof." Such legal tender could be used to pay off all obligations. This system was considered self-regulating in that the supply of currency in the economy would not grow without an increase in the supply of the precious metal on which it was based. As such, the Founders contemplated no other regulatory device. But the Constitution was better designed to maintain political stability than economic stability, and economic interests were rarely content to rely solely on the benefits of self-regulation.

The supply of precious metals was not a reliable source of economic stability. The monetary history of the nineteenth century is one of severe dislocation wrought by the bank panics of the 1830s, 1870s, and 1890s, when depositors lost confidence in the banks' ability to deliver their cash. The money supply, tied to the supply of gold, was not flexible enough to meet spikes in demand, such as those triggered by droughts and floods. Large numbers of businesses failed and individual savings were wiped out in "runs" on the banks. Political conflict over how the currency should be valued was nearly continuous.[18] Farmers in the South and West fought to expand the definition of which metals could be exchanged for cash in an effort to create easier credit, while merchants and bankers in the East fought for the more restrictive stability and predictability of "sound money" based on gold. The Federal Reserve has its direct roots in the Panic of 1893 and the resulting economic crisis. In the wake of this panic and the resulting years of economic instability, an alliance of reform-minded bankers, businessmen, and economists called for an "elastic currency" that could be mobilized in financial crisis when cash was in short supply. This idea was critical to the birth of central banking in the United States.[19]

Bureaucratic Control. The Panic of 1907, in which J. P. Morgan famously tried to mobilize the urgently needed monetary liquidity, provided the critical incentive needed for the creation of a central bank. Morgan announced that he could no longer be expected to rescue the banking system in a panic. Reform-minded businessmen and bankers designed a central bank that would allow them to build their firms while avoiding unmanageable panics. In the final legislation, enacted in 1913, a system of eight to twelve regional Reserve Banks was to be created and run by the regional bankers, overseen by a board of governors in Washington. Although the degree of banker control was to erode over the course of the twentieth century, the long efforts of the banking community paid off with the creation of a central bank that could furnish an elastic currency that could be expanded when needed, thereby creating enhanced financial stability.

In its early years, the Board in Washington was weak and the regional Reserve Banks, run by the private bankers, took the lead in controlling the Federal Reserve System. The efficacy of the system, as well as the distribution of power between the Board and the twelve Reserve Banks, was somewhat ambiguous and contested. From the beginning, the New York Reserve Bank, located at the center of American finance, asserted its preeminence among the other eleven regional banks and the Board in Washington. But the retirement of Benjamin Strong as governor of the New York Reserve Bank in 1928 left a leadership vacuum in the system.[20]

During the numerous bank failures of the early 1930s, when banks were unable to meet their obligations to clients, the Fed remained passive. Economists Milton Friedman and Anna Schwartz famously blamed this passivity on the leadership vacuum left by Strong in New York and the organizational ineptitude of the Board in Washington.[21] More recently Allan Meltzer explained the Fed's inept behavior based on the widespread acceptance of a misguided economic idea, the "real bills doctrine."[22] According to this doctrine, the underlying cause of bank failures was loans made for speculative purposes, and the proper response was to purge the economic system of its excesses by letting banks fail. With this approach, a chain reaction of bank failures ensued. The Great Depression was its consequence.[23]

As a result of the Fed's failure to mitigate the financial crisis, Congress turned to reforming the Fed itself. In keeping with other New Deal reforms, it chose to strengthen the government's hand in the market. The Banking Act of 1935 both changed the structure and broadened the power of the Fed. The ambiguities over the distribution of power between the regional banks and the Board in Washington were resolved in favor of the Board in Washington. The Federal Reserve Board was renamed the Board of Governors of the Federal Reserve System, and members were given higher salaries and fourteen-year terms. At the same time, the Secretary of the Treasury and the Comptroller of the Currency were removed from the Board in an effort to make it less political and "independent within the government." All the pieces were in place to make the Fed an independent regulator of the money supply. But monetary policy had taken a back seat to fiscal policy in the New Deal, which focused on using government revenue to influence the economy. The Fed became the servant of policy set at the Treasury Department.

Technocratic Control. The Federal Reserve chafed under Treasury control. By the early 1950s, many in Washington believed it was time for an effective monetary policy that did more than maintain a low price for government securities in support of the recovery from the Great Depression. The Treasury–Federal Reserve Accord in March 1951 allowed the Fed to use the discretion over monetary policy it had been given in the Banking Act of 1935. Another significant but subtle shift occurred in 1952. Congress affirmed the expectation of an activist Fed. Rather than being an adjunct of the self-regulating gold standard, which had been abandoned by Congress in 1933, the Fed was expected to adapt to the cycle of economic expansion and contraction using its discretion to identify turning points in those cycles and create policy that would inhibit the unwanted effects of both phases, excessive inflation and deep recession. The automatic discipline of the gold standard was to be replaced by what Allan Sproul, president of the Federal Reserve Bank of New York, referred to as "the discipline of competent and responsible men."[24] This conferral of power meant that the Fed would rely on *technical expertise* to "tame" the fluctuations in the market for money and credit. With this and the earlier structural reform of 1935, Congress laid the groundwork for the technocratic, relatively autonomous Fed of modern times. Competence as a central banker was increasingly associated with one's knowledge of economic theory and one's career experience in analyzing the macroeconomic situation. In 1960, none of the seven governors were economists. In 1970, four of the seven were, and by 1980, all but one was an economist.

Over the course of its history, the Fed has increasingly come to stand for technical rationality: the application of scientific thought to the solution of policy problems. The policymakers' action is grounded in a knowledge of monetary economics that very few people share. As Karl Brunner, himself a renowned monetary economist, wrote, "The possession of wisdom, perception, and relevant knowledge is naturally attributed to the management of central banks. . . . The mystique thrives on a pervasive impression that central banking is an esoteric art. Access to this art and its proper execution is confined to the initiated elite."[25] John Kenneth Galbraith wrote, "Because the meanings of their actions are not understood by the great majority of the people, they can reasonably be assumed to have superior wisdom."[26]

The Fed's opacity and the esoteric nature of its operations facilitates a mythic representation of its technical rationality. The "scientization" of central banks has allowed them to "gain legitimacy and authority basing their views on, and applying, the language of science."[27] It has allowed their analyses to become objectified and reified in the marketplace. But it has not allowed the control of the money supply to become "scientifically" managed in the sense that the major uncertainties of monetary policy, especially in the midst of financial crisis, are now well-understood operations. Rather, the aura of technical rationality that surrounds central banking disguises the bounds to rationality: a policy process based on a tool kit of cues, concepts, and practices that, unsurprisingly, have cognitive, informational, and epistemological limits. In this study, our focus on sensemaking will disenchant some of the mystique surrounding technical rationality, examining how the FOMC interprets an ambiguous and changing environment.

Making Policy

The predominant focus of this study is on the closed meetings of the FOMC and how this group made sense of the emerging financial crisis. The transcripts offer little insight into other parts of the Fed, but the presence of the seven governors of the Fed, twelve presidents of regional Reserve Banks, and more than twenty staff members in the FOMC meetings suggests that the transcripts offer a fair representation of their sensemaking during the financial crisis.[28] The FOMC meets at regular intervals for one or two days to discuss current conditions and set monetary policy for the coming period. The FOMC has twelve voting members. Seven are the members of the Board of Governors of the Federal Reserve appointed by the president of the United States and confirmed by the Senate for terms of fourteen years. The other five voting members are presidents of one of the twelve regional Reserve Banks and are elected by boards of directors representing their home regions. The presidents of all twelve regional Reserve Banks participate in the meetings and four of them rotate onto the FOMC as voting members for terms of one year. The president of the Federal Reserve Bank of New York is a permanent voting member and serves as the vice chair of the FOMC. The names, affiliations, and work histories of the FOMC members serving during the period under study are presented in Appendix A.[29]

The FOMC, as its name implies, oversees open market operations. These operations involve the buying and selling of government securities to influence the price and therefore the supply of money and credit in the economy. The FOMC directs the Open Market Desk at the New York Fed to buy or sell government instruments, short-term bonds, to influence the fed funds rate, which is the interest rate at which banks lend their funds maintained at the Fed to each other. If the Fed directs the desk to buy, this lowers rates and increases the supply of money in the economy. If the desk sells, rates go up and the money supply contracts. Although this description simplifies the process by which Fed action influences the economy, it gives some sense of what the FOMC does. Targeting a specific short-term interest rate, the fed funds rate, is the FOMC's major policy tool and the object of its policy process.

FOMC meetings begin with short presentations from staff economists and the managers of domestic and international operations, followed by questions from the committee members. The meeting then moves on to a roundtable discussion of current economic conditions in which the chair calls on the members. Most of the statements of the members are prepared beforehand, but as we learn in this study, they became increasingly extemporaneous as the crisis proceeded. Once every FOMC member has presented a position, the chair opens a discussion of current policy choices. These choices are generally limited to moving the fed funds rate incrementally up, incrementally down, or not at all. There is a strong push for consensus in the group as members try to present a clear signal to the market about their intentions. This discussion continues until the chair identifies a central tendency in the discussion and calls for a vote on policy.[30] Members are acutely aware that every word and action issuing from their committee is closely watched and interpreted by corporations and investors as well as various government bodies. They often fine-tune the language of the policy statement to increase the probability that their intentions are understood.

Sensemaking, Culture, and the Policy Process

My experience as a member of the FOMC left me with a strong
feeling that the theoretical fiction that monetary policy is made

by a single individual maximizing a well-defined preference
function misses something important. In my opinion monetary
theorists should start paying some attention to the nature
of decisionmaking by committee, which is rarely mentioned
in the academic literature.

—ALAN BLINDER, *CENTRAL BANKING IN THEORY AND PRACTICE*

Most prior work on policymaking at the FOMC has been argued from a
rational choice perspective. This work assumed that FOMC policy was an
aggregation of the individual preferences of its members.[31] It sought to explain the preferences of members for tighter or easier monetary policy as a
function of individual maximizing behavior. This book examines policymaking at the FOMC from a different perspective—that of a group of actors faced with the ambiguities of their situation. This book shifts our attention to the groups' adaptive response by focusing on the sensemaking that
preceded the group's vote on policy. Our subjects, members of an elite policymaking committee, engage in hours of deliberation trying to extract the
salient cues in that situation, develop a shared narrative that characterizes
the situation, and match that narrative with a policy that seems appropriate.
This sensemaking process transfers our analytic attention from the individual
pursuit of preferences to the social process by which a group interprets its
shared circumstances.[32] This process is embedded in the expert culture that
characterizes central banking. This culture is grounded in the language and
logic of macroeconomics, but also includes the Fed's history of policy prece-
dents and, at a more abstract level, the ongoing debate over the role of the
state in the market. As such, the perspective developed here links the group
process of sensemaking to the cultural contexts in which it is embedded.

Another underlying theme in this analysis is the scientific limits to rationality in policymaking. Much of the story to be told is about what happens
when the limits of scientific knowledge are reached in a crisis, when the
usefulness of standard answers and normal procedure is exceeded. We will
explore a long period of doubt and confusion, as well as moments of experimentation and learning. The process was not linear, but it does suggest institutional resilience.

This book is not a history of the financial crisis. It will not explore the
causes of the meltdown. There are many good analyses explaining the various
causal factors involved.[33] It is also not another prescription for greater Fed
transparency or greater Fed independence. There are many excellent books

that do that well.[34] Rather, this book is a study of one group of policymakers doing their jobs in the midst of a crisis. It stands in the long line of studies intended to give the reader a sense of a modern organizational setting that is somewhat mysterious: a work unit of software engineers, scientists in a laboratory, or traders in an investment bank. It explores these policymakers' practices, conflicts, conundrums, and the social and cultural factors that shaped their enigmatic world. We will investigate these mysteries by listening in on the policy deliberations of these Federal Reserve officials as they navigated the financial crisis.

1

No Crystal Ball

AUGUST 2007

By the August 7, 2007, meeting of the Federal Open Market Committee (FOMC), there was considerable reason for concern about the direction of the US economy. Freddie Mac, the government-sponsored buyer of home mortgages, had stopped purchasing subprime mortgages in February; New Century, a leading subprime lender, had filed for bankruptcy in April; rating agencies had downgraded 100 bonds backed by subprime mortgages in June; Bear Stearns, an investment bank, had stopped redemptions and then liquidated two of its investment funds in July; and American Home Mortgage, another mortgage lender, filed for bankruptcy on August 6, the day before the meeting. All of this could be traced back to the growing number of subprime mortgage defaults. These defaults in the subprime mortgage market began distressing the collateralized debt obligation (CDO) market that had been created to hedge mortgage-backed securities. As adjustable rate mortgages began to reset at higher rates because of increased risk perceptions, delinquent payments climbed. Home foreclosures rose dramatically.[1] The financial turmoil was clearly spreading.

Earlier in 2007, the FOMC had been primarily concerned with inflation, believing that the events in the housing and mortgage markets would not upset the ongoing expansion. But at the August 7 meeting, the FOMC was discussing the situation in financial markets with growing anxiety. Within a few minutes of the beginning of the meeting, a staff member, Bill Dudley, made the following report to the committee:

As you all know, there has been considerable financial market turbulence since the last meeting: Problems in subprime mortgage credit have persisted and intensified; credit-rating agencies have begun to downgrade asset-backed securities and CDOs [collateralized debt obligations] that reference subprime debt; . . . corporate credit has been infected, with high-yield bond and loan spreads moving out sharply; and stock prices have faltered.[2]

Given this report, we might expect that at least some of the people in the room would favor action to mitigate the kinds of problems we now know occurred and show concern for a broad-based financial crisis. But if we flip to the end of the transcript, jumping over several hours of discussion, we find the policy directive that they voted on that day. The following statement reflects the FOMC's decision to keep interest rates where they had been since July of 2006:

> To further its long-run objectives, the Committee in the immediate future seeks conditions in reserve markets consistent with maintaining the federal funds rate at an average of around 5.25 percent. Although the downside risks to growth have increased somewhat, the Committee's *predominant policy concern remains the risk that inflation will fail to moderate* as expected. Future policy adjustments will depend on the outlook for both inflation and economic growth, as implied by incoming information.[3]

The vote in favor of this policy directive was unanimous. Clearly, FOMC members decided not to act on the growing financial turbulence. They saw the downside risk to growth, including the possibility of recession, increasing only "somewhat." Rather, their predominant policy concern was still on inflation. They did not foresee the emerging crisis or its consequence, the looming Great Recession. But given all the warning signals, it seems appropriate to ask why they couldn't see the tsunami approaching or why they so underestimated the effects of the problems that were already visible.[4]

Competing Cues

We begin by taking a close look at the FOMC members' sensemaking work that day. The first and most obvious question is, "What cues were they looking at?" Cues are commonly used indicators, or as Karl Weick described them, "simple, familiar structures that are seeds from which people develop a larger sense of what may be occurring."[5] There were a variety of favored, conventional cues available to them as well as cues that were unique to the moment. FOMC members manage the process of extracting cues from the blizzard of information available to them through dialogue and consensus. Each member spends the six weeks between meetings discussing conditions with people inside and outside the Fed. They are exposed to a variety of internal Fed reports, media outlets, and other data sources. They extract the cues they find most salient. Finally, they arrive at the meeting ready to present their take on economic conditions and to hear and evaluate the views of their peers. From all this emerges the focal cues for policymaking, the reference points from which group interpretation takes off.

Following the staff presentations, there was a "go-round," during which committee members, sitting around a long table, offered their assessment of the macroeconomic situation, highlighting what they viewed as the most significant facts. Most members echoed Bill Dudley's concern, acknowledging the conditions in the financial markets as the major point of reference getting their attention. Their focus within financial markets was drawn to two related cues: the "re-pricing of risk" and the "loss of confidence among investors." Re-pricing refers to the higher risk premiums demanded by investors for instruments that were once believed to be safer. These premiums reflected market participants' concern about defaults in the subprime mortgages, the tightening credit standards in housing, and the consequent deterioration of markets in mortgage-backed securities and related derivatives.

Some members of the FOMC acknowledged the re-pricing of risk issue but were unsure of its consequence. To the extent that it discouraged investment and consumption, re-pricing could choke off demand, affecting the performance of the economy. One member, Gary Stern, felt that the situation had become unusually "dramatic" and was concerned about its effect. "Of course, the big headlines have been the turbulence in the financial markets and all the uncertainty associated with the duration of the re-pricing and the adjustments that are under way and their quantitative significance for the performance of the economy going forward. This turbulence in the financial markets is likely the most significant development for short-term performance of the economy and possibly for policy."[6] Others acknowledged the cue's visibility but were more optimistic that it was a beneficial development for these markets. As Chairman Ben Bernanke put it, "There has been a widespread re-pricing of risk. That is, obviously, a healthy development, particularly if there is no overshoot."[7] The prevailing economic logic here is that re-pricing is the sign of a well-functioning market. If such a re-pricing is going on, then the market must have been overpriced and this is a beneficial correction.

> THOMAS HOENIG: I am not yet convinced, however, that recent financial market volatility and re-pricing of credit risk will have significant implications for the growth outlook. It is still reasonable at this point to think that the recent volatility will prove transitory, and the re-pricing of credit risk is, in that sense, desirable.[8]

> CHARLES PLOSSER: The biggest economic news headlines since our last meeting have focused on the volatility of the financial markets and the re-pricing of risk. I am inclined to put minimal weight on the current financial conditions for a slowdown in the pace of economic activity going forward.[9]

The second widely mentioned cue, the issue of investor confidence, receives deeper concern. It refers to a loss of confidence in the credit-rating agencies (Moody's, Standard & Poor's, Fitch) and their ability to assess risk. The specific concern is confidence in the new "structured products," the derivative instruments that were created at investment banks and had since become huge speculative markets. It was increasingly clear to investors that the ratings given to many of these instruments by the ratings agencies were simply wrong. Many CDOs depended on mortgage-backed securities that contained a significant number of subprime mortgages that were in default. Eric Rosengren, the president of the Federal Reserve Bank of Boston, was one of many to cautiously articulate this concern.

> If investors have lost confidence in the rating agencies to accurately assess credit risk for structured products, the market could be impeded until confidence is restored. Since similar structures are used for financial instruments besides mortgages, getting secondary market financing for a broader range of financing needs could be difficult, and external financing for some borrowers could be affected.[10]

This loss of confidence was particularly disturbing for several reasons. First, it meant that those making investment decisions did not trust the information provided by ratings. There was no available measure for this lack of confidence in credit ratings other than that inferred from falling prices, but the members seemed in little doubt that it was a real threat. At a deeper level, it suggested that investors may have lost faith in financial instruments more generally, and it is an ominous threat to an economy when investors lose faith not only in the worth of assets but in the credibility of the market's self-regulatory system and its ability to mediate the overpricing or underpricing of an asset. For members of the FOMC, as guardians of economic stability, such a loss of credibility would suggest a significant threat of systemic failure.

But the financial turbulence was not the only cue that FOMC members extracted from the flow of economic information in which they were immersed. Although the turbulence in financial markets and the erosion of trust had grabbed their attention, raising red flags, policymakers at the Fed are in the habit of observing a standard set of cues. As they speak during the go-round, the members of the FOMC are likely to address key indicators such as growth and inflation. These indicators have the legitimacy of being taken for granted as measures of economic welfare as well as reflecting the legal mandate of the Fed to maximize growth while minimizing inflation. The trend of these indicators, unlike the financial situation, had not changed significantly since the last meeting. In fact, in the key areas of economic growth and controlling inflation, members saw things getting better.

RICHARD FISHER: Mr. Chairman, at the past few meetings I have spoken about my District as having strong growth. I have asked questions about the strength of the growth in the national economy, and I have described the global economy from the standpoint of the way the staff here writes about it and the way we do our own work as "hotter than a $2 pistol." Nothing has really changed since my last intervention.[11]

GARY STERN: Thank you, Mr. Chairman. Well, as best I can judge, recent readings on the economy are generally consistent with anticipation of moderate growth and some gradual diminution or at least no deterioration in inflation. Second-quarter GDP [gross domestic product] readings, as far as I can tell, contain no big surprises.[12]

JEFFREY LACKER: At the national level, we continued to receive fairly good news on inflation. After annualized rates of monthly core PCE [personal consumption expenditure] inflation above 2 percent at the beginning of the year, we've now had four months of readings below 2 [percent].[13]

These quotes, in contrast to the earlier ones, are the kind found in a routine meeting.[14] In these cues there are no big surprises, just continuing good news. There is none of the sense of foreboding and doubt that we saw earlier.[15] Both growth and inflation are moving in the right direction at a gradual but acceptable rate in most of the country. The global economy is "hotter than a $2 pistol." This is good news in contrast to the competing cues from the financial markets.[16] But the identification of resonant cues by the FOMC members is only the beginning of the politics of interpretation. It is the policymakers' way of establishing the "facts." In this meeting, as we have seen, there are disparate facts. They were chosen from a repertoire of accessible indicators because they are deemed salient and appropriate in the current situation. The object is to assemble a story that is suggestive of appropriate policy.

Narratives

Substantial Damage: The Contagion Narrative

The cues themselves are an inchoate form of explanation. They offer inadequate causal accounts for the conditions in the environment and little basis for extrapolation to policy. Rather, these facts must be assembled and an explanatory order imposed on them. This order takes the form of a narrative, a story about events that contains agency, context, and a temporal ordering of the events that suggest a plot or story line. Narrative construction is the social process that policymakers use to translate their individual cognitions into shared understanding.[17] At the FOMC, the narrative emerges in a collective process of formulation, editing, and agreement or disagreement. At the August 7 meeting, the FOMC used these competing cues to construct competing narratives to explain the available facts and resolve the tension between the competing cues. This process is not one of calculation or computation, but argument and negotiation. The narratives are in constant flux as the conversation proceeds. They are constructed from bits and pieces of cues, anecdotes, existing fragments of story lines from previous meetings, staff and media analyses, and especially favored operating models.

> TIM GEITHNER: These developments in financial markets, even though they represent a necessary adjustment, a generally healthy development, have the *potential to cause substantial damage* through the effects on asset prices, market liquidity, and credit; through the potential failure of more-consequential financial institutions; and through a general erosion of con-

fidence among businesses and households. If this situation were to materialize and these effects were to persist, they could have significant effects on the strength of aggregate demand going forward.[18]

Geithner, who was president of the New York Federal Reserve Bank and therefore vice chairman of the FOMC at the time, knit together elements of the available cues from the financial markets to form a plausible predictive plot that goes beyond Dudley's earlier statement of the facts. This plot is predicated on an old but familiar contagion story in which falling asset prices undermine financial institutions as well as the confidence of firms and consumers.[19] Each consequence is a credible direct effect of the trouble in mortgages and mortgage-backed securities. Nothing in this narrative seems implausible. The narrative seems both clear and dramatic. What is left out of Geithner's story are the dimensions of time and space—that is, how long this erosion will take and how far beyond the mortgage markets it will spread into the economy.

A plot such as Geithner's is not a significant part of the policymaking process until it is glossed or reconstructed by other members. They not only offer their support for the narrative, but they often include further explanatory elements. The reconstruction is done socially through argument and reasoning. The outcome reflects a negotiated analysis of the situation. At the August 7 meeting, although members were comfortable discussing the turbulence in financial markets, few members seemed inclined to construct a pessimistic story about the potential damage of the financial turmoil. Certainly it was outside their customary discussion of monetary policy. But Geithner was not alone in suggesting heightened risk. For those who did, the first concern was temporal—how long it might last. Gary Stern, president of the Minneapolis Reserve Bank, acknowledged the significance of the financial conditions but seemed unwilling to predict their duration or consequence. "At this point, it is very difficult, to put it mildly, to assess its effects for reasons I alluded to earlier—namely, that we don't know how long this will last and what will follow in its wake."[20]

Stern is not only contributing the element of time to the plot, he is expressing considerable uneasiness that without some idea of how long the financial turmoil will last, its effects cannot be evaluated. Whereas predictive narratives should add confidence to the policymaking process, the contagion narrative is full of uncertainty and caution. It suggests an impediment in the sensemaking process based on lack of information and knowledge. Another

FOMC member provides a gloss on this narrative that corroborates the sense of uncertainty.[21]

> DONALD KOHN: But we can't know how the market situation will evolve. I also believe that there's a non-negligible chance of a *prolonged* and very messy adjustment period that would feed back substantially on confidence, wealth, and spending. With the rating agencies discredited and markets vulnerable to adverse news on the economy, the period of unusual uncertainty could be *prolonged*. The greatest risk is in the household sector, where uncertainty about valuations of mortgages could continue to feed back on credit availability, housing demand, and prices in a self-reinforcing cycle.[22]

Kohn's gloss on the contagion narrative expresses some of the same uneasiness found in Stern's quote and offers an explanation. His gloss articulates a temporal model of causality with multiple feedback loops that suggest how the negative effects of re-pricing might affect other parts of the economy. In this case, the period of "unusual uncertainty" may be drawn out.

A second element of concern suggested by the narrative of contagion was spatial: how far the turmoil would spread to other markets in the economy. Such turmoil may be confined within a few arcane financial markets or may spread like a communicable disease. A re-pricing of assets, particularly when risk is being reassessed, may also spread to other instruments. The momentum in such stories suggests a downward spiral, each stage a precipitant to the next. This is a familiar causal story line. It is especially familiar because it characterizes the Great Depression, among other economic disasters. Financial markets are notorious for such irrational collective behaviors, as suggested by the terms "mania" and "panic." Economists do not really have the tools to assess the probability of such behaviors. Their models are not designed to predict such crises, and the predominant theory, which states that market behavior is efficient, would suggest that the market will correct for such problems before they spread.[23] The contagion narrative is inherently unsettling, even confusing in this context. Several members note the discrepancy between a professional economist's predictions and an investor's fears.

> JANET YELLEN: Of course, the big developments since our last meeting were in financial markets. . . . We seem to be repeatedly surprised with the depth and duration of the deterioration in these markets; and the financial fallout from developments in the subprime markets, *which I now perceive to be spreading beyond that sector,* is a source of appreciable angst.[24]

ERIC ROSENGREN: It is notable that the rather benign outlook of the forecasters is in marked contrast to the angst I hear when talking to asset and hedge fund managers in Boston. The angst is new and reflects heightened concerns with the financial ramifications stemming from subprime mortgages.[25]

Ben Bernanke wondered aloud that "what looks like $100 billion in credit losses in the subprime market has been reflected in multiple trillions of dollars of losses in paper wealth."[26] Why, he asks, has it spread to other markets? His answer, a classic contagion scenario, refers to "concern about the macroeconomic implications of what is happening. In particular, there is a fear that subprime losses, re-pricing, and the tightening of underwriting standards will have adverse effects on the housing market and will feed through to consumption, and we will get into a vicious cycle."[27] Bernanke, like his colleagues, plots a narrative of contagion. But each of them notes either surprise or contradiction in this plot. There is clearly a sense of uneasiness or even exposure over the uncertain prediction of both time and space in this narrative. This makes the contagion narrative unsatisfying, tentative, and undeveloped. Such a narrative is likely to be replaced if one with greater assurance is found.

A Fundamentally Healthy Situation:
The Narrative of Restoration

At the same time that the contagion narrative was being plotted and glossed, a narrative of restoration was being constructed. This narrative takes many of the same cues but interprets them differently. We have already seen the re-pricing of risk referred to as "desirable" and "a healthy development." This reflects the speakers' understanding that there is an alternative story line in which the financial turmoil is limited and has positive consequences. As Frederic Mishkin explains:

> The media are making the subprime market into the whole story, but I think it is just not the right story. The subprime market is really a very small percentage of the total credit markets. . . . Basically what I think is happening is quite a good thing . . . the parts of the market that are having the problem are the most opaque parts, [and] it is not clear that they are particularly important to the things we really care about in terms of our policies.[28]

If the contagion narrative was grounded in the imagery of a system of negative causal loops leading to a regressive spiral, the restoration narrative is grounded in the imagery of self-interested economic agents. The agents are astute investors who sight an opportunity to profit from assets they believe have become underpriced. In this plot, it is these investors who will restore the markets and prevent contagion to other parts of the economy. Kevin Warsh offered a basic version of this narrative:

> Opportunistic capital is a key here to a smooth transition. It's key to ensuring that what happened in the financial markets doesn't seep its way into the real economy. Of the equity investors that were using loose credit markets to get equity returns, the most sophisticated are focusing on and looking for equity returns in the debt markets. So many investors previously investing in equity are now looking to the debt markets, where they see a risk-reward tradeoff that is better than it has been in a long time. That gives me some confidence that opportunistic capital will come back to some of these markets.[29]

At the heart of this predictive narrative is a belief that markets are self-correcting mechanisms, like a thermostat, and that market actors exist who will initiate the correction by seizing the available opportunity for profit. This assumes that as investors become aware of better returns in the debt markets, such as securitized mortgages, they will optimize their utility, thereby supporting the price. Donald Kohn adds a temporal dimension to the restoration narrative saying, "The most likely outcome is that it will be limited in duration and effect, and that's what I assume for my forecast. Well-capitalized banks and opportunistic investors will come in and fill the gap, *restoring* credit flows to nonfinancial businesses and to the vast majority of households that can service their debts."[30] Randall Kroszner glosses the restoration narrative further by citing historical precedent and specifying the role of banks in supporting the restoration:

> The major banks have very high, relative to historical trends, capital-to-asset ratios in excess of the required minimums. . . . That is extremely important because the banking system can provide a critical automatic stabilizing mechanism, as it did in 1998, when there are liquidity challenges. . . . So the banks do act as liquidity providers and liquidity insurers, and I think we're starting to see a bit of that now with people pulling out of some of these instruments and so more is flowing into the banks.[31]

Whereas the contagion narrative seems to be asking "Why is this happening?" the restoration narrative asks, "How will it stop?" It is notable that the answers to the first question were full of angst and uncertainty. The answers to the second seem full of confidence. What was being restored was "order." They replaced a harder question about causality with an easier one about the solution. As Daniel Kahneman points out, this sort of substitution makes judgment on difficult questions possible.[32] The solution is based on the observation that financial markets are efficient. This observation engenders a widespread faith among economists in the markets' resilience, their ability to self-adjust. But the restoration narrative is only significant as an answer to the angst-laden questions created by the contagion narrative. As Frederic Mishkin protested, the financial turmoil in credit markets is not the "right" story. For that story, we turn to a third and final narrative constructed at this meeting.

Natural Tendencies: The Growth/Inflation Narrative

Although the financial turmoil was the most dramatic feature in the Fed's environment, it was not considered the most salient for policymaking. Our earlier discussion of competing cues noted that FOMC members routinely review a standard set of measures for determining monetary policy. Most prominent among those are economic growth and inflation. Based on its "dual mandate," the Fed is legislatively required to promote the goals of maximum employment and stable prices.[33] In the first half of 2007, the FOMC was predominantly focused on price stability and the dominant narrative was an optimistic story about growth. At the meeting on June 28, 2007, six weeks before the August meeting, the committee released a statement saying that growth had been moderate during the first half of the year, but that inflation pressures still existed. By August the financial turmoil had created risks to economic growth. Yet the dominant narrative put minimal weight on those risks, telling a story about what is "natural" in the economic world.[34]

DONALD KOHN: I see a number of reasons to think that moderate growth remains the most likely outcome going forward. First, as President Stern has stressed from time to time, is the *natural resilience* of the economy, its tendency to grow near potential unless something is pushing it one way or another. If anything, this resilience has probably increased over the past couple of decades, reflecting more-flexible labor and product markets.

Second, global growth remains strong, supporting the growth of exports . . . . Third, the most likely factor to throw the economy off its potential is the financial markets. My most likely forecast assumed that the credit markets would begin to settle down over coming weeks with some, but limited, net tightening of conditions.[35]

In this plot, the economy is a natural system. Like a plant or other organism, economies will tend to grow, to reach a point near their systemic potential, unless prevented by their environment. This resilience has been enhanced by the increasing flexibility of constituent parts of the natural system—labor and product markets. Growth of other organisms (foreign economies) on which the focal organism is dependent has been strong. Finally, the forces threatening the organism are expected to abate, leaving little damage. The growth narrative is embedded in a metaphor of "natural" equilibrium that can be expected to reassert itself. As Gary Stern explains, referring to recent dynamics, markets are expected to recover. "Second-quarter GDP readings, as far as I can tell, contain no big surprises. In particular, the components of aggregate demand that were expected to bounce back after periods of sluggishness or, in some cases, correction—inventory accumulation, spending on equipment and software, and federal government outlays—all in fact did bounce back as anticipated."[36] Or, in a more predictive vane, Frederic Mishkin says, "My forecast is basically similar to my forecast at the last FOMC meeting and is consistent with the Greenbook forecast—that we would have a return to trend growth a bit later than we had expected but by mid-2008 and 2009."[37] The narrative of growth is characterized by a belief that the economy is not fragile but rather resilient.[38]

Given the optimism about growth, the greatest risk continued to be inflation. FOMC members had been hypervigilant about inflation since the high rates of the 1970s. By the August 2007 meeting, despite the fact that inflation indicators had been improving, members retained a desire to either reduce inflation or inflation expectations. As Ben Bernanke said when summarizing what he has heard from those around the table, the members believed that some "upside" inflation risk remained:

> Views on inflation are similar to those in previous meetings. Recent readings are viewed as reasonably favorable. However, risks to inflation remain, including the possible reversal of transitory factors, tight labor markets, the high price of commodities, and higher unit labor costs resulting from lower productivity growth. In all, the risks to inflation

remain to the upside. That is my summary of what I heard. I'm sure a lot more could be said.[39]

Bernanke, performing the role of the chair, identifies the central tendency among the group's concerns. That is, that the progress on inflation may be transitory. The narrative of growth/inflation was the least elaborated, most sketchy of the narratives. It had been dominant in previous meetings for some time and so could be discussed in shorthand at the August meeting. Members again expressed their satisfaction with the continuing growth and their concern with inflation. In contrast to the chaos suggested by the contagion narrative, the emotional tenor of the growth narrative was relaxed, almost routine. The narrative of growth/inflation suggests no surprises, just moderation and order.

The members of the FOMC evaluated each of the three narratives—contagion, restoration, and growth—on its own in terms of its coherence and persuasiveness. There was little or no comparison of narratives. The contagion narrative was rejected as incomplete and uncertain, lacking sufficient information about duration and impact. The restoration narrative offered a familiar and reassuring plot about the financial turmoil and the growth/inflation narrative fit easily with the group's prior and continuing expectations for the economy. As Janet Yellen noted, they are repeatedly surprised by the market deterioration. Expert policymakers are most likely to see what they expect to see.[40] They turned, instead, to the more familiar and understood restoration and growth narratives as more coherent, complete, and certain. It is these narratives that constitute their sense of the situation. Given the broad consensus on the restoration and growth narratives, the FOMC moved on to a discussion of appropriate policy.

Matching: Finding the Appropriate Response

To this point in the meeting the policy options have not been systematically discussed and no decisions have been made. The consensus around explanatory narratives challenges the FOMC members to identify an appropriate solution. Normative decision theory suggests that the policymakers should array the alternatives and compare them in an effort to find the optimal solution.[41] This is not what happened.[42] Instead, they invoked a "logic of appropriateness" to match their analysis of the situation to a solution.[43] They asked what action would be appropriate for the FOMC in a situation like this one. As William Poole said to his colleagues, "It's clear that the markets are very skittish. . . . So what should our *response rule* be to events like this, not how should we respond to this particular case?"[44] Poole invoked a part of their policy routine, a process of matching situation to action using a general, situation-appropriate operating model.[45]

More abstractly, the policymaking process reflects an implicit question, "What does a person like me (a central banker) and an organization like this (the central bank of the United States) do in a situation like this?"[46] This question has two important elements to it: organizational/professional identity and a logical principle that is derived from a repertoire of such principles. The two are interrelated in the recognition of appropriate action. Every identity or role in an organization comes with tacit scripts about how the incumbent ought to act. For the central banker, who has been socialized into an identity by years of graduate training in economics and/or by service in a variety of economic policy jobs inside and outside the Fed, a response rule, or appropriate script, is recalled once the situation has been identified. The interweaving of identity with such scripts is suggested in the following quote from Richard Fisher, who was concerned about how the FOMC should respond to the financial turmoil:

> The best guidance would be that we must not ourselves become a tripwire. I think we have to show a steady hand. I rather liked the reference to the Hippocratic oath earlier, "Do no harm." I think we can best accomplish this by acknowledging market turbulence and yet not implying that we are given to a reaction that might create a moral hazard. I'm particularly mindful of the discussion in the press and by security analysts of a so-called Bernanke put, and I want to make sure that we do not take any action or say anything that might give rise to an expectation that such is to occur.[47]

Fisher is concerned about their identity as responsible stewards of the economy. Since he, like his colleagues, accepts the restoration narrative, he believes the market will self-correct and that the FOMC members must avoid giving the impression that they plan to prop up financial markets, thereby rescuing failing investors. The "Bernanke put" was a reference to former chairman Alan Greenspan's supposed effort to prop up markets during the dot.com bubble, an effort that was believed to induce greater risk-taking by investors. An important objective at the August meeting was to discourage any additional risky behavior by investors while the markets were recovering. The reference to the Hippocratic notion of "do no harm" is tied to the restoration narrative's plot suggesting that no treatment is necessary and the patient will recover on its own. Fisher is supplying Poole with the desired "response rule."

Chairman Bernanke confirms their primary identity as stewards of the economy stating, "In the longer term, of course, our policy should be directed not toward protecting financial investors, but, rather, toward our macroeconomic objectives."[48] Bernanke is reminding his colleagues that their professional role as central bankers is not to bail out financial markets but to maximize employment and stabilize prices. Financial markets should be left to restore themselves, and appropriate action remains focused on that mandate.

The match between the restoration narrative and the prescription of no treatment for the financial disorder is more fully elaborated by Dennis Lockhart:

> I believe that the correct policy posture is to let the markets work through the changes in risk appetite and pricing that are under way. . . . The traditional investors are still out there with substantial liquidity, and they are just temporarily on the sidelines for understandable reasons and, barring further shocks, should return to the markets in force later this fall. The dislocations in the financial markets call for a posture of *vigilant monitoring* of developments but nothing more for now.[49]

This solution sounds straightforward, but as we will see in subsequent chapters, Fed action is never that simple. The policymakers must consider not only the economics of the situation but the market psychology as well. They must assess market participants' expectations and how those participants will react to the Fed's decision. At the time of the August 2007 meeting, market actors are, as Poole said, "skittish." Many are expecting Fed action in response to the financial markets or at least a reassuring signal that the Fed is aware of the situation. At the same time, policymakers do not want to communicate undue concern with a situation they don't yet see as contagious.

> TIM GEITHENER: The challenge, of course, is to figure out a way to acknowledge and to show some awareness of these changes in market dynamics without feeding the concern, without overreacting, about underlying strength in the fundamentals of the economy as a whole or in the financial system. That is a difficult balance, but I think it requires some softening of the asymmetry in our assessment of the balance of risks now.[50]

Geithner is suggesting that the wording of the policy directive soften its focus on inflation risks and acknowledge the changes in the financial markets. Managing market psychology is a subtle craft. Identifying a response rule to match the growth narrative is more straightforward. The Fed's target interest rate was raised to 5.25 percent in June 2006 and held there. In a growing economy, this rate was intended to inhibit inflation while still allowing for moderate growth. The growth/inflation narrative shows that this has been successful and the members are content to continue on this path. Janet Yellen explained the logic of this response rule: "I consider it *appropriate* for policy to aim at holding growth just slightly below potential to produce enough slack in labor and credit markets to help bring about a further gradual reduction in inflation toward a level consistent with price stability."[51] Dennis Lockhart, president of the Federal Reserve Bank of Atlanta, reinforces the idea that inflation remains the primary concern.

> Thank you, Mr. Chairman. My basic view of *appropriate* policy is little changed from the previous meeting. None of the intermeeting developments yet compel me to change my view that our focus should remain on reducing inflation and inflation expectations. . . . Evidence within the Sixth District is consistent with this basically stable and positive outlook. . . . Just like the Greenbook, we view the fundamentals of the economy to be stable.[52]

Both Yellen and Lockhart explicitly employed a "logic of appropriateness," matching the current situation to continuing the anti-inflation/moderate growth policy. This was, in some sense, a comfortable place for a central banker to be. The economy was growing and the inflation rate was moving in the right direction. If the turmoil in financial markets hadn't been creating uncertainty, this meeting would have been routine. Gary Stern put the financial (restoration) and macroeconomic (growth) stories together in matching the situation to a solution that justifies no change in policy.

> Thank you, Mr. Chairman. Well, I guess the thing that strikes me first about the current situation is that the incoming news on core inflation has been promising. At least as far as I'm concerned, the inflation outlook is satisfactory. So that, in and of itself, suggests no change in policy. Now, if we append to that the financial market turmoil and the adjustment that is under way there, that does raise the risk to real growth. I think we have pretty well acknowledged that in this discussion. But in my view, that

shouldn't prompt a change in the federal funds rate target at this meeting
for the reasons I cited earlier having to do with the substantial uncertainties associated with all of this and, of course, I would be lax if I didn't men-
tion the *resilience* of the underlying economy that has been demonstrated
through the period of the great moderation.[53]

Stern's reference to resilience not only glosses the restoration narrative, it
aligns with the growth / inflation narrative. He notes that resilience is representative of the Great Moderation, a term used to describe the period of
low inflation and modest growth that had been in place since the mid-1980s.
This sense of the "natural" resilience of the economy was about to end.[54]

Cultural Blinders

The foregoing analysis suggests that there is an overarching explanation for
why the FOMC members underestimated the effects of the growing financial turbulence. This explanation accounts for the rejection of the contagion
narrative. It accounts for why the restoration and growth narratives were selected and other narratives were not. It suggests that these narratives and
the subsequent response rules were not spontaneous interpretations of the
moment, but that this consensus reading of the situation was done through
culture-shaded lenses. This culture consists of the repertoire of favored cues,
familiar stories, salient metaphors, and preferred logic that members bring
to the narrative construction process.[55] But culture is not a straitjacket that
determines interpretation; rather, it is a tool kit that members draw on more
or less skillfully.[56] Members used these tools to make sense of the situation
in August 2007.

   The group decision process at the August meeting was shaped primarily
by the logic of modern finance: a faith in the resilience of financial markets
and therefore a trained incapacity to sense their frailties.[57] This logic evoked
an idealized version of the pricing mechanism in financial markets that dominated the field of finance. Its diffusion and adoption among policymakers
reflected the success of the neoliberal revolution of the 1980s. In this idealized version of financial markets, their inherent efficiency became a taken-
for-granted assumption.[58] The influence of this belief on FOMC culture is
exhibited most vividly in the restoration narrative, where it is expressed as a
faith that self-interested economic actors would surely intervene and take

advantage of opportunities created by the market instability. There is a confidence not only in the rationality of investors, but also in the self-regulating ability of financial markets. This led to the belief that the instability was only a "correction" and, as Frederic Mishkin says, "quite a good thing."[59]

At the same time that cultural blinders privileged a restoration narrative, they disadvantaged unorthodox explanations. This is exhibited in the under-rating of the contagion scenario, a narrative that is antithetical to the logic of self-correction. Contagion's imagery of a crowd or herd mentality is at odds with the image of rational, self-interested individuals who would intervene to restore the market. Although a small number of prophetic voices outside the Fed were predicting a financial crisis based on subprime mortgages and related derivatives, they were too few to undermine the restoration narrative.[60] The pervasive influence of a deep faith in self-correcting markets made the contagion narrative harder to believe. Given the focus of the dominant logic, the contagion narrative had little chance of acceptance.

The chances for the contagion narrative were further eroded by the Fed's customary predisposition for inflation control. This has been the dominant logic of Fed policy during the careers of all the FOMC members.[61] Bernanke's reminder to the members that their policy should be directed toward these macroeconomic objectives, rather than financial investors, is an activation of a cultural assumption that often remains tacit. Under routine circumstances it is rare that the Fed chair would find it necessary to offer such a reminder that the stability of the "real economy" takes precedence over the financial sector. Their return to the growth/inflation narrative suggests the power of the "real economy" norm as a basis for action, the members' greater comfort with its assumptions, and perhaps, a reluctance to contemplate the disorder of contagion.

In rejecting contagion, the FOMC activated the Fed's default response rule, its operating model, known as "counter-cyclical policy." This simple model of appropriate policy was succinctly characterized by William McChesney Martin, chairman of the Federal Reserve from 1951 to 1970, as "leaning against the winds . . . whichever way they are blowing."[62] When the economy is contracting, the Fed increases the supply of money and credit to stimulate it. When the economy is expanding, they restrain the supply of money to inhibit inflation. In the August meeting, Janet Yellen's response rule, holding back growth to inhibit inflation, is a clear application of the restraint phase of this model. Members actively use these operating models. The models, of course, cannot control for all the variables in the economic environment. They are terse constructs whose very simplicity makes them cognitively and socially useful. They both enable and constrain the thinking and action of policymakers.

Finally, the FOMC, like any ongoing policymaking body, has a heritage of stories from its history that shapes action. The stories are told and remembered because of their resonance. Members use these stories as sensemaking tools. In the August meeting, members were concerned with moral hazard, the possibility that any easing of monetary policy might encourage further risk-taking by investors. Richard Fisher's allusion to a "Bernanke put" was a cultural reference and a cautionary tale from the Greenspan era about actions and consequences that should be avoided.[63] This is in keeping with the related theme of "do no harm." As a response rule for the financial turmoil it says that "when the diagnosis is ambiguous, action should be limited to vigilant monitoring." This conservative message is in keeping with the culture of maintaining order and stability in the "real" economy as opposed to the financial markets.

It is possible to look at the influence of culture on policymaking at the FOMC as a dimension with ideology on one end and pragmatism on the other. At the ideological end the cultural repertoire may deeply constrain what is "thinkable," and on the pragmatic end it may offer tools for coping and even innovating in a difficult situation.[64] At the August meeting, the members of the FOMC were confronted by, as Tim Geithner put it, "challenges in information and diagnosing what is happening in the market."[65] Given the ambiguity, it is perhaps not surprising that they relied heavily on familiar cultural guides. In the remainder of this book we will be looking for the point at which these cultural guides are recognized as an obvious hindrance and the members of the FOMC move toward the pragmatic end of the dimension, using their tools to creatively innovate a response.

2

Textures of Doubt

SEPTEMBER–DECEMBER 2007

Doubt is an uneasy and dissatisfied state from which we struggle
to free ourselves and pass into the state of belief.

—CHARLES SANDERS PEIRCE, "THE FIXATION OF BELIEF"

Between September and December 2007, a greater sense of doubt crept
into discussions at the Federal Open Market Committee (FOMC). One
example of this doubt was a growing skepticism about the Fed's ability to
forecast economic conditions in the face of the financial turbulence. The Fed
is known for the sophistication of its forecasting models, but even the most
complex econometric models available did not capture the consequences of
what was occurring in the credit markets, such as those in subprime mortgages and credit default obligations. David Stockton, a staff economist, raised
the issue early in the September meeting in his report to the FOMC. Janet
Yellen, among others, elaborated on it.

DAVID STOCKTON: The difficulty we confronted in this forecast is that,
even after decades worth of research on credit channels and financial
accelerators—much of it done by economists at all levels in the Federal Reserve System—the financial transmission mechanisms in most of the
workhorse macro models that we use for forecasting are still rudimentary.
As a result, much of what has occurred doesn't even directly feed into our
models.[1]

JANET YELLEN: The simplest approach is to rely on our usual forecasting
models. However, as David emphasized in his remarks, the shock has not
affected, to any great extent, the financial variables that are typically included in our macro models. . . . But, of course, an evaluation of the likely

economic impact from the financial shock must also take into account changes in credit availability and lending terms even though these variables rarely appear explicitly in forecasting models.[2]

At the September 2007 meeting, as at the August meeting before it, the forecasting models of the Fed staff continued to be optimistic about growth into 2008 and 2009. All of the regional bank presidents reported that their staff was forecasting continued growth in their own regions. The doubt conveyed by Stockton and Yellen reflects the uncertainty created by unreliable information and missing data. The models in use simply didn't account for the changes in financial markets.[3] The sense of discomfort is one of acknowledged ignorance in the face of a knowledge-intensive task. While such discomfort is common in FOMC discussions, the magnitude of the discomfort was unusual.

There was another kind of doubt that was implicit in these statements. Rather than uncertainty caused by an incomplete picture with too little information, this was the ambiguity caused by a complicated picture with too much information.[4] An example of this kind of doubt was conveyed by the dissonance between the consensus forecast on growth into 2008 and 2009 and the rising threat the FOMC saw from the financial markets. The sense of discomfort was not one of ignorance but of confusion. How is one to make sense of opposing predictions? As Charles Evans, president of the Federal Reserve Bank of Chicago, pointed out to the FOMC members, their interpretive capacities had been exceeded:

> In the early 1990s, restrictive credit . . . had a significant impact on real economic activity. In contrast, in the fall of 1998, we thought financial conditions would impinge a good deal on the economy, but 1999 turned out to be a very strong year for growth. Bottom line—and we all recognize this—we need to be careful how we react to the current financial situation.[5]

Evans was suggesting that similar historical situations can lead to different outcomes and that the current situation in late 2007 was, at best, confusing. Sometimes financial disruptions affect the "real" (nonfinancial) economy; sometimes they don't. The FOMC members did not have a theory to explain which situation they were in now, nor a good track record on predicting which way it would go. Again, the problem here was not too little information, but too many plausible causal narratives. Neither the individual members nor the committee as a whole can confidently determine which narrative is most likely. For the FOMC, and sometimes for individual members, it was unclear which story to favor. Richard Fisher, president of the Dallas Reserve Bank, affirmed this sense of confusion and its import using an allusion to *The Odyssey:*

> I'd like to suggest that we're navigating a very narrow passage here in something of a fog. . . . So on the starboard shore we hear a siren called "Very Large Financial Institutions," which infer that a reduction in the fed funds rate will rescue them from peril, however self-inflicted that peril may have been and despite the fact that they're well capitalized according to the reports that we have put together. On the other shore, we are relying on navigational charts or uncertain landmarks or—as you said, David— rudimentary tools that are giving us mixed readings.[6]

As a result, concern shifted between the uncertainty of unreliable indicators and the ambiguity of their own interpretive confusion.[7] The members of the FOMC are usually comfortable moving between quantitative and narrative-based approaches to policy analysis. Unfortunately, neither of these approaches provided a clear reading of the situation and neither allowed them to see the systemic failure awaiting them.

Uncertainty and ambiguity, although more extreme in periods of crisis, are built into the policymaking task facing the FOMC. The salience and validity of economic facts are often in dispute and the interpretations of those facts are often contested. This chapter shows how members of the FOMC employed diverse approaches to understand their situation. In addition to facts and interpretations, the policymakers employed action as a means to clarify the situation. Ultimately, we shall see that a fluctuating pattern of doubt and varied approaches to resolving that doubt prevailed in the autumn of 2007.

Navigating in a Fog: September 18, 2007

The six weeks following the August meeting were calamitous ones in the financial markets. On August 9, just two days after the meeting, BNP Paribas, France's largest bank, halted redemptions in three investment funds.[8] This event, on top of the wider losses in subprime mortgages and collateralized debt obligations (CDOs) led to a seizing-up in a number of related debt markets. Investors lost confidence that these securities could be valued properly, and buyers could not be found for the sellers of these securities. On September 14, the British Treasury announced it was providing support for Northern Rock, the United Kingdom's fifth largest mortgage lender. Although most FOMC members saw an increased "downside risk" to the economy from these events, only one member, Janet Yellen, expressed significant concern about the growing plausibility of the contagion narrative. Yellen plotted the narrative clearly:

> A big worry is that a significant drop in house prices might occur in the context of job losses, and this could lead to a vicious spiral of foreclosures, further weakness in housing markets, and further reductions in consumer spending . . . So at this point I am concerned that the potential effects of the developing credit crunch could be substantial.[9]

There was some tendency to minimize the contagion narrative. Main Street had been far less affected than Wall Street, and housing and mortgages were only one sector of a broad economy. As Charles Plosser explained:

> The national economy looks more vulnerable to me than it did six weeks ago, but it would be a mistake . . . to count out the *resiliency* of the U.S. economy at this early stage. I think there can be a tendency in the midst of financial disruptions, uncertainty, and volatility to overestimate the amount of spillover that they will exert on the broader economy.[10]

Tim Geithner affirmed the restoration narrative even more explicitly, adding the injunction that participants in these markets should not be bailed out. "The process of adjustment and deleveraging that is under way in markets, in asset prices and risk premiums, is necessary," he said, "and we should not direct policy at interrupting or arresting that process or at insulating investors or institutions from the consequences of the decisions that got us to this point."[11]

The impulse to avoid "insulating investors and institutions" suggests the conflict at the heart of the FOMC members' efforts to match the emerging narratives with an appropriate policy option. This conflict is nascent at this point but would grow throughout the financial crisis. The members generally agreed that the appropriate solution was to lower interest rates in response to the changes in the outlook for risk. But they were also concerned that the Fed should not be seen as "bailing out" investors and institutions.

As the September meeting moved into its policy phase, members promoted competing frames to justify favored options on the size of the reduction in the FOMC's target interest rate—the fed funds rate. The members engaged in an interpretive politics, or rhetorical competition, to support their positions and cast doubt on each other's frames. Ultimately, framing moves, or justifications, were about different kinds of outcome uncertainty, which is what the FOMC members most often meant when they talked about "risk."[12] The first frame, which members labeled as *insurance,* referred to reducing the probability that financial shocks would influence the nonfinancial (real) economy. This was frequently described with a statistical reference to "tail risk"—the risk of a rare event. While few members were willing to plot a contagion narrative at this meeting, most of them wanted insurance against rare events.

> ERIC ROSENGREN: The tail risk of liquidity problems and economic problems has grown, and we clearly want to avoid outcomes by which declines in prices for houses and for financial assets tied to the housing sector could create more-severe economic outcomes. The fact is that we do not have much experience with periods of extended illiquidity, especially when the housing sector is so weak. So taking out insurance against these risks seems entirely appropriate.[13]

> TIM GEITHNER: By reducing the probability of an extremely bad outcome on the real side, monetary policy can help mitigate some of the coordination problems that are hampering financial market functioning and delaying the necessary re-pricing of risk that needs to take place. . . . Policy needs to provide a convincing degree of insurance against a more adverse outcome.[14]

Insurance seems to be a metaphor suggesting protection against an event that they don't really expect to happen. Despite the fact that insurance was the dominant response to the increasing downside risk, quite a few of those supporting the frame still believed that continued growth was the more likely outcome.

> CHARLES EVANS: I'd just like to take a minute to talk about risk management. We talked a lot about that in terms of tail risk and nonlinearities and insurance, and I think this is quite appropriate in the current environment. But we have to continue to ask, "What happens in the more likely event that things turn out better than these tail events?" That's why they're called tail events. So I agree with Governor [Frederic] Mishkin that we have to be very careful to think about taking them back.[15]

BEN BERNANKE: There seem to be significant tail risks, and I think some insurance is worthwhile. . . . I also want to agree with Rick and others who have noted that we should be prepared to take this back, and I state that for the record.[16]

The alternative frame that received attention was one that troubled some members throughout the crisis. They referred to "moral hazard"—the threat that investors would perceive the Fed as willing to rescue those actors most responsible for the crisis. If the Fed's action to reduce interest rates were interpreted in that way, it could increase risk-taking and the problems in the financial markets. Investors would bid up asset prices, confident in the knowledge that the Fed would intervene if asset prices declined. Adherents of this view were loath to be pushed into lowering interest rates by "bad actors." Lowering the fed funds rate could send the wrong signal, as Charles Plosser explained: "I think this has the potential to confuse people—that our move is being taken as a desire to bail out bad actors—and that could feed into moral hazard."[17] This concern with not rewarding the "bad actors" was expressed most strongly by Richard Fisher.

> I'm very concerned that we're leaning the tiller too far to the side to compensate risk-takers when we should be disciplining them. So I'm going to conclude not with a sailing analogy but with a football analogy. I don't think it's time to throw a "Hail Mary" pass. I think it's time just to continue to move up the field, running the ball as we've been doing, and I would strongly recommend a rate cut of only 25 basis points and no more.[18]

In the end, the arguments against the moral hazard frame and in favor of the insurance frame were interpreted through the lens of professional identity. Those who argued for a reduction of 50 points in the fed funds rate as insurance against unknown risks referred repeatedly to their responsibility and credibility as central bankers to maintain stability in the economy. As Don Kohn explained, "I'm not concerned about the moral hazard issues. I think *our job* is to keep the economy at full employment and price stability and let asset markets fluctuate around that. There will be winners and losers. That's fine. The Congress told us to have maximum employment and stable prices, and that's what we should be about here."[19] Chairman Bernanke reinforced this sentiment, implying that his opponents were misusing the term "moral hazard." "I just want to say that I think that moral hazard is a terribly misunderstood idea and that as the central bank *we have a responsibility* to help markets function normally and to promote economic stability broadly speaking," he said.[20] Kohn and Bernanke invoke stability and responsibility as what is expected of them. The identity of central bankers as guardians of monetary order is used here as a cultural tool, a norm that guides action, to argue for the insurance frame.

As the meeting came to an end, several members made the argument that the uncertainty about the future was too high to make any definitive policy statement in the public announcement that would be released after the meeting. In the following passages, members complained that they could not calculate the uncertainty, leaving them uncomfortable about announcing policy. As Don Kohn made clear, "There's a huge amount of uncertainty about how things are going to evolve. . . . I don't feel as though I know enough to say that the risks are balanced. I *don't* know. The range of outcomes is just too wide, and there's very little central tendency in it."[21] Janet Yellen echoed Kohn's discomfort about the policy statement. "I don't like the idea of putting out a statement today that says there are continuing asymmetric downside risks," she said. "It leaves us open to the question, 'If you think that, then why didn't you do more?' I agree with Governor Kohn. I like the risk assessment (in the statement) because I honestly don't know exactly what the risks are."[22]

Going beyond the analytic inconvenience of uncertainty, one member, Randall Kroszner, seemed to intuit that the uncertainty caused by missing information about the financial system posed a bigger problem than they had acknowledged. According to Kroszner's perceptive analysis, the problem lay in the bundling of disparate mortgages of unknown risk, the creation of instruments to hedge these new risks, and the institutions that trade them. This innovation, referred to as *securitization,* created interconnections in the financial system and, therefore, vulnerabilities that were unexpected. Risks were held not just by the big commercial banks regulated by the Fed, but in a shadow market for debt, a diverse set of investment banks, bond insurers, and other financial firms. Not only did the Fed not have variables in its models to predict the system's operation, but the system was now designed in such a way that the Fed didn't really comprehend the risks.

RANDALL KROSZNER: I think we have a much greater challenge today because the source of uncertainty is really a change in the whole model of how these markets are operating. In the old days, we used to know where the risks were; unfortunately, we knew that they were all on the bank balance sheets. With the originate-to-distribute model and securitization, we have been able to move to a different model in which the risks are much more dispersed. Not all of them are on the bank balance sheets, although some of them are certainly going to be coming onto the bank balance sheets, so the banks never fully get out of this. But it leads to potential pockets of uncertainty, and that is exactly what has come up.[23]

The dynamics of these new "pockets of uncertainty" were previewed earlier in the meeting by staff economist Karen Johnson. Referring to the Bank of England's rescue efforts toward one of the United Kingdom's largest holders of securitized instruments, Northern Rock, she concisely said, "It was just, if you will, one thing after another, all of which are interacting."[24]

But no one picked up on either Kroszner's or Johnson's observations about unpredicted interactions in the system. The meeting ended with a decision to "buy the insurance" afforded by a reduction of 50 points in the fed funds rate to 4.75 percent.

A Close Call: October 30–31, 2007

A sense of relief pervaded the October meeting. Both the financial markets and the "real" economy were improving. FOMC members believed that their action in September had reduced the economy's vulnerability to mortgage-related asset markets. The disruption did not seem to be spreading to additional financial instruments or the broader economy. As Janet Yellen put it, "I think we have roughly neutralized the shock,"[25] and as Charles Evans said, "I still think the problems in financial markets are likely to remain largely walled off from the nonfinancial economy."[26] The staff was now more confident that the shock would not undermine commercial banks' ability to make loans in any substantial way, thereby avoiding a "credit crunch." Tim Geithner, one of those who raised the possibility of contagion in the August meeting, now believed that the mortgage-related shock would only result in "several quarters of growth modestly below trend."[27] There was a clear preference for minimizing the painful doubts of the September meeting. As Eric Rosengren put it, "While I am worried about downside risks, I am reminded that forecasters have frequently overestimated the consequences of liquidity problems in the past."[28]

The favored narrative in this hiatus from doubt was, of course, restoration. Efficient markets were seen to be working and expectations were high. As Kevin Warsh explained, "All things considered, as a function of both time and Fed policy, there is, indeed, better sentiment; bid-asked spreads have narrowed, price discovery is at work."[29] Confidence in the restoration narrative was reflected in the injection of humor into its plotting by one of its strongest adherents.

RICHARD FISHER: I would add only the following—that with regard to credit markets, the hardening of the arteries or the blockage of the aorta or whatever cardiovascular analogy we want to choose to describe what happened is no longer as severe and life-threatening as it appeared to be in August. . . . Imagine that. Investors are coming home from lala land. To be sure, we're not out of the woods quite yet, as President Plosser and President Rosengren mentioned. The situation remains real, but we've gone beyond suspended reality. If you will forgive me, you might say we have gone from the ridiculous to the subprime.

JEFFREY LACKER: Let the transcript say "groan" [*laughter*].

RICHARD FISHER: By that I mean, by the way, that the subprime market is a focus of angst, which it should be, but the ridiculous practice of the suspension of reason in valuing all asset classes, if not over, is in remission.[30]

The doubt in the October meeting resided much less in the analysis of the situation, which everyone agreed was improving, than it did in possible future shocks. The policy choice in this meeting seemed particularly equivocal. It was between holding the target fed funds interest rate steady versus lowering it by a quarter of a point. This kind of equivocal doubt could not be influenced by facts since there are no facts about future states. Rather, the discussion was based on the best estimate of plausible consequences. As Randall Kroszner explained in support of lowering the interest rate, "It provides perhaps a bit more insurance against some of the negative shocks that we may be hearing about. If those other shoes do drop over the next few months, then we have a lower downside risk for broader financial turbulence."[31]

Although "easing" was the dominant policy position, Thomas Hoenig, Charles Plosser, and Richard Fisher all favored holding the interest rate where it was. This position was framed in terms of inflationary risks. These members argued that lowering the rate might ignite inflationary expectations, setting off an inflationary spiral that would be hard to control. Plosser invoked the need for discipline to justify his position. Not surprisingly, other members experienced this as a rebuke. Tim Geithner's irritation was thinly veiled.

CHARLES PLOSSER: I would prefer to keep my own approach to discipline-based policymaking by looking at the forecast and waiting for the data to tell me whether my forecast deteriorated significantly. . . . On net, I am troubled by a cut today. I would much prefer to wait until December and to assess the data that come in.

TIM GEITHNER: Let the record show I am asking this with a smile. President Plosser, you are not really suggesting that your colleagues, if they have evolved in their view, are undisciplined, unsystematic, or capricious in their rationale for that evolution, are you?

CHARLES PLOSSER: No, I am just saying that the communication of that rationale is tricky, and I did say that people are making their best efforts to make their forecast.[32]

Despite Geithner's smile for the record, it was clear that the group was more divided than at the earlier meetings. As the argument proceeded, it focused on a disagreement over two things: what firms and investors were expecting them to do and how further easing would be perceived. Those in favor of easing, among them Janet Yellen, were concerned that the market had already figured in the anticipated rate reduction and that a failure to do so might actually make borrowing more expensive. "In other words," Yellen said, "if we don't ease today as the market expects, then rates may move up, and that raises concern to my mind about whether we will have accomplished the goal of offsetting the restrictive effects of the recent financial shock."[33] The alternative position reflected the concern that another rate move, after September's, would be perceived as too much stimulus to the economy. As Richard Fisher put it:

I'm tempted to consider the value of another cut as insurance against weakness. Yet we took a huge step last time—we took out a double-barreled shotgun—and it seems to be reflected in the data that the staff projected. I'm a little worried not so much of being accused of being asleep at the wheel but of having our foot too heavily on the accelerator if we cut 25 basis points.[34]

Given the degree of uncertainty about the future, the disagreement was more about the FOMC's signal to firms, investors, and consumers, and the significance of that signal, than it was about interpretations of the data.[35] In the end, they voted to ease by a quarter point to 4.50 percent. The markets were improving, but the fallout from the financial shock in the summer was still impossible to calculate. Kevin Warsh summed up the doubts in the group well: "So I think we're in the realm of a close call and we shouldn't completely rue that situation. Again, that's probably a function of the resilience of the economy, the resilience in the markets, some time and patience, and maybe even a little good monetary policy. So I'm okay with that, I think."[36]

"Anybody Who Isn't Confused . . .": December 2007

By December, the US economy had already moved into recession, according to a subsequent analysis by the National Bureau for Economic Research. Housing prices were in steep decline, delinquency on mortgages and foreclosures had moved up sharply. Unemployment had risen to 5 percent. The broader economy was clearly slowing down. Nevertheless, the Fed's models still had the economy missing recession before continuing its growth in 2008. Such projections, based on existing data, inherently lag the real economy as it descends into crisis. According to David Stockton, the staff economist, the forecast "could still be read as painting a pretty benign picture."[37] Even among the more concerned members there was little sense of the magnitude of the impending adversity. As Frederic Mishkin explained, "You don't like to use the R word, but the probability of recession is, I think, nearing 50 percent, and that really worries me very much. I also think that there's even a possibility that a recession could be reasonably severe, though not a disaster."[38]

Most policymakers recognized the financial turmoil but did not yet see the systemic risk. In the week before the December meeting of the FOMC, the Board of Governors had approved the creation of a Term Auction Facility (TAF). TAF was designed as a temporary program to address the growing reluctance to lend and borrow in the short-term funding market that banks used for daily operations. The Fed would auction twenty-eight-day loans to all banks eligible with good collateral. The amounts eventually loaned to US and foreign banks through TAF and an expanding list of other facilities was in the trillions of dollars. The creation of this facility was among the earliest signs of the Fed's willingness to expand its balance sheet and reflected its growing concern with the lack of liquid funds available to banks. Even if the forecast for the larger economy could still be read as "pretty benign," the Fed was preparing to "backstop" the credit markets.

The texture of doubt in the December meeting was interwoven with threads of conflict as contradictory interpretations gained increasing prominence. At the same time, these interpretations were often prefaced with a caution about the difficulties of getting clarity, as in Dennis Lockhart's prologue to his analysis: "The current situation is extremely difficult to read."[39] The result was circumspect and conflictual sensemaking. The character of this interpretive conflict is reflected in Richard Fisher's summary of the discussion. "Well, Mr. Chairman," he said, "having listened to various views starting with President Yellen, on the one end, and President Plosser, on the other, and President Hoenig on inflation, I was thinking that Edward R. Murrow said that anybody who isn't confused really doesn't understand the situation [*laughter*]. I'm confused, and I don't understand the situation."[40]

Early in the meeting Janet Yellen gave the strongest and most prescient assessment of the situation based on her observation that financial contagion was spreading to the broader economy:

> At the time of our last meeting, I held out hope that the financial turmoil would gradually ebb and the economy might escape without serious damage. Subsequent developments have severely shaken that belief. . . . I am particularly concerned that we may now be seeing the first signs of spillovers from the housing and financial sectors to the broader economy.[41]

Yellen's beliefs are among the most strongly held at the meeting. Most of the other participants continued to hedge their positions.

The position of the most pessimistic members is marked by a direct attack on the restoration narrative. Kevin Warsh skeptically questioned whether the theory that there will always be opportunistic financial actors to buy up low-priced assets, returning the market to equilibrium, was credible at this point: "Is there enough opportunistic credit from those institutions that distinguish themselves—large foreign banks, U.S. branches, super-regional banks, mid-sized banks, community banks, credit units, the GSEs, the Home Loan Banks—to pick up market share and take advantage of that slack that's been left for a period? I think in a word the answer is "no."[42] Don Kohn expressed a similar concern, stating that "the losses are large enough to call into question the ability of some very essential intermediaries to provide support for markets or to extend much additional credit. Those intermediaries include Fannie and Freddie and the financial guarantors, as well as some investment and commercial banks."[43]

At the same time, some of the strongest adherents of the restoration narrative began to sound a little less certain, relying on the long run to sort out the problems in the market.

WILLIAM POOLE: I have an inherent optimism about the economy, which is hard to put any real flesh on the bones I guess, but I think that the economy in the longer run is inherently strong and resilient. A lot of the adjustments in the credit markets I believe are under way. . . . There are a lot of smart people with sharp pencils who are digging into their situations, deciding what to write off, and then getting on with things; and they are past the initial scramble. So those things together give me some sense of optimism.[44]

CHARLES PLOSSER: Overall, the recent financial developments suggest that it will take longer before conditions are "back to normal" in all segments of the market. As I've said before, I continue to believe that price discovery still plagues many of these markets. It now looks as though it will take a little longer before these markets can sort things out and return to normal. Financial institutions continue to write off some of the investments and take losses. I view these write-downs as a necessary and healthy part of the process toward stabilization.[45]

The restoration narrative was still dominant, but the contagion narrative was gaining traction. The outcomes expected in the contagion scenario were now more openly contemplated. Although only Janet Yellen appeared ready to say that she expected serious damage to the real economy, Tim Geithner understood that economic actors were vacillating between these narratives:

We need to be cognizant that the market is torn between two quite plausible scenarios. In one, we just grow below potential for a given period of time as credit conditions adjust to this new equilibrium; in the other, we have a deep and protracted recession driven as much by financial headwinds as by other fundamentals. There are good arguments for the former, the more benign scenario, but we need to set policy in a way that reduces the probability of the latter, the more adverse scenario.[46]

As one might expect, the December 2007 discussion matching the situation analysis with an appropriate policy was more contentious than in the previous meetings. It was not just participants in the market who were torn; the FOMC was divided in its analysis of the situation. The conflict of opposing narratives was transported into the conflict of opposing solutions. The policy positions taken by the contagion narrators, and justifications for these positions, were more vehement than in past meetings. The debate now focused on the size of the interest rate reduction or, put another way, "how much insurance do we really need?" The policy recommendation of Janet Yellen reflected this vehemence:

> To my mind, the risk to the forecast and the risk of a vicious cycle, in which deteriorating financial conditions and a weakening economy and house prices feed on each other, argue for adopting a risk-management strategy that, at the very minimum, moves our policy stance to the low end of neutral—namely, a cut of 50 basis points—and I think it argues for doing so now rather than taking a "wait and see" approach and lowering it only grudgingly. This may not be enough to avoid a recession—we may soon need outright accommodation—but it would at least help cushion the blow and lessen the risk of a prolonged downturn.[47]

The opposing policy recommendation, a .25 easing of the fed funds rate, captured a larger range of positions in the group. It included those who felt ambivalent about the choice between narratives and those who felt that rising inflation and/or inflation expectations might compel the FOMC members to reverse the direction of their policy and tighten monetary policy in the coming months. They framed the discussion in terms of being "nimble." While most agreed that a reduction was appropriate at this meeting, those who supported the restoration narrative and foresaw continued growth were staking a claim for a near-term about-face. As Eric Rosengren explained, "This seems to be the appropriate time to take significant further action, knowing that, should the economy perform much better than we currently anticipate, we could be equally nimble in raising rates as appropriate."[48] Frederic Mishkin expressed a deeper level of concern, invoking the fear of a cardinal mistake.

> You have to be *nimble*. What do I mean by that? Well, as all of us completely agree, keeping inflation expectations contained is the most critical thing that we do. We do need to worry about the real side of the economy; but we know that, if you unravel inflation expectations, then the jig is up, and you get very bad monetary policy outcomes, not just for inflation but

also for the real side of the economy. That is one of the key lessons that we have learned in the past fifty years about monetary policy.[49]

Mishkin is alluding to the fact that fighting inflation has been the sine qua non of monetary policy during the careers of these FOMC members. Before the Great Recession, the greatest crisis during the careers of this generation of policymakers was the Great Inflation of the 1970s. The primacy of inflation prevention is so baked into the culture as a primary logic of action that even when a new crisis was upon them and real inflation appeared well controlled, its cause carried resonance.

At the end of the meeting, we find the Fed chairman trying to thread the needle between the opposing positions. There is no clear central tendency in the group. Bernanke uses the "nimble" frame to say that policy could go either way in the future as knowledge develops:

> You can tell that I am quite conflicted about it, and I think there is a good chance that we may have to move further at subsequent meetings. In that respect, it is very important that both in our statement and in our inter-meeting communications that we signal our flexibility, our nimbleness: We are not locked in, we are responsive to conditions on both sides of the mandate, and we are alert to new developments.[50]

Being responsive on both sides of the mandate, inflation control and employment maximization, may seem like an equivocal solution, as it is hard to lean against the wind in both directions. But then, equivocal knowledge generates equivocal solutions. The FOMC compromised on a quarter-point reduction in the fed funds rate to 4.25 percent.

Textures of Doubt and Epistemic Failure

The meetings of the FOMC in the fall of 2007 reveal a committee aware that it was navigating in heavy fog. By December, the doubt attached to cues, narratives, and matching solutions created the conditions for conflict and confusion that challenged the policymakers' confidence. The ability of the group to interpret the situation was inhibited by cognitive limits, the limits of their predictive models, as well as the complexity created by a cascade of failing markets. By December, the FOMC members agreed that it was very difficult to know what was happening. Nevertheless, they were obliged to make policy.

The meetings reviewed here suggest three main approaches to dealing with doubt at the FOMC. The three approaches are deeply embedded in FOMC culture and therefore part of the shared tool kit of all members. The most common and explicit approach referenced the reliability and validity of economic facts. For the members, the sources of uncertainty included imprecise forecasts, unreliable or missing information, and a situation that did not closely resemble the theoretical model that guided their thinking about financial market behavior. The term "risk," which was used nearly as frequently as uncertainty, generally referred to the costs associated with the uncertain facts. This version of doubt reflected a *positivist* epistemology, a "way of knowing" in which only empirical evidence can be used to validate knowledge. There is an underlying assumption that it is the absence of facts that is the problem. With better information, the problem would be workable. This suggests belief in a world that is concrete and ultimately knowable. These are the assumptions of the field of economics and are manifest in the language and professional culture of the members of the FOMC.

The meetings also revealed a more tacit form of doubt. This doubt was reflected in the increasingly contradictory narrative choices facing the members. The source of this doubt lay less in the absence of "facts" than it did in the interpretation of equivocal information. Everyone agreed that the financial markets were roiled and that inflation was controlled for the present. The disagreement was over what those facts meant at this juncture. Members introduced anecdotes from contacts in the business community suggesting that the statistics were misleading and that alternative interpretations existed. Narrative construction is the default approach to knowledge construction when statistical "facts" are inadequate or unreliable. It was an *interpretivist* way of knowing in which members attempted to reduce the ambiguity of the situation. Interpretation was accomplished with familiar causal stories that seemed to fit the circumstances. This suggests a way of knowing in which "objective" facts may be inconclusive, in which causality is unclear, and in which interpretations of both facts and causality may be contested through argument and consensual validation. The world is apprehended through culturally available constructions (e.g., the contagion and restoration narratives). This way of knowing, although it is part of every meeting, became more significant and more conflictual as doubt increased. The more equivocal the facts, the greater the interpretive contest.

At an even more tacit, taken-for-granted level, there was a third approach to doubt employed at the FOMC. This was a *pragmatist* approach that was focused on the transformation of a problematic situation.[51] It was less about understanding the cause than learning from the outcome of action. The FOMC, convening every six weeks, acts on the economy and then evaluates the ongoing result. It is a feedback generator. It is overtly performative.[52] In this way of knowing, action and understanding are inseparable. It is an approach to knowledge requiring both interaction with the environment and active analysis of the consequence. The continuing purchase of "insurance" and the assessment of its effect is a good example. In the December meeting Kevin Warsh refers to the FOMC's policy choice as "a natural experiment to help us figure out what the diagnosis of the patient really is."[53] The frame of "nimbleness" employed in the same meeting suggested that the chosen treatment might well be followed by a reversal, depending on outcomes. In this way of knowing, the members are concerned with the practical effects of their action and what those effects might tell them about future action.

The "ways of knowing" employed by the FOMC in fall 2007 resulted in epistemic failure. The positivist failure was vested in the continuing faith in predictive models of the economy and statistical facts that were inadequate for predicting financial shocks. The interpretive failure rested on the deep cultural embeddedness of a conceptual model of financial markets as self-correcting that caused members to have undue faith in the restorative power of markets. The pragmatic failure lay in the assumption that taking out "insurance" was an adequate response to a problem of much greater proportion than they were able to imagine.

The three ways of knowing described here were part of the culture of the FOMC, providing tools for making sense of the economy. They guided the practice of FOMC members and helped to reduce the anguish associated with doubt. They are ways of knowing that exist in the face of doubt. Critics of the FOMC have referred to Fed policymaking as idiosyncratic and ad hoc, implying that good policymaking requires a single, consistent way of knowing.[54] The FOMC has resisted calls to apply a purely positivist epistemology based on an economic rule, such as agreeing not to exceed some inflation target. The seemingly promiscuous mingling of epistemologies by the FOMC members reflected the complexity of causal factors in the economy, their situational salience at particular moments, and the organizational imperative to make sense of the complexity. The rejection of a purely positivist epistemology suggests their limited confidence in the predictive capacity of existing information and models. Rather, their policymaking reflected their identity as central bankers who make an earnest effort to solve problems, moving between their training in economics, their interpretive insights based on experience as monetary policy experts, and their sense of urgent responsibility based on their mandate to maintain economic stability in a changing environment. The culture of knowing at the FOMC is a complicated and intricate tool kit with approaches that are applied in ways the members see appropriate to the situation. But, as this mingling of epistemologies suggests, the cultural tools available are incomplete and members must skillfully employ them, especially when so many elements of the financial markets were spiraling out of control, as they were in late 2007.

The limits of scientific knowledge elicit a culture that eschews any single way of knowing. As Knorr-Cetina explained in her study of epistemic culture among scientists, there are multiple ways of producing scientific knowledge; a variety of "construction machineries."[55] The policymakers are committed to the conventional cues, but they resort to narrative and metaphor to understand the action and causality of these cues. All of these, as well as economic logic, are part of scientific instrumental reason. Positivism and interpretivism are not opposites; rather, as Andrew Abbott put it, in scientific rationality they are interwoven, "they are different moments in one process."[56] But each approach had its limits. Positivism worked until statistical facts were inadequate to tell a plausible story. Interpretivism worked until its stories were misleading. Pragmatism worked until the scope of the problem to be solved exceeded the treatment. In the financial crisis, the context was sufficiently "transient, shifting, disconcerting, and ambiguous" that the individual ways of knowing became what James Scott referred to as "thin simplifications."[57]

The culture of the Fed divides the economy into the "real economy" and the financial economy. It divides the financial sector into commercial banks, a variety of other intermediaries such as investment banks and hedge funds, and a plethora of markets. Staff members each have their regions and markets of specialization. This division of labor is designed for an orderly world where Main Street and Wall Street are discussed separately. This is a world in which the subprime mortgage market does not bring down the US economy. But in an era of financial innovation that produced unexpected interactions, this worldview was archaic. Interconnection was, of course, implicit in the contagion model, but it was understood more as a collective hysteria than a systemic weakness created by new financial instruments and new financial markets that were interconnected with the older, more stable system. Contagion was considered a "tail risk" against which the FOMC bought "insurance" policies that were inadequate to prevent the coming credit crunch on Main Street. There were no formal models, no theories of system interconnectedness and fragility that were a part of the discourse. The focus in economic thinking was on the individual actors in the system and the self-interest of those actors as a mechanism of price equilibrium and restoration. Only one member, Randall Kroszner, noted that systemic risk had shifted away from the commercial banks under their regulatory control. In fact, this kind of questioning of system boundaries and exploration of systemic connections, as a way of knowing, was a missing part of the culture of the FOMC.

Even complex systemic thinking that included diverse interconnections could not have smoothed the texture of doubt into confident certainty. Data would still be missing or unreliable; narratives would still be only terse, abbreviated, and contestable; and the complexity of interactions in the economic system would still be beyond our current and foreseeable modeling abilities. Given this assessment, the FOMC's attempt to smooth out the texture of doubt in autumn 2007 should be understood as the effort of a group of technical experts to agree on effective policy. This effort was not based in rules or standard procedures. It was a social process grounded in the group's enduring epistemic culture, the multiple ways of knowing that informed its sensemaking practice.[58] The policymaking process at the FOMC in the fall of 2007 was a resourceful attempt to reduce doubt. Members were engaged in an iterative process of inquiry to find an explanation of events that would suggest appropriate policy. That goal was to remain elusive until the depth of the financial disruption was clear.

3

A Learning Moment?

A Conference Call: January 21, 2008

By the third week in January there had been significant erosion in confidence among participants in the financial markets and in the wider economy. This presented the policymakers at the Federal Open Market Committee (FOMC) with a critical choice of whether to exercise their ability to interrupt the downward spiral of market psychology through their policy actions. Late on the afternoon of January 21, 2008, Ben Bernanke assembled an unplanned meeting of the FOMC members via conference call. It happened to be the Martin Luther King holiday. He apologized for not waiting for the regularly scheduled meeting, which was just nine days away, but explained that "there are times when things are just moving too fast for us to wait for the regular meeting."[1] The chairman's sense of urgency reflected rapidly deteriorating conditions and set the emotional tone for the meeting. Bill Dudley, a senior staff member, gave the Committee an update on financial markets.

> The macro outlook and broader financial market conditions have continued to deteriorate quite sharply. The S&P 500 index, for example, fell 5.4 percent last week; it is down almost 10 percent so far this year. Today it fell another 60 points, or 4.5 percent, so that means that the cumulative decline in the S&P 500, if it opens near where the futures markets closed today,

will be nearly 15 percent since the start of the year. Global stock markets were also down very sharply today—Monday. Depending on where you look, the range of decline was anywhere from 3 percent to 7½ percent, pretty much across the board.[2]

Stock markets were not the only cue cited by Bill Dudley. He noted that credit ratings had been downgraded for monoline guarantors, a relatively obscure but significant sector of the insurance industry. They provide insurance for mortgage-backed securities and collateralized debt obligations, among other instruments. In fact, Merrill Lynch had announced a multibillion-dollar charge for its exposure to the most fragile of these firms, ACA. In retrospect, we can see that the trouble among monoline insurers was a foreshadowing of the wider systemic failure that awaited mortgage-related debt markets. Dudley cited another decisive cue: traders of fed funds rate futures contracts had priced in a dramatic rate cut to the January contract and an even deeper cut to the March contract. As it turned out, the futures traders underestimated how far the members of the FOMC would be willing to go in adapting to the precarious situation in the financial markets. At this meeting and the regularly scheduled meeting nine days later, the FOMC dropped the fed funds rate from 4.25 to 3.0 percent, nearly a third of its value. This is unusually dramatic policy action in a little more than a week suggesting that the definition of the situation, the meaning given to cues and narratives, had changed. So, how had the group's collective understanding changed, and what had the members learned that elicited this uncommon policy response?

Redefining Contagion

In a regularly scheduled meeting, following Dudley's remarks the chairman would solicit each member's take on the current situation. He did not do so. Rather, he explicitly took control, saying, "Let me just talk about the issue here." Chairman Bernanke called this meeting because he wanted an immediate cut in the fed funds rate. To get support for an intermeeting cut he needed to overcome the members' attachment to the restoration narrative; the idea that markets would restore their own equilibrium. To Bernanke it was increasingly clear that "opportunistic investors" were not coming into the markets as prices dropped. In fact, as he says below, there was a "withdrawal from risk." He needed to coax the group toward redefining the contagion narrative as an existing menace rather than just a dangerous possibility. Bernanke now saw contagion as not just price volatility moving beyond mortgage markets: it was a psychological state of fear that was spreading and needed to be confronted.

> BEN BERNANKE: I think there is a general sense—I certainly feel in talking to market participants—that it is not just subprime anymore and that there are real concerns about other kinds of consumer credit—credit cards, autos, and home equity loans—and that there is fear of housing prices falling enough that contagion will infect prime mortgage loans. There is building in the market a real dynamic of withdrawal from risk, withdrawal from normal credit extension, which I think is very worrisome.[3]

In the very careful language of economic policymakers, Bernanke was laying out an argument for immediate action. In concluding his justification for calling the meeting, a monologue that ran over 1,300 words, he seemed to abandon his usual caution, redefining the contagion as a crisis.

> At this point we are facing, potentially, a broad-based *crisis*. We can no longer temporize. We have to address this crisis. We have to try to get it under control. If we can't do that, then we are just going to *lose control of the whole situation*. . . . I think we really have no choice but to try to get ahead of this.[4]

Bernanke left little room for misinterpreting the depth of his apprehension in this statement. What had previously been referred to only as financial turbulence, turmoil, or shock was now a crisis. This term clearly dramatized the situation. It is the statement of a committee chairman who, up to this point, has seemed more like a group facilitator than an opinion leader. Having departed from custom by calling the meeting on a holiday and speaking before rather than after the other members, Bernanke had attempted to reinterpret the situation as critical. By doing so, he defined the issue to be whether the committee was ready to share this reinterpretation. The ensuing discussion was a negotiation among the members about how far to follow Bernanke's interpretive lead.

Although few members were willing to follow the chairman in using the word "crisis" to define the existing situation, several members echoed Bernanke's implicit claim that the contagion narrative was ascendant. The narrative was elaborated with increasing force, using words like "fear" and "panic" to describe the psychological dynamics in the marketplace.

DON KOHN: We have a vicious cycle in housing between the financial markets and the housing markets, where the decline in the housing markets is feeding into the credit markets, which is feeding back on the housing market . . . I agree that the equity markets per se aren't our goal, but declines in equity prices destroy wealth. I think they are symptomatic, as you indicated, Mr. Chairman, of a fear and a declining confidence in where this economy is going.[5]

KEVIN WARSH: First, during the discussions on this call, we have described these financial markets as fragile. That strikes me as rather euphemistic for what we have been witnessing really since the first of this year, particularly what is being witnessed overseas today. . . . Panic appears to be begetting further pullbacks by investors, retail and institutional alike. There seems to be continued interest in the safest currencies, and this pullback strikes me as quite non-discriminate, geographically and in terms of sectors, companies, and even entire asset classes.[6]

The rhetorical intensification of the contagion narrative could be expected to have implications for expectations about the continued growth of the economy. This, in turn, would suggest a revision of the growth narrative. Once again Bernanke took the lead in reinterpreting the cues to project a more dire narrative: "The data and the information that we can glean from financial markets reflect a growing belief that the United States is in for a deep and protracted recession," he said.[7] Janet Yellin came closest to supporting this redefinition of growth potential. She framed her interpretation in terms of increased risk: "I think the risk of a severe recession and credit crisis is unacceptably high," she said, "and it is being clearly priced now into not only domestic but also global markets."[8] Eric Rosengren, using anecdotal evidence, seemed to share the redefinition, noting, "It is widely viewed in the business community that we are slipping into a recession. Problems with consumer debt are growing. I am concerned not only that we might be in, or about to be in, a recession. I am concerned also how severe a recession could be."[9]

But a revision of the growth narrative did not go unchallenged. In fact, it was not widely accepted. The staff, both in Washington and at the regional banks, was still forecasting that the economy would avoid recession. Most members were still not ready to get ahead of these forecasts and avoided the word recession. Richard Fisher, characteristically, was quite explicit in rejecting the claim for a protracted or severe recession:

I am only about 30 percent of my way through my CEO calls in preparing for the (regularly scheduled) meeting. I don't hear a widespread expectation of recession. I do hear a concern about slowing down, and we have seen that in all of the indexes that I like to talk about in the meetings from the credit card payables, delinquencies in payments, the Baltic index, et cetera, et cetera. But the words "severe recession" I have yet to hear from the lips of anybody but those in the housing business, and for them, it gets more severe with each passing moment.[10]

The scarce use of the word "recession," if not its outright rejection, suggests that members were not willing to accept Bernanke's revision of the growth narrative and did not share his concern for a protracted recession. In fact, many members were still worried about inflation and Bernanke agreed that these were "valid concerns."[11] But the members had accepted that financial contagion was the immediate problem and that action was needed to inhibit panic in financial markets. The largest part of the policy discussion, matching narratives with action, was taken up with a debate about how the financial markets might interpret the action being suggested by the chairman.

Framing a Solution

Bernanke stated his policy recommendation early in the conference call. "I think we have to take a meaningful action—something that will have an important effect. Therefore, I am proposing a cut of 75 basis points. I recognize that this is a very large change. I would not do that if I thought that the size of the cut was inconsistent with our medium-term macroeconomic objectives."[12] His initial framing or justification for this aggressive action was that they had only lowered the fed funds rate 100 basis points, from 5.25 to 4.25 percent, since they began lowering it in September 2007. This, he believed, was not yet an accommodative position for monetary policy. It was not really making a dent in the contagion nor was it supporting the macroeconomic objective of growth. "Importantly, of course, we have lowered the funds rate only 100 basis points so far," Bernanke said, "so I think at first approximation we are about 100 basis points *behind the curve*—something in that general area—in terms of the neutral rate, and that itself doesn't even take into account what I believe at this point is a legitimate need for risk management."[13] This assertion that they were "behind the curve" was a provocative rhetorical strategy for coaxing action. It was time to catch up with the declining conditions in markets.

Since most members did not see recession as an immediate threat, there was little discussion of the broader economy. Most of the discussion about Bernanke's recommendation did not focus on macroeconomic objectives but on the financial markets and the spreading contagion. The concern was about how the financial markets would interpret the move. The justification given for immediate action was to inhibit the panic by reassuring markets that the Fed was, in the Chairman Bernanke's words, "in touch with the situation."[14] As Tim Geithner put it, "Conditions are so fragile and so tenuous now that by not acting tomorrow morning we would be taking an irresponsible risk that we would see substantial further erosion in confidence."[15] The argument was that immediate and dramatic action might change market psychology. As Dennis Lockhart put it, "I think the psychology here is bordering on, shall we say, a spiral quality. A preemptive move like this—preemptive on two dimensions, the rate dimension and the timing dimension—has a shot at changing the overall psychology of the moment."[16]

Nevertheless, there was significant skepticism that the move was necessary, predominantly among the presidents of regional Reserve Banks. The skeptics were focused on future expectations about the actions of the Fed if conditions continued to decline. They invoked a deeply held cultural trope that monetary policy was not designed to "rescue" financial markets but to stabilize the wider economy. The Fed famously resisted responding to the stock market Crash of 1929 to avoid "bailing out" irresponsible speculators. A response to market declines in January 2008 elicited similar concerns. The skeptics identified two related problems. The first was the problem of frequency. Would the markets expect a response to every jolt in the market? The second was a problem of reputation. What drives Fed policy: financial markets or the wider economy?

WILIAM POOLE: First of all, whenever we act between meetings, we set a precedent, and what this will do in the future, maybe even in the very near future, is that whenever we have a stock market decline of this magnitude, if we get some more of them—and we could easily—or whenever we have some bad economic data—and we certainly could have some—there will be speculation in the market as to whether the FOMC is going to jump in with an intermeeting policy action. So we have to be confident in our own minds that we are not setting a precedent that we will live to regret.[17]

JEFFREY LACKER: Like President Poole, I have real reservations about moving now rather than waiting until our meeting. I think that in the situation this is inevitably going to be viewed as a reaction to the falloff in equity markets. . . . I worry about the message that this tactical choice sends about our strategy. I worry about what it says about what drives our reaction function and what we believe that we can control or offset.[18]

CHARLES PLOSSER: I am very concerned that we are going to be interpreted as reacting to the stock market declines, and I think my concern is that lowering the funds rate terribly rapidly with intermeeting moves is going to set up a dynamic that is going to drive us into more and more of these and drive the markets into expecting more and more from us. It is not clear to me that the fragility that exists in the market in fact will be solved by rapid cuts in the funds rate.[19]

This policy discussion reflected fundamental differences among members on the appropriate degree of Fed activism. The interventionists favored immediate action to inhibit the effects of the financial turmoil. The skeptics, only one of whom was a voting member at this meeting, resisted action based on a slippery slope argument about market expectations. The concern of the skeptics, as it was at the time of the Great Depression, was about giving financial market actors the impression that the Fed would bail them out of their failed risks. The activists were more concerned with contagion from these markets to the wider economy. Echoing American political ideology, the participants were divided on the appropriate role for the state in economic management. With the interpretation of "crisis" in a liminal state, the justification for action was contested terrain and group learning was inhibited.

Learning as Reproduction

In the end, the vote was 8 to 1 to support the chairman's recommendation for a 75-point reduction in the fed funds rate.[20] The skeptics, having expressed their concerns, were mostly willing to get out in front of the spiraling panic and show a united front. So, what can we say was learned by the FOMC? Learning by the individual members of the Committee is a cognitive process involving inquiry, information processing, and interpretation. The transcript suggests that the members had been processing and interpreting large amounts of disturbing information in the weeks before the meeting. But this sidesteps whether the group itself changed how it discussed and defined the situation.

To show signs of learning, the group must indicate significant reformulation of its policy reflecting the changed and turbulent conditions. But the group does not have a brain to do the processing. Rather, it moves its collective definition of the situation by negotiating over the meaning of cues and by renegotiating narratives. This group learning is not cognitive but social. The group is redefining the meaning of certain key artifacts, such as the inflation rate, the growth forecast, and the fed funds rate.[21] They are not negotiating the numbers themselves—those are already given. They are negotiating what meaning they will attribute to those numbers in the context of policymaking. They are negotiating the plausible causal reasoning behind the narratives that guide policy.

In the January conference call, Ben Bernanke opened the negotiation with an effort to redefine the existing cues and narratives in a fairly radical way as he attempted to classify the contagion as a crisis in which they might "lose control of the whole situation." The members' willingness to support a 75-basis-point cut in the fed funds rate between meetings suggests that the contagion had been redefined as imminent. In this interpretation, a "vicious cycle" was in motion and "panic" in financial markets was spreading.

But even as Bernanke raised the threat of disorder (loss of control), the dialogue repeatedly returned to issues associated with the normal order of things. In framing a solution, a policy to match the emerging narrative, members countered Bernanke's efforts with concerns about precedent, market expectations, and reputation. The members were still more concerned with reproducing the normal order than transforming it. They were habituated to a shared sensemaking process that occurred at regular intervals, done in relatively small increments. The learning done in the conference call was *reproductive learning*, an adaptive updating of the contagion narrative and a matching policy that increased the amount of insurance they would take out against the narrative's implications. This learning reflected a shared understanding that they were "behind the curve." In this kind of learning, the FOMC measured the economic situation against a standard or norm and acted to maintain that norm. Adaptive learning is part of the routine of the FOMC. According to Bernanke, a 75-basis-point reduction in the fed funds rate would bring them to a neutral policy position, neither accommodative nor restrictive. This seemed a modest goal.

The alternative to reproductive learning, *transformative learning,* would interrupt the flow of existing routines and their standards and norms. It would question the validity of the norms. Such learning is more likely when the existing narratives are clearly inadequate to the situation or the system is seen as threatened with failure. Adaptive practices are unlikely to change unless they are severely challenged. The practitioners must be convinced that their practices are maladaptive in relation to some significant part of their institutional environment. Typically, a redefinition of appropriate practice must be available, sponsored, and persuasive. The FOMC was not ready for transformative learning. Such learning might have explored more aggressively Bernanke's attempted redefinition of a growth narrative that was still based on avoiding recession.[22] This exploration might have foreseen how the interconnectedness of the financial crisis and the wider economy could lead to a "protracted" and "severe" event.

JANUARY 29–30, 2008

Contradictory Cues

After Chairman Bernanke opened the regularly scheduled January meeting, Bill Dudley gave the FOMC members his overview of economic conditions. He described one of the few things everyone could agree on: a widening contagion. The turmoil was no longer limited to subprime mortgage markets or even declines in global stock markets. The consequences were now firmly felt in the provision of credit to both firms and individuals. This could be expected to inevitably affect investment and consumer spending.

BILL DUDLEY: The bigger story remains the continued pressure on bank balance sheets, the tightening of credit availability, and the impact of this tightening on the outlook for economic activity. The travails of the monoline financial guarantors—some of which have already been downgraded by one or more of the rating agencies—have exacerbated the worries about the potential for further bank writedowns.[23]

Despite the negative indicators, the forecasting models still had the US economy avoiding recession. Although conditions looked worse, the Fed staff and its regional bank staffs were unaware the economy was already in recession. They continued to foresee moderate growth. As David Reifschneider, associate director of the Fed's Division of Research and Statistics, told the members, "As you know, we are not forecasting a recession. While the model estimates of the probability of recession have moved up, they are not uniform in their assessment that a recession is at hand."[24] Summarizing the forecasts of the twelve regional banks, staff economist Brian Madigan told them, "Looking ahead to next year, your forecasts indicate that you expect economic growth to pick up as the drag from the housing sector dissipates and credit conditions improve. . . . Your growth forecasts for next year are mostly above the staff's forecast of 2.2 percent."[25]

Later in the meeting, Randall Kroszner called the rosy forecasts into question. He did this in the context of the historic difficulty the forecasters and the FOMC had predicting the turn in the economy from expansion to contraction and the absence in the predictive models of key financial indicators.

> Our models have never been successful at assessing turning points, and that is true whether they are the typical linear models, nonlinear models, probit models, Markov switching models, or other things like that. We sort of know once we've switched, but it's hard to get that transition. As many people have suggested, there are an awful lot of indicators that would go into those kinds of models that would flash for contraction being likely. I think that is correct, but that makes it very difficult for us to assess what will happen.[26]

Governor Kroszner is telling his colleagues that their understanding of the economy's transition from growth to contraction is based on statistical models that have never been satisfactory predictors. This is reminiscent of Janet Yellen's and David Stockton's remarks in the September 2007 meeting, noting that Fed models did not take into account the shocks to the financial markets and how they might feed through to the larger economy. As we have seen, learning at the FOMC is based in the redefinition of cues and narratives, the central artifacts of the culture. Learning that the economy has transitioned—that it is in a downturn—is based on cues that are famously unreliable. Yet, trust in data is what allows economic policy committees like the FOMC to operate. It is part of every central banker's identity and tends toward persistence. Without it, analysis would be impossible. It is this persistence and the contradictions between cues that make learning so difficult at transitional moments.

Among the cues discussed on January 29 were an unusually high number of anecdotes brought by members of the Committee based on their personal contacts. These contacts are mostly business groups and business leaders with whom the members communicate during the six weeks between FOMC meetings.[27] Although PhD-trained economists are not supposed to credit anecdotes based on a small sample of opinions with much significance, these anecdotes are often more current than the statistics gathered by the staff. They reflect the expectations and plans of firms for the near future in a way that retrospective statistics cannot.[28] Anecdotes, therefore, carry valued information that is unavailable in staff statistics. This suggests a paradox in which the Fed technocrats are trying to be scientific but are compelled by the informational limits of data to be less systematic. As Jeffrey Lacker put it, "One can be skeptical about the incremental value of anecdotal reports in typical times, but at times like these, I believe they can and do provide a more timely read on what is going on."[29]

> SANDRA PIANALTO: Taken as a whole, the stories that have been relayed to me by my Fourth District business contacts have been downbeat, and several of the contacts are concerned that we may be slipping into a recession. I'm hearing that consumer spending has declined appreciably since the soft December retail sales numbers were reported.[30]

> JANET YELLEN: My contacts have turned decidedly negative in the past six to eight weeks, and further financial turmoil may still ensue. On consumer spending, two large retailers report very subdued expectations going forward following the weak holiday season, which involved a lot of discounting. On hiring and capital spending, my contacts have emphasized restraint in their plans due to fears that the economy will continue to slow.[31]

Richard Fisher challenged the value and use of the negative anecdotes offered by his colleagues:

> Basically, what we are doing at this time of transition is almost cheating on the data by looking at the anecdotal evidence. . . . The point is that, while there are tales of woe, none of the 30 CEOs to whom I talked, outside of housing, see the economy trending into negative territory. None of them at this juncture . . . see us going into recession.[32]

The use of competing and contradictory cues, both statistical and anecdotal, suggests that the transition to crisis is a moment when order and disorder are being juxtaposed.[33] The meaning of key artifacts is in question and their meaning for policy is contested. It was hard for members to know whether they should be guided by expectations for continued growth or for a contraction produced by the financial shock. The narrative construction phase of the meeting contested precisely these questions.

Dissonant Narratives

Advocates of the contagion narrative became increasingly confident by the end of January. At the same time, their accounts of the contagion varied in plot details and continued to be stated as projected concerns rather than as existing facts. They discussed a process of social hysteria whose trajectory into the wider economy was not well understood. Nevertheless, for these members, the hope that investors would come into the markets restoring stability had become dimmer. Dennis Lockhart knit anecdotal evidence into his contagion narrative:

> I made a number of calls to financial market players, and my counterparts cited a variety of concerns relevant to overall financial stability. . . . (One) also indicated that, even though there are real money investors—as he called them—interested in return to the structured-finance securities markets but currently on the sidelines, they are reluctant to expose themselves to volatility that arises . . . in such illiquid markets. These anecdotal inputs simply point to the continuing uncertainty and risk to financial stability with some potential, I think, for self-feeding hysteria.[34]

An alternative form of the contagion narrative was tied more specifically to the housing market and its relationship to the wider economy.

> ERIC ROSENGREN: While our forecast assumes a gradual decline in real estate prices, it does not have a substantial feedback between rising unemployment rates causing further downward pressure on real estate prices and the health of financial institutions. Were we to reach a tipping point of higher unemployment, higher home foreclosures, increased financial duress, and falling housing prices, we would likely have to ease far more than if we were to act preemptively to insure against this risk.[35]

The disorder projected by these contagion narratives was countered and outweighed by the optimism of the growth narrative across the policy group. As in the contagion narratives, the causal mechanisms in the plots of the growth narratives differed, although they all purported to explain why the economy might slow but not stall in response to the financial turmoil: Firms would not cut spending drastically, other national economies would stay strong, and restoration was already under way. All three examples below reflect the self-repairing imagery that is at the heart of the restoration narrative. At this point in the ongoing narrative construction, the restoration and growth narratives have merged. Growth will continue because of the repair and adjustments in the financial markets. This economic logic seemed, to some of the members, a bit forced, an obligatory faith in market efficiency. The overall impression is of economic policymakers, as Frederic Mishkin put it, "trying to be cheery."[36]

CHARLES EVANS: I expect that we will eke out positive growth in the first half of 2008. This expectation largely reflects the judgment that businesses have not begun to ratchet down spending plans in the nonlinear fashion that characterizes a recession. . . . For the second half of 2008, I see growth increasing toward potential by year-end. . . . In addition, the financial system should continue to sort through its difficulties, making further headway in price discovery and repairing capital positions.[37]

TIM GEITHNER: Let me just start by saying it's not all dark [*laughter*].

FREDERIC MISHKIN: Don't worry; be happy?

TIM GEITHNER: I'm going to end dark, but it's not all dark. The world still seems likely to be a source of strength. You know, we have the implausible kind of Goldilocks view of the world, which is it's going to be a little slower, taking some of the edge off inflation risk, without being so slow that it's going to amplify downside risks to growth in the United States. That may be too optimistic, but the world still is looking pretty good. . . . In the financial markets, I think it is true that there is some sign that the process of repair is starting.[38]

WILLIAM POOLE: I'm very much of the view that the natural state of the U.S. economy is full employment and output growth at potential. That's where the economy tends to gravitate, and firms and markets respond relatively quickly on the whole to shocks. . . . Firms and markets are making many necessary adjustments. Housing starts are down. House prices are falling, which I think they have to do. Banks are raising more capital. Risk spreads are rising from abnormally low levels, and lots of other kinds of adjustments are occurring that need to be made and are ongoing.[39]

If the construction of both the contagion and growth narratives seems multivocal, arriving at the same conclusion with slightly different reasoning, the negotiation of the inflation narrative is more like a dual over competing stories. These stories reflect not only different readings of the inflation cues but different theories of market operation. According to the dominant theory in the group, based on the concept of market discipline, the slowing economy will keep pressure for price increases under control. As Frederic Mishkin explained, "Given that inflation expectations plus expectations about future slack in the economy are the primary drivers of inflation dynamics, I actually think that inflation will come down."[40] Stated more assertively and technically by Don Kohn, "Greater slack in resource utilization and product markets should discipline increases in costs and prices."[41]

The alternative logic was that inflation would not come down on its own as slack increased in the economy; that it required the raising of interest rates by the Fed. This reflects the idea that inflation will rise only if the Fed allows it to rise.[42] In this view the Fed must inhibit inflation and the expectation of inflation. According to this logic, it is not market discipline but Fed discipline that is needed. Its adherents, the inflation hawks, seek to inhibit inflation before there is evidence for it. As Jeffrey Lacker put it, "I am not optimistic about inflation coming down in a sustained way on its own. As a result, I believe that, in order to keep expectations from drifting up and to bring inflation down, we will need to raise rates later this year, even if that means a longer and slower recovery."[43] This concern is exacerbated by the inflation hawks' skepticism about their colleagues' willingness to reverse course—that is, raise interest rates expeditiously. As William Poole explained, "I think that we are at risk that inflation expectations might rise. We monitor them closely, but once we start to see inflation expectations rising, it's going to be difficult and costly to rein them in. It's going to create a big problem for us."[44]

These competing narratives reflect a long-standing conflict between inflation hawks and inflations doves. Maintaining price stability, or fighting inflation, is at the core of the central bankers' identity. Most central bankers in the world do not have a dual mandate to maintain both growth (maximum employment) *and* price stability. The Fed has been accused of favoring the price stability side of its mandate and at least since the high inflation of the

1970s, it has been hypervigilant in that regard. In this meeting, the strongest inflation hawks included Governor Warsh and Reserve Bank presidents Plosser, Lacker, Poole, and Fisher.

Chairman Bernanke, in summarizing the policymakers' statements, credited both narratives:

> Everyone has talked about inflation, as should be the case. I am also concerned. The pickup in core inflation is disappointing. . . . The hope is that energy and food prices will moderate; in fact, if oil prices do rise by less than the two-thirds increase of last year, it would obviously be helpful. Nominal wages don't seem to be reflecting high inflation expectations at this point. So I think there are some reasons for optimism.[45]

A Bipolar Solution

As one might expect, after the contentious narrative construction phase of the meeting, the policy discussion was similarly dissonant. The members gave clear justifications for their favored policy solutions, but their foci of attention were different. For most members, the financial turmoil was generating cues that made the recession narrative salient, calling for easing. For other members, the Fed's easing itself, the prior easing of interest rates, was the cue to activate anti-inflation vigilance. Staff economist Brian Madigan laid out the basic conundrum facing the FOMC, recognizing both positions:

> Although aggressive policy easing would help mitigate economic weakness, it would also raise the risk that policy could add unduly to inflation pressures should recessionary weakness not develop, . . . [and] the cost of an aggressive near-term easing in the *absence* of a recession could be limited if policymakers were to recognize quickly that the economy was not weakening to the degree feared and boosted the federal funds rate rapidly.[46]

The policy discussion developed precisely along the lines suggested by Madigan. Some members expressed an explicit fear that further easing, even in the midst of a slowing economy, would lead to inflation. Other members, the supporters of further easing, framed their argument in terms of risk reduction in the face of financial instability. They argued that a further lowering of the fed funds rate was needed to "catch-up" with the state of the economy and to provide more insurance against further financial

64

shock. The supporters of this position, including Don Kohn, saw the financial situation as a greater risk than inflation at this point:

> In these circumstances, we need to concentrate on addressing the economic and financial stability issues that we're facing. That's the bigger risk to economic welfare at this time than the risk that inflation might go higher, and the 50 basis points in my mind is just catching up with the deterioration in the economic outlook and the financial situation since the end of October. We are just getting to something that barely takes account of what has happened, with very little insurance.[47]

Some supporters of the catch-up frame felt even more strongly than Kohn that the Fed should go further in easing its policy. Janet Yellen explained, "We need to be absolutely clear, to state clearly today, that we recognize the continued existence of downside risk and communicate that we stand ready to cut further if necessary. . . . Today's move and the intermeeting move are essentially catch-up."[48] Several members made the argument that a 50-basis-point reduction in the fed funds rate would *only* bring them to a neutral position, neither restrictive nor accommodative. These members argued that it was time to take the financial situation and its potential consequences a bit more seriously. As Frederic Mishkin put it, "So all else being equal, I would actually advocate a 75 basis point cut at this meeting because I do think there is a need to take out insurance. . . . I think that insurance is warranted, and I get nervous that we are not getting sufficiently ahead of the curve."[49]

The counterargument to the catch-up frame came from the inflation hawks. They echoed concerns that further easing would fuel inflation and require a rapid reversal by the FOMC, a reversal the Committee members might be hesitant to make. The argument was supported by the claim that the asset bubble in housing was caused by the Fed holding interest rates too low for too long in the early part of the decade. As Thomas Hoenig said, "To stimulate the economy further at our current inflation rate is to invite, or at least to increase the probability of, higher inflation or encourage the next asset bubble or both, and it will undermine our credibility in the long run."[50] Charles Plosser elaborated this theme repeatedly and emphatically throughout the meeting:

> Lowering rates too aggressively in today's situation would seem to me a risky strategy, fueling inflation; possibly setting up the next boom-bust

cycle, which I worry about; . . . I think we need to be very cautious not to get carried away in our insurance strategies with lowering rates too much. In my view, we are on the verge of overshooting, and I worry about the broad range of consequences for our credibility and the expectations of our future actions such behavior may have.[51]

The competing frames left more than a few members conflicted. Kevin Warsh tried to see both sides: "There are clearly risks on both sides of the mandate, and for folks who are of differing opinions, I don't think that they would either deny the tough spot we're in or say that we have a lack of worries on either side."[52] Other members were equally unsure. Jeffrey Lacker, Charles Evans, and Tim Geithner all talked about the need for humility in the face of the choice. Dennis Lockhart used humor to characterize the opposed interpretations of the Committee:

> I've heard cogent arguments that 50 basis points would be restrictive and likewise accommodative. Yesterday I had a chance to look at the disabilities-related display in the elevator lobby on the Concourse Level, and I took some comfort in the fact that many great people are or were bipolar. So whether it's restrictive or accommodative, I can be convinced either way.[53]

In the end, most of the inflation hawks, who were presidents of regional Reserve Banks, were not voting members of the FOMC in 2008. With only one dissenting vote, Richard Fisher, the FOMC voted to continue in its accommodative direction, lowering the fed funds rate another 50 basis points to 3.0 percent.

Contested Logics of Control

As discussed in the Introduction, monetary policy in the United States has passed through three modes of control: market control, bureaucratic control, and technocratic control. Technocratic control refers to the application of scientific ideas to the solution of administrative and policy problems.[54] The competing cues and dissonant narratives in the January 29 meeting reveal the paradoxical nature of technocratic control in this moment. The FOMC's action is intendedly rational and scientific, but the data and even the scientific principles are ambiguous. Some FOMC members believe that the slowing economy will inhibit inflation, others believe that only Fed action to raise interest rates can do that. Some believe that the contagion in financial markets will induce a recession, others believe that restoration through the action of efficient markets will lead to continued growth in the second half of 2008. Policymakers are caught between contested rationales for the operation of the economy. These rationales are the seedbed from which conflicting analyses germinate, providing competing narratives and competing solutions.

The Fed sits at the intersection of three institutional orders: the state, the market, and the profession of economics. There is a tension within the Fed over the balance between state and market logics as guides to technocratic policymaking. The Fed is an institution of the state, created by Congress and designed to pursue the societal values of price stability and maximum employment. To serve this mandate, it operates as a central bank that participates directly in the financial markets. It buys and sells large quantities of financial instruments in an effort to influence interest rates in the credit markets, makes short-term loans to banks at its discount window, and is a lender of last resort to banks and other financial institutions. It is an integral part of the markets for money and credit. Finally, the Fed is a creature of modern economics. Economists prepare the staff reports and policy options, almost all the members of the FOMC have PhDs in economics (see Appendix A), and the cues, narratives, and solutions are couched in the logics of economic theory. Much of the legitimacy of the Fed's policymaking comes from the members' ability to apply their expert and esoteric knowledge to their decisions.

Each of the institutional orders—the state, the market, and the profession of economics—are reflected in the technocratic tool kit that FOMC members bring to policymaking. Thus, the members construct interpretations from available institutional logics that offer a set of key organizing principles.[55] These logics are not uniform belief systems but rather a cluster of rationales to which each member of the FOMC has access. They guide both interpretation of the situation and behavioral practices. Members elaborate these logics as suggested by the prevailing situation. In January 2008, the strongest proponent of the state logic was the Fed chairman, Ben Bernanke. The master rationale of the state logic is the maintenance of order; it assumes that the Fed is both responsible and accountable for price stability and maximum employment. The state is deeply implicated in market stability. In Bernanke's interpretation, state logic, therefore, argued for strong action:

So long as house prices keep falling, we cannot rule out some extremely serious downside risks to our economy and to our financial system. We need to be proactive and forceful, not tentative and indecisive, in addressing this risk. Conveying the message that the Fed will be active and willing to mitigate tail risk is critical for achieving financial stabilization, which in turn is necessary for achieving economic stabilization.[56]

Bernanke was arguing not only that the Fed is responsible for maintaining economic stability, but that to fulfill this mandate the Fed needs to convince the markets that it understands the problem and that it is willing to act. As Tim Geithner explained, it is a matter of market participants' confidence in the abilities of the FOMC: "The scale of financial market fragility we now face, you could even say solvency in parts of the financial system, is a function of the confidence we create in our willingness to get policy to a point that provides meaningful protection against an adverse outcome."[57] According to this logic, markets must be confident that the state will play its role in maintaining order.

This argument about responsibility and the efficacy of state action extended to countering the inflation hawks' concern that the FOMC will not reverse its accommodative interest rate policy should inflation become a problem. Eric Rosengren, among others, countered the inflation hawks' argument, stating, "As a Committee, we seem to have consensus on the importance of maintaining low inflation rates, and I am confident we have the will to raise rates with the same alacrity that we reduced them, should economic conditions warrant such action."[58]

On the other hand, the market logic, in its purest form, is skeptical of the efficacy of the state and favors market solutions to market problems. The master rationale of market logic is the market's superior ability to restore equilibrium efficiently. As Charles Plosser explained, "I don't believe that enough time has elapsed for us to realize the full effect of the cuts that we have already put in place. I share President Hoenig's concern that *only the market* can solve many of the problems that we see out there, and we must give the market time and patience to do so."[59] Richard Fischer extends this argument, saying that the state is not capable of intervening effectively in the contagion problem: "When the market is in the depressive phase of what President Lockhart referred to as a bipolar disorder, crafting policy to satisfy it is like feeding Jabba the Hutt—doing so is fruitless, if not dangerous, because it simply will insist upon more."[60] Fisher takes the reasoning still further, arguing that the FOMC is itself becoming the problem, not the solution.

> My CEO contacts tell me that we're very close to the "creating panic" line. They wonder if we know something that they do not know, and the result is, in the words of the CEO of AT&T, Randall Stephenson, "You guys are talking us into a recession." . . . I'm going to quote Tim Eller, . . . who told me, "We had just begun to feel that we were getting somewhat close to at least a sandy bottom. Then you cut 75 basis points and add 'appreciable downside risks to economic growth remain' in your statement, and it scares the 'beep' out of us." He didn't use the word "beep."[61]

There is a conflict between the state and market logics that permeates FOMC sensemaking and policy. In times of crisis this conflict can be the arbiter of transformative learning. It is decisive in triggering state action and determining the scope of that action. In attempting to distinguish between these logics, Tim Geithner fell back on one of the ultimate questions of central banker identity: "What is our job?" Geithner reminded the competing factions of the mediating role of the central bank.

> As many of you said, markets have to go through a further set of adjustments, and I think that has to work through the system. *Our job*, again, is not to artificially interfere with that process or to substitute our judgment for what the new equilibrium should be in that context. *Our job* should be to make sure that adjustment happens without taking too much risk that it tips the financial system and the economy into a much more perilous state that would be harder for us to correct and require much more policy response.[62]

Members of the FOMC find themselves caught between state and market logics. The creation of the Fed was premised on the idea that the market and the state are interdependent. Nevertheless, members of the FOMC apply different interpretations of that interdependency. Those employing the state logic seem to see an interdependency of the state and the market in which the state tames the excesses of the market economy while the economy affords productivity and efficiency, supporting the state's legitimacy. It is in crises that these interdependencies become most obvious and the state logic of stability comes to the fore. Those more inclined to the market logic have a stronger faith in the market economy's ability to regulate itself. Even in turbulent times, they remain optimistic about the market's robust ability to restore equilibrium. They are more concerned with the Fed's vigilance in restraining the expansion of the money supply. These competing logics are more like rationales for action than scientific principles. They contain assumptions about the role of the state, the efficiency of the market, and the relationship between the two that go beyond scientific knowledge.

The competing logics reveal a differentiated culture that has been at the core of the Fed since its founding. They reflect a fundamental conflict over the competing priorities of employment and price stability. When the state logic is dominant, the Fed defines its responsibility broadly in terms of maintaining economic order. Economic growth or economic decline are the primary generators of action and recession is the primary nemesis. When market logic is dominant, then the Fed's responsibility is more limited.[63] It is the maintenance of price stability that is the primary concern, and inflation is the nemesis. In recent decades, when market logic was dominant in the political zeitgeist, it was only in the midst of crisis that the state logic could dominate.[64]

The competing logics echo the conflict discussed in this book's introduction between farmers and bankers in the nineteenth century. These logics were reflected in the compromise between Democrats and Republicans that produced the Federal Reserve Act in 1913. The conflict is still playing out in the technocratic era. Whereas clear material interests drove the beliefs of farmers and bankers, the technocrats' logics echo contemporary American politics in which beliefs about both the market and the state often seem imperfectly correlated or even decoupled from material interests. Rather, policymakers' positions reflect academic debates within economics between Keynesian and neoclassical theories.[65] The FOMC, with its cues, narratives, and solutions, is a creature of the professional logic of economics. The profession remains conflicted over the appropriate balance of market and state logics, and this affects the repertoire of narratives and policy tools of FOMC members, as we will see in successive chapters.[66]

A Learning Moment?

The logics described above are the most abstract components of the FOMC's cultural tool kit. They facilitate the translation of conventionalized cues into triggers for action. In theory, this action may be incremental and reproductive or substantial and transformative. In practice, it is usually incremental, based on minor modifications in the dominant narrative. The growth fore-cast, for example, is based on a forecasting model that is designed to capture incremental moves in a relatively stable economy. This, in turn, is shaped by a conventionalized market logic assuming that the market adjusts in minor increments toward or away from equilibrium. As several members of the FOMC have observed, the model does not capture the effect of the finan-cial shock on the wider economy. Members of the FOMC exploit the ex-isting cultural tools to refine their understanding of the situation in the in-terest of adaptive updating, a routine and measured response that is well designed for the normal fluctuations of the business cycle. But adaptive up-dating of cues and narratives is a barrier to the discovery of systemic prob-lems, reproducing the status quo and making it harder to enact the trans-formative meanings that Bernanke was suggesting. Reproductive learning is designed to maintain a stable equilibrium, a goal that will become increas-ingly difficult as the situation worsens.

4

Improvising in a Liquidity Crisis

MARCH 2008

This is a crisis, I admit, and I just want to make sure that we are
clear on what it is we are initiating here.

—THOMAS HOENIG, FOMC TRANSCRIPT, MARCH 10, 2008, 10

Conference Call: March 10, 2008

The opening quote suggests two sensemaking puzzles that the members of
the Federal Open Market Committee (FOMC) faced in March 2008. First,
are the members of the Committee ready to acknowledge that a crisis had
begun? As we have seen, the policymakers faced significant barriers to such
recognition. Second, what kind of action is called for in dealing with such a
situation? The acknowledgment of crisis generally calls for transformative
learning—a questioning of existing assumptions that provokes inventive action. As to the first question, Hoenig's admission reflects a set of cues that
were like flashing red warning lights in the policy environment. Primary
among these cues were the deterioration in financial markets and the resulting shortage of cash for financial institutions to pay off their creditors and
cover their losses. This shortage of cash exemplified a liquidity crisis. Banks
and investment firms that employed a large number of mortgage-backed
securities as collateral for short-term funding were particularly short of
cash. Some of these short-term markets—really, overnight loans—had become frozen as financial institutions became unwilling to accept the troubled
assets of other institutions as collateral. It is exactly this dynamic that was
about to bring down Bear Stearns, the nation's fifth largest investment bank.

The second question implied in Hoenig's admission asks whether the
acknowledgment of crisis called for a new form of action, one that went

beyond incremental adaptive updating and the reproductive learning of recent meetings. The action being contemplated was outside existing FOMC
routines and beyond prior sensemaking about the financial turmoil. It was
in the context of these questions that Chairman Bernanke called together
another unscheduled meeting of the FOMC via conference call to discuss
such action. He opened the meeting with a review of the most salient cues.

> BEN BERNANKE: Good evening, everybody. I am sorry, once again, to
> have to call you together on short notice. We live in a very special time.
> We have seen, as you know, significant deterioration in (short) term funding
> markets and more broadly in the financial markets in the last few days.
> Some of this is credit deterioration, certainly, given increased expectations
> of recession; but there also seem to be some self-feeding liquidity dynamics
> at work as well. So the question before us is whether there are actions we
> can take, other than monetary policy, to break or mitigate this adverse
> dynamic.[1]

Bernanke described the liquidity crisis as a self-feeding cycle that needed
to be broken. He wanted to replace the fear on the part of short-term lenders
with confidence that borrowers would have access to cash. Failure to stem
the fear could result in a run on the borrowing institutions. Short-term loans
would not be renewed and other financial institutions would become reluctant to transact with the borrowers. The concern was that if a financial institution was forced to sell its stronger assets at fire-sale prices to cover losses,
then its liabilities might come to exceed its assets, making it insolvent and
in need of bankruptcy protection. Bill Dudley, a senior staff member, laid
out a revised contagion narrative—a narrative that was developing into a
crisis narrative. The crisis narrative added a plotline that projected the disruptive consequences of the contagion dynamic.

> If the vicious circle were to continue unabated, the liquidity issues could
> become solvency issues, and major financial intermediaries could conceiv-
> ably fail. I don't want to be alarmist, but even today we saw double-digit
> stock price declines for Fannie Mae and Freddie Mac. There were rumors
> today that Bear Stearns was having funding difficulties: At one point today,
> its stock was down 14 percent before recovering a bit.[2]

Don Kohn, a member of the FOMC who had just returned from a meeting
with European central bankers, described the crisis narrative he heard there.

It was quite similar to the one that Dudley had constructed. Janet Yellen glossed this narrative, drawing the conclusion that the financial system was threatened and clarifying what risks for the Fed might be involved.

DON KOHN: Liquidity has dried up in London and other European markets in particular, but elsewhere as well. There is really no price discovery. There is aggressive deleveraging and a flight to safety and soundness. . . . Liquidity and solvency were becoming intertwined. The dysfunction in the securities markets and the banking sector were intertwined, and there was just a very vicious spiral going on in many financial markets.[3]

JANET YELLEN: I certainly agree that we face a situation in which systemic risk is large, and it's escalating very quickly. . . . I think financial stability is truly at stake here, and although there are financial and reputational risks in pursuing this approach, it is a creative and well-targeted approach, and it is worth taking these risks to try to arrest the downward spiral in market conditions. . . . I think it is absolutely right to worry that liquidity problems are escalating into solvency problems.[4]

As a solution to this liquidity crisis, the Fed staff had developed, and Bernanke was proposing, two forms of action. The first increased "swap lines" to the European Central Bank and other foreign central banks, providing them with dollars in return for foreign currency. The need for the swap lines had been created by foreign banks that had borrowed in dollars to purchase US mortgage-backed securities. The foreign banks were now overextended. The swap lines allowed them to borrow dollars from their central banks to cover losses. The swap lines mostly created liquidity abroad but also supported the mortgage-backed securities market in the United States.[5]

The second and more innovative action was the creation of the Term Securities Lending Facility (TSLF).[6] The TSLF allowed an expansion of lending to a group of twenty financial firms known as the primary dealers. These were the five largest investment banks in the United States and fifteen commercial banks that regularly bought and sold Treasury securities with the New York Federal Reserve Bank. These firms needed Treasury securities to use as collateral in the short-term funding market. The TSLF expanded the amount of Treasury securities the dealers could borrow from the Fed by extending the forms of collateral the Fed would accept to include

AAA-rated mortgage-backed securities. It also extended the loans from overnight to twenty-eight days. The firms could use the Treasury securities as collateral in the short-term funding markets, and the Fed hoped that this injection of liquidity would, in turn, extend the banks' ability to lend.

Accepting as collateral the mortgage-backed securities written by private firms, in addition to those written by government entities like Fannie Mae and Freddie Mac, was not part of the Fed's normal operation. Neither was lending to investment banks, firms that were regulated by the Securities and Exchange Commission rather than the Fed. It required the invocation of section 13(3) of the Federal Reserve Act. Section 13(3) had been added to the Federal Reserve Act in 1932 as part of the response to the Great Depression. It allowed the Fed to lend to virtually any borrower if the circumstances were "unusual and exigent." There were three conditions attached to this emergency power. First, there had to be evidence that the borrower could not secure a loan from any private institution. Second, at least five of the seven members of the Board of Governors of the Fed had to vote in favor of such action. Finally, the loan had to be "secured to the satisfaction" of the lending Reserve Bank, in this case the New York Federal Reserve, meaning that the borrower's collateral was sound enough that the Fed could realistically expect to collect on the debt.

The invocation of section 13(3) was a critical moment in the Fed's response to the financial crisis. The TSLF was an innovative policy response that recognized the "unusual and exigent" situation and employed a tool that had not been used in seventy-two years. The rapid deterioration in the mortgage-backed securities market and its effect on short-term funding for those commercial and investment banks with large portfolios of these assets required immediate action. Bill Dudley justified the unusual measure to the FOMC members in the typical measured tones of a central banker:

> The staff believes that it is important to take this additional step because the level of dysfunction in the non-agency mortgage-backed securities market is pronounced, this market is large, and steps to improve market function in this asset class are likely to have positive consequences for the availability and the cost of mortgage finance. In other words, improvement in this area would make monetary policy more effective and would likely generate significant macroeconomic benefits.[7]

Dudley's framing of the need for action suggests a break in the operating norms of central banking. The standard routines of monetary policy were interrupted by the dramatic failure of the market mechanism, the matching of buyers and sellers, in a significant market. The TSLF was the transformative response, the creative enactment of a rarely invoked identity: lender of last resort. Dudley was also making the case that dysfunction in the mortgage-backed securities market was serious enough to be highly consequential for the liquidity of interconnected institutions. Members understood that the failure of these markets left many large financial institutions with a shortage of cash, exactly the kind of shortage that leads to a panic. Many members expressed the hope that the TSLF would help to arrest the accelerating downward spiral described in the contagion/crisis narrative. Thus, the liquidity and solvency issues among the primary dealers were enough to define the situation as a crisis, a major rupture in normal conditions. A smaller number shared Dudley's hope that it might reduce the need for further monetary easing. As Charles Evans put it, "I hope that, after these actions, market conditions might improve somewhat so that ultimately fewer adjustments in the funds rate might be called for. If so, then it's possible that the inflation risks that come with those adjustments might be more limited."[8]

But FOMC members' support for the unusual and exigent action was not without reservation. They exhibited two major concerns with the proposed initiatives: proper authority and risk. The first was expressed tentatively but early in the conference call by a question from Thomas Hoenig. "If I understand this, the ability to go outside our normal collateral . . . is based upon section 13(3) in the Federal Reserve Act. Am I right on that?"[9] The invocation of section 13(3) began to be referred to as "crossing a line." Members were aware that their action might be viewed in the markets as setting a precedent, creating the expectation of further action. They were intervening in troubled markets and coming to the aid of those primary dealers, especially investment banks, most invested in the mortgage-backed securities market. Randall Kroszner characterized the discomfort that was being more widely expressed:

Are we crossing certain lines? Are we going a bit further than we might feel comfortable doing? Those questions are very serious ones, and the questions that have been raised about the program are quite valid. But given the conditions in the market and, at least as far as I'm concerned, the clear connection between solvency issues and liquidity issues and the fact that the only way we have to get indirectly at the solvency issues is through these liquidity provision mechanisms, I think that we should go forward with something like this.[10]

Both Tim Geithner and Ben Bernanke tried to ease the concerns about authority and precedent. Section 13(3) authority had not been used since 1936. The largest such use at that time had involved a $300,000 loan to a typewriter manufacturer.[11] The TSLF initially made available as much as $200 billion. Would there be pressure to provide even more? Geithner admitted that he expected there would be, but that the crisis demanded such action.

> The important thing is that the Congress gave us the authority, although they may not fully have envisioned the world we live in today, to do a range of things to address these kinds of pressures. Not to use that authority in carefully designed, responsible ways because of the fear that we could not resist pressure to expand is not, in my view, a good argument not to do things that we think would be sensible in mitigating these pressures.[12]

Bernanke's response to the concern was to reassure members that these were indeed "unusual and exigent" circumstances. "The section 13(3) legal basis for this operation requires an affirmation that market conditions are significantly impaired," he said. "If we couldn't honestly make that affirmation, our legal basis would disappear"[13]

A second area of concern was over the risks that the Fed was taking in setting up the lending facility. There was a significant financial risk in accepting mortgage-backed securities as collateral given that they might continue to decline in value and never fully recover. Related to this concern was the risk of dealing with investment banks over which the Fed had no regulatory control and about which they had to depend on the Securities and Exchange Commission (SEC) for information because the SEC was the primary supervisor of the investment banks. The skepticism was expressed clearly by Randall Kroszner, who said, "We have pretty good relations with the SEC, but it's always different to be having good relations with the supervisor as opposed to actually being the supervisor or having the experience of supervising those institutions. So I think that is an important issue."[14]

Richard Fisher refined the concern. Given that the Fed did not regulate the investment banks, could it evaluate the risk it was taking and could it refuse access to the TSLF to one of them? Both Bill Dudley and Tim Geithner from the New York Fed attempted to address these concerns.

RICHARD FISHER: Do we have the capacity, for example, going back to your introductory comments on what happened in the markets, to evaluate Bear Stearns as a participant in this program and to say, "No, you can't participate"? If we did that, what would that do to Bear Stearns?

BILL DUDLEY: Well, the first thing is that almost all of these primary dealers have the SEC as their primary consolidated supervisor. So it is important to understand that it is not as though there isn't an entity looking at the financial strength and stability of these institutions. We have the right not to accept collateral from any of the primary dealers, should we decide to do that. It is not going to be public. We are not going to be making a statement. This is just going to be a bilateral arrangement between us and the given primary dealer.[15]

TIM GEITHNER: I agree that we face that risk. As many of us have learned over the past six to nine months, even the primary supervisors of these institutions have limits around their capacity to understand in real time what is actually happening. So we face that vulnerability—I agree with you—and that will limit, realistically, how much protection we are going to be able to take for ourselves in this context.[16]

Geithner's statement seems particularly revealing for the admission that the internal affairs of banks dealing in mortgage-backed securities and other related assets were opaque to their regulators and that their understanding of the actual level of risk involved was limited. This rather cryptic statement about primary supervisors gets to the heart of the regulatory failure associated with the mortgage-backed securities held by investment banks. The SEC, the regulator of investment banks, had insufficient capacity to understand what was going on inside those institutions. It was designed to monitor legal compliance rather than financial soundness and safety. The Fed, it seems, was dependent on the SEC and was operating in the twilight, if not in the dark. This was a design flaw in the regulation of investment banks whose consequences would become increasingly evident as the crisis evolved.

Despite their concerns about the investment banks and especially the weakest of the five, Bear Stearns, by the end of the conference call the FOMC members voted unanimously to support the proposed initiatives. The vote was 9 to 0 because two appointments to the Fed Board of Governors were held up in Congress and one member was not available on short notice. The Fed was about to make its first but not its last use of its section 13(3) authority in the financial crisis.

Improvising on a Theme by Bagehot

> In a panic the holders of the ultimate Bank reserve ... should lend to all that bring good securities quickly, freely, and readily. By that policy they allay panic; by every other policy they intensify it. The public have a right to know whether the Bank of England—the holders of our ultimate bank reserve— acknowledge this duty, and are ready to perform it.
>
> —WALTER BAGEHOT, 1873, IN BAGEHOT, *LOMBARD STREET*

The idea expressed in this quote has become known as Bagehot's Dictum. Bagehot, a nineteenth-century British economist and journalist, was laying out the principles by which a central bank, in this case the Bank of England, should operate as a lender of last resort, providing liquidity during a panic. According to Bagehot, in the midst of a financial panic, a central bank had the duty to lend by every possible means, even adopting new modes of lending, taking in forms of collateral it had never accepted before.[17] These modes must be consistent with the safety and soundness of the central bank, meaning that adequate collateral against the loan is secured from the borrower. It remains implicit that these tactics cannot be invoked until the moment a crisis is fully recognized.

Bagehot's Dictum was part of the culture of central banking and was used as an operating model by central bankers. In fact, both Geithner and Bernanke refer repeatedly to Bagehot in their published memoirs of the crisis.[18] But such a dictum is a vague model on which to manage a crisis. It says little about how one manages the lending, how one knows that it is time to employ the last resort, or how one deals with the issues of authority and risk. The TSLF was an improvisation on Bagehot's theme. It was elicited by the transformation of contagion into crisis. It reflected a change in the narrative that implied a breakdown or failure in the system. The chairman first gave the narrative voice, calling it a "self-feeding liquidity crisis." Don Kohn elaborated the crisis narrative saying, "There is really no price discovery" and "liquidity and solvency were being intertwined." In such a situation, the standard actions associated with monetary policy were insufficient. A continual lowering of interest rates would not restore price discovery in the markets, nor would it speak to the panic that was overtaking participants in the financial markets. Only an intervention of unprecedented dimension would match these conditions. As Don Kohn said, quoting a colleague in Europe, "Sometimes it's time to think the unthinkable and I think that time is here for us right now."[19]

As we have seen in earlier chapters, the FOMC employed a relatively standardized routine in most of its meetings. Its sensemaking process followed a pattern of identifying salient cues and constructing a narrative. Its policy actions reflect the identification of matching incremental solutions tied to that narrative. But in the March 10 conference call, the FOMC members were voting on a policy that was experimental and risky. They were compelled to improvise on a rarely used version of their authority as well as reevaluating their tolerance for new forms of risk. They were voting under pressure to counteract the cues of extreme instability in the financial markets. In switching from their role as monetary policymakers to lenders of last resort, they were obliged to be far more spontaneous and intuitive than usual.[20] Their discomfort with this improvisatory role was obvious, but they also seemed to understand that this lender-of-last-resort role was exactly why the Fed was created.

> DON KOHN: There are no guarantees that this will work. We're not addressing the solvency issues that are to a certain extent at the heart of this. But I do think liquidity and solvency are interacting in a particularly difficult and vicious way right now. To the extent that we have even a chance of breaking that spiral by intervening on the liquidity side—which is what the central banks are here for—and can help at least stabilize the situation, it may encourage the dealers to make markets.[21]

> BEN BERNANKE: So, there are different ways to look at this. We're crossing certain lines. We're doing things we haven't done before. On the other hand, this financial crisis is now in its eighth month, and the economic outlook has worsened quite significantly. We are coming to the limits of our monetary policy capability. . . . But right now I agree with Vice Chairman Geithner that this is probably the best option that we have, and it comes at a critical time in terms of where the markets are.[22]

In a policy group accustomed to the incremental movement of an interest rate target, even the TLSF's strongest advocates were uneasy. Not only was this improvisation risky and experimental, it reflected a dramatic change, nearly an inversion, in the theories guiding action since the August 2007 meeting, the starting point for this book. In the August meeting, the FOMC members voted to take no action because they believed that despite the turmoil in financial markets, these markets were highly efficient and they would restore themselves. As Don Kohn explained on the conference call, they had been forced by circumstances to give up on the restoration narrative:

> If I thought that price discovery was occurring in these markets, I would be hesitant to do anything that might interfere with it. But there isn't any real price discovery happening. So I don't think this is a case that, if we could only get out of the way, the markets would find their prices, and then the prices would be low enough, and people would step in, and price and liquidity would be restored. That's not what's happening. The markets just aren't operating.[23]

In fact, there was only one voice on the conference call willing to argue that the market was still functioning and that a lender-of-last-resort intervention was inappropriate at this point. Jeffrey Lacker, president of the Richmond Reserve Bank, was a nonvoting member of the FOMC in 2008.[24] Lacker's strong dissent was unambiguous.

> As all of you know, throughout this episode I have opposed measures using our balance sheet to attempt to arrest credit market developments, and so it will come as no surprise that I oppose, respectfully, this measure as well—and for similar reasons. These measures are all aimed, one way or another, at altering the relative prices of some financial claims. I think the burden of proof ought to be on those who are advocating such measures to provide evidence of some sort of market failure. I have yet to see a plausible case for market failure that would warrant such intervention by a central bank here.[25]

Lacker appears to be waiting for the market to restore stability. He continues to be guided by an economic logic in which the action of self-interested investors will restore equilibrium. But Lacker was a minority of one. Everyone else who spoke in the meeting agreed that the financial markets were in a liquidity crisis and that the role of a central bank in such a situation was to lend "boldly," as Bagehot prescribed.[26] For these members, the time had come for a state-based logic, in which the Fed takes responsibility for financial stability, to prevail. The conflict between the state's role and the market's role in resolving the crisis has been decided for the moment. The state, as represented by the central bank, was deemed the last resort for taming the market. As Thomas Hoenig, one of the inflation hawks, explained, "We are extending the safety net to a group with the goal of settling the markets . . . we have opened the safety net to a broader group for the purposes of managing this crisis."[27] Or, as Don Kohn described the Fed's responsibility, "We are in dysfunctional markets, and we have to try what we can to help them along."[28]

Crises often demand creative and innovative action. When the Fed finally recognized the situation as a classic liquidity crisis, it was transformative in its response. The threats to the liquidity and solvency of major financial firms were potent cues to these central bankers, a radical disruption in the system they were overseeing. There was near consensus on the appropriate action for central banks in that situation. They interrupted their monetary policy routines and enacted fluid roles as lenders of last resort. The form that action took was not fully scripted and it was not fully confident. The TLSF was an educated and creative leap of faith. The Fed, in early March 2008, was capable of designing and implementing such an improvisation. By the end of that week, its leaders would be called on to improvise even further, composing a Bagehot-themed solution in the moment.

The Bear Stearns Variations

Rumors about the instability of Bear Stearns, the smallest of the big five investment banks, began circulating on Wall Street and in the media on Monday, March 10, the day of the FOMC conference call. It was well known that Bear Stearns was a major participant in the mortgage-backed securities market. It ranked in the top-three firms underwriting these securities from 2000 to 2007.[29] It was also deeply exposed in the short-term funding markets. Unfortunately, the TSLF that had just been established in the conference call would not be up and running for two weeks. By Wednesday, March 12, Alan Schwartz, the CEO of Bear Stearns, went on CNBC to deny the rumors that lenders and counterparties were shunning his bank. Such protests tend to come too late and only make things worse. Bear's cash reserves fell from $18 billion on Monday to $12 billion on Wednesday. Lenders were refusing to renew Bear's short-term loans and counterparties in the derivatives markets were canceling contracts. By Thursday night, Bear was down to $2 billion in cash. It was the modern-day equivalent of an old-fashioned bank run, a liquidity crisis.

On Thursday night, Alan Schwartz called Tim Geithner, president of the New York Fed, to tell him that Bear might have to file for bankruptcy in the morning. He also called Jamie Dimon, the CEO of JPMorgan, to request a loan that would allow Bear to open on Friday morning.[30] Both Geithner and Dimon sent teams to Bear Stearns to assess its books.[31] By 2:00 a.m. they knew that Bear's books were full of toxic assets. At 4:00 a.m., Geithner's staff called him back into the office. The news had gotten even worse. Bear's failure would devastate the already fragile mortgage-backed securities market because Bear's lenders would unload its collateral, thereby depressing the price of Bear's securities as well as other borrowers' collateral. Also, Bear had 750,000 open derivatives contracts. Participants in these markets would not only lose confidence in Bear, but in any party that might have exposure to Bear. As Tim Geithner and Ben Bernanke both put it, Bear was "too inter-connected to fail."[32]

Tom Baxter, the general counsel at the New York Fed, proposed an idea that was designed to keep Bear Stearns from bankruptcy through the weekend while they searched for a buyer for Bear's assets. The New York Fed would make a loan to JPMorgan. JPMorgan would then lend the cash to Bear and the Fed would stand behind the loan. The general counsel in Washington added that they would have to invoke section 13(3) because, although they were loaning to JPMorgan, the loan was effectively for Bear. This was the first loan by the Fed to an investment bank. Geithner referred to Baxter's plan as "creative and intrepid."[33] It was a classic improvisation on Bagehot's Dictum.

Now that there was an arrangement to get Bear through Friday, Geithner and Secretary of the Treasury Henry Paulson told Alan Schwartz, the CEO at Bear, that he had until Sunday night, when financial markets opened in Asia, to find a buyer. JPMorgan was interested but wary of Bear's portfolio of mortgage-backed securities. On Saturday, JPMorgan's CEO, Jamie Dimon, said he was prepared to pay $8 to $12 per share for Bear's stock, but he withdrew the offer on Sunday morning.[34] JPMorgan had discovered that 75 percent of the assets were subprime or only marginally safer.[35] A deal was struck after marathon phone calls between Dimon, Geithner, Bernanke, and Paulson. The New York Fed agreed to lend JPMorgan up to $30 billion collateralized by Bear's assets, mostly mortgage-related securities. JPMorgan would buy Bear Stearns for $2 per share and would immediately stand behind Bear's obligations, even before the deal went through with the shareholders. JPMorgan accepted the deal because the Fed agreed to take on some of Bear's riskiest assets as collateral, accepting the risk of those assets and once again using its section 13(3) authority.

The sale of Bear Stearns did not end the liquidity crisis. Many of the other primary dealers also held large portfolios of mortgage-backed securities that were used as collateral in the short-term funding market. Late Sunday afternoon the Fed's Board of Governors voted to use its section 13(3) authority yet again by creating the Primary Dealer Credit Facility (PDCF). It allowed the primary dealers, especially the four largest surviving investment banks, to borrow from the Fed "just as commercial banks had always been able to do."[36] The acceptable collateral had been extended even beyond that accepted by the TSLF. The borrower got cash rather than Treasury securities, as it did with the TSLF. The objective was to interrupt the panic that was paralyzing the short-term funding markets. For the third time in a week, the Fed was improvising in a liquidity crisis.

The rescue of Bear Stearns from bankruptcy was justified by the phrase "too interconnected to fail." That is, the fallout from Bear Stearns for other major financial institutions could have a domino effect. The PDCF was a further acknowledgment that these institutions were interconnected and susceptible to the same system-threatening pressures. Lending boldly followed Bagehot's Dictum on how to contain a financial panic. The Fed's actions of early March 2008 provided a temporary backstop for those institutions, especially Lehman Brothers, whose capitalization was higher than Bear's but smaller than capitalization at Merrill Lynch, Morgan Stanley, and Goldman Sachs. The Fed had performed its role as lender of last resort. The state logic of order and stability had trumped the market logic of competition as a guide to sensemaking and intervention. The policymakers waited to see if the safety net worked and if the markets settled.

The March 18, 2008, Meeting: Contested Terrain

The reality is that we are in the worst financial crisis that we've experienced in the post–World War II era. I don't think we should be shy about saying it. . . . I will not use "financial crisis" in public. "Financial disruption" is still a good phrase to use in public, but I really do think that this is a financial crisis. It is surely going to be called that in the next edition of my textbook.

—FREDERIC MISHKIN, FOMC TRANSCRIPT, MARCH 18, 2008, 69

After the meltdown of Bear Stearns the previous week, there was little disagreement among FOMC members that the "disruption" was now a financial crisis, even though they were reluctant to label it publicly as such for fear of spreading panic. But when the group looked beyond the financial sector to the broader economy, its consensus dissolved. This was evident early in the meeting with the attempt to construct a consensus narrative. The members could agree on the existence of contagion, the increased chance of recession, and the rise in inflation expectations, but there was little agreement on the severity or scope of any these narratives. Even their relative significance was in contention.

The "unusual and exigent" circumstances of the previous week lent themselves to improvisation, but the making of monetary policy was more bound by the standard operating procedures we have observed in earlier meetings. The regularly scheduled meeting of the FOMC was a return to more routine monetary policy. Nevertheless, the failure of Bear Stearns could not be ignored. Bill Dudley addressed the elephant in the room right away in his report to the members. Later, Kevin Warsh generalized the problem to other investment banks that employed their capital in similar risky ways.

BILL DUDLEY: Before talking about what markets have been doing over the six weeks since the last FOMC meeting, I'm going to talk a bit about the Bear Stearns situation. In my view, an old-fashioned bank run is what really led to Bear Stearns's demise. But in this case it wasn't depositors lining up to make withdrawals; it was customers moving their business elsewhere and investors' unwillingness to roll over their collateralized loans to Bear. The rapidity of the Bear Stearns collapse has had significant contagion effects to the other major U.S. broker-dealers.[37]

KEVIN WARSH: Financial institutions, more broadly than financial markets, are having a hard time finding their way. . . . The old model, at least in investment banking, of high imputed leverage works incredibly well in a world of high liquidity and doesn't work as well when liquidity is in short supply. . . . These institutions are spending all their time and attention on their own business models, figuring out how they can survive this period, not on providing credit to the real economy. So I don't look to financial institutions to be very good shock absorbers or very good catalysts going forward.[38]

Warsh's statement is a prescient description of what was to come with the failure of Lehman Brothers and the massive loans to the nation's largest investment and commercial banks. Other members looked beyond the financial markets to contagion in the broader economy. Frederic Mishkin talked about an "adverse feedback loop" that was weakening the economy, and other members picked up on the phrase.

SANDRA PIANALTO: Pessimism over economic prospects is now prevalent among the CEOs that I talked with, and many are scaling back their business plans for 2008 by a considerable amount. The faltering business prospects are making the financial environment even more uncertain—a pattern that conforms to the adverse feedback loop that Governor Mishkin and others have been warning about.[39]

RANDALL KROSZNER: I've talked many times before about the slow burn from the financial markets that is spreading out elsewhere. Unfortunately, I think the fire is a bit hotter than I had expected in my earlier discussions, and it comes particularly through capital pressures in the financial institutions. What we're seeing now is the simultaneity of stress in the housing market and stress in the financial markets, . . . Whether we have tools to address those directly is something we continue to discuss, but I think it is this direct connection that potentially leads to the negative feedback loop that we have discussed quite a bit.[40]

BEN BERNANKE: We won't have a recovery until financial markets stabilize, and the financial markets won't stabilize until house prices stabilize, and there is simply no particular reason to choose a time for that to happen. So I do think that the downside risks are quite significant and that this so-called adverse feedback loop is currently in full play. At some point, of course, either things will stabilize or there will be some kind of massive governmental intervention, but I just don't have much confidence about the timing of that.[41]

Of course, these adverse feedback loops were worse than they imagined, and it *was* a "massive governmental intervention" that came to pass. But in March 2008, members held out hope that markets would steady and the staff shifted its forecast to recession, without great conviction. Despite the limited ability of the forecasting models to capture events in the financial markets, the macroeconomy did appear to be slowing. As staff economist David Stockton revealed, the reevaluation came with some doubt:

At this point, we've seen enough to make us think that recession is now more likely than a period of weak growth, and that is what we are forecasting. . . . I want to impress upon the Committee just how much this remains a *forecast* of recession; a lot has to happen that we haven't seen yet to be confident of this call.[42]

The construction of a recession narrative generated less accord than the contagion narrative's "adverse feedback loop." Members of the FOMC exhibited a range of recession narratives, from mild to severe, although all of them expressed a high degree of uncertainty.

JANET YELLEN: The bottom line is that, like nearly everyone else, I have downgraded my economic outlook substantially. Assuming that the stance of policy is eased substantially at this meeting and additionally by mid-year, I see the economy as essentially in recession during the first half before picking up somewhat in the second because of the effects of monetary and fiscal policy.[43]

GARY STERN: Well, the baseline forecast in the Greenbook looked to me a lot like the 2001 recession experience—very brief and very mild. If things turn out that way, we will have been very fortunate, frankly. The forecast I submitted at the last meeting was lower than most around the table, and now my bottom line is that I think the recession that, if we are not in, we are confronting is more likely to resemble that of 1990–91, which, while brief, wasn't that mild.[44]

ERIC ROSENGREN: The potential for a further episode of financial market dysfunction and for runs on additional financial firms is significant. My primary concern at this time is that we could suffer a severe recession. Falling collateral values and impaired financial institutions can significantly exacerbate economic downturns.[45]

Despite lengthy discussion, there was no real consensus on the scope of the recession they believed they were facing. The group was even further divided on the subject of inflation. Members saw immediate threat in the increasing expectations of inflation, but there was no agreement on the scope of the problem these expectations suggested. At one end of the spectrum were those who believed that the recession would take care of inflation expectations as firms and individuals spent less. As Charles Evans explained, "I think we're in a situation where this is most likely a recession. I expect that it will reduce pressures on inflation. That's my forecast. I think it's consistent with the earlier period, and it's hard to know exactly how much it will bring inflation down, but I think that it will lower inflation."[46]

Other members of the group saw inflation concerns and recession concerns as presenting the group with daunting alternatives. These members were responding to the rise of the inflation indicator above the Fed's 2 percent target and the expectation that inflation would continue to rise in 2008. As Frederic Mishkin described it, "My view in general is that we are facing an incredibly unpleasant tradeoff. We basically have the risk of the economy turning very sharply and the risk of inflation getting somewhat unhinged."[47] Tim Geithner characterized the tradeoff more acutely, stating, "We can't be facing both the most serious risk of a financial crisis and of a deep, prolonged recession in 50, 30, or 20 years and at the same time the risk of having a very substantial rise in underlying inflation over the medium term."[48] Both Mishkin and Geithner were clear that in a tradeoff between these risks, they preferred to deal with the risk of inflation rather than a prolonged recession.

The inflation hawks in the group were more protective of the credibility the FOMC had gained for maintaining price stability. In Fed jargon, expectations of inflation were "anchored." In theory, this anchoring was a result of the confidence the Fed had created in its determination to keep inflation down. Any loss of confidence could lead firms to raise prices. But, as the financial crisis compelled the FOMC to lower interest rates further as "insurance," the concern was that those expectations would become unanchored. As Thomas Hoenig put it, "I am increasingly concerned that, in our need to respond to signs of economic weakness, we risk losing our hard-won credibility on inflation."[49] Hoenig was expressing the view of the inflation hawks who saw the risks of inflation as not merely part of an unpleasant tradeoff, but rather as a result of misplaced priorities. The vigorous easing of the fed funds rate that began in September 2007 was seen as threatening the Fed's reputation for keeping inflation low—a reputation the Fed had lost in the 1970s, when most of the FOMC members were entering the profession, regained in the 1980s, and maintained ever since.

JEFFREY LACKER: I believe inflation expectations no longer qualify as well anchored. Moreover, they no longer seem consistent with the credibility of even a 2 percent inflation objective. I believe that this substantial erosion in our credibility is occurring because of our aggressive policy moves and the perception that the hierarchy of our macroeconomic priorities has changed.[50]

The charge of Fed culpability for unhinging inflation expectations was just too much for Tim Geithner. His response is unusual in its vehemence in a group that is notably restrained and affable. It is also an example of how carefully Fed officials try to control how firms and consumers interpret their actions.

> Some of you at this table may believe that we are losing credibility, and you may be losing confidence in the capacity of this Committee to mitigate the risk to our long-term inflation objectives. If you say that in public, you will magnify that problem, and just because you believe it does not make it true. I believe that you should have more confidence in the commitment of this Committee to do what is necessary to keep those expectations stable over time.[51]

When the FOMC members moved into the policy discussion, the justifications for a policy action that would match the situation were even more diverse than the explanatory narratives they had constructed. It was clear that the problems in housing and banking were creating a drag on the broader economy, but the estimates of risk varied widely. The advocates for a vigorous easing of the fed funds rate talked about the continuing risks across the economy. Bernanke supported lowering the rate from 3.0 to 2.25 percent, saying, "When I spoke about the downside risks in the Congress and in speeches, I cited three categories of risks: housing, finance, and labor markets. All of those have transpired in that direction. So I do think we have to respond effectively against that. For that reason I would recommend the 75 basis point reduction."[52] This concern with macroeconomic risks was reinforced by Don Kohn: "As long as the economy is weakening the way it is and we have these risks, that easing monetary policy will be helpful. . . . We need to ease to compensate for the substantial headwinds that we are facing."[53]

For Bernanke and Kohn, it was evident that the economy needed even easier access to credit. Lowering interest rates would facilitate that. Other advocates of a .75 easing of the funds rate returned to the insurance frame. These members were mindful of still-unforeseen threats in the financial markets that now seemed more likely since the failure of Bear Stearns.

> GARY STERN: There are a lot of things I don't know, and it's likely that some events are going to occur in the next couple of weeks or sometime in the future that may disturb things, and as a little insurance for that, 2½

would be a good idea. Well, those events—I'm talking about Bear Stearns and other disruptions—occurred sooner rather than later, so it seems to me that we need to go to 2½ and then ask ourselves whether we want some additional insurance. My answer to that is "yes."[54]

FREDERIC MISHKIN: I strongly support the Chairman's proposal. I should say, by the way, that even so, the 75 basis point cut, which I don't think takes out enough insurance, does pose some risk that long-run inflation expectations will rise. But we have to realize that there is a lot of risk of really bad things happening that could mean that things really get out of control. The discomfort is that we now have a tough tradeoff. But then, when I think about the tradeoff, I am willing to say that we have to take the risk because otherwise the consequences could be very problematic.[55]

The inflation hawks were, predictably, in opposition to the .75 percent easing. They rejected the cut in the fed funds rate with several arguments. Richard Fisher and Tim Geithner had a polite but contentious exchange on the efficacy of interest rate cuts as a response to the liquidity crisis. Fisher and others made the point that lower rates would not address the collapse in mortgage-backed securities and other related markets.

RICHARD FISHER: I don't believe, as Mr. Evans said, that monetary policy is addressing the root problem. . . . We are the water main, and yet the grass is turning brown. The water is not getting to the grass because the piping is clogged with all the hair and residue and all of the ugly stuff that has been building up in this Rube Goldberg piping device that we allowed to happen over a long period of time. I don't believe that cutting the fed funds rate addresses the issue.

TIM GEITHNER: Just to make sure that I didn't misinterpret you, did you say the efficacy of "any" further cut?

RICHARD FISHER: I think it is pretty clear that I am not going to vote for further cuts.

VICE CHAIRMAN GEITHNER: No further cuts.

MR. FISHER: At this juncture. Look, Tim, we cut rates 50 basis points last time. Everything that we wanted to go down went up, and everything that we wanted to go up went down. So I just wonder about the efficacy of the cuts as opposed to the measures that we have undertaken.[56]

Thomas Hoenig and Charles Plosser contended that the easing would stimulate inflation expectations and inflation itself. Hoenig argued, using the restoration narrative, that buyers must be given a chance to enter the market. Plosser argued that it was time to defend the Fed's reputation as an inflation fighter.

> THOMAS HOENIG: Two and a quarter will stimulate the economy forward and introduce other significant risks both to speculative activity and to inflation, and that's why I think we should be more careful in going forward. . . . There are a lot of people on the sidelines waiting for us to stop so that they can come in and take advantage of the situation.[57]

> CHARLES PLOSSER: Ultimately, if we wish inflation expectations to be well anchored, we must act in a way that is consistent with such an outcome. Words are simply not enough. Reputational capital, whether it be for a central bank, an academic institution, or the brand capital of a firm, is very hard to build. But most of us know, in the private sector and in other sectors, that capital can be easily squandered. We must not let that happen.[58]

The dramatic policy action contemplated in the immediate wake of the Bear Stearns failure had elicited strong emotions. But these emotions also accentuated the fundamental difference in views about the role of the Fed in the midst of the financial crisis. The chairman ended the meeting on a conciliatory note saying, "These are very, very difficult decisions. We are all people working in good faith, and we are all doing the best we can. I appreciate the candor and the honest comments, and we will continue to work together and to address these very, very difficult issues that we have."[59] The final vote was 8 to 2. Richard Fisher and Charles Plosser, the two inflation hawks with votes at this meeting, were in opposition to the reduction in the fed funds rate from 3.0 to 2.25 percent.

Insufficient Capacity?

If performance of the Fed's lender-of-last-resort role required improvisation, its monetary policy role in March 2008 was a variation on a more familiar tune.[60] In both cases, the Fed exhibited its capacities to deal with its immediate situation. These capacities included authority, financial resources, and knowledge, but most important, sensemaking or interpretive capacity—the ability to make sense of new information, assimilate it, and act on it.[61] This capacity was guided by the existence of policy ideas and practices that were embedded in the structure and culture of the Fed as a central bank.

The lender-of-last-resort identity, as represented in Bagehot's Dictum, provided a script for reacting to the liquidity crisis facing the largest investment banks. This crisis was quite different from the more gradual decline in the housing and mortgage-backed securities markets. The catastrophic consequences of a bankruptcy at Bear Stearns were unpredictable and frightening. The intolerable nature of those consequences was reflected in the phrase "too interconnected to fail." Although reproductive learning is the result of clear and regular feedback, transformative learning is often enabled by ambiguous, irregular, but highly threatening and often surprising information from the environment. The transformative learning observed here was triggered by menacing cues and the threat of an imminent liquidity crisis. The probability that such learning will occur is greatly enhanced by the importance of a culturally embedded identity, like lender of last resort, that offered a guide for the kind of innovative action that could be taken under such unsettled conditions.

The Fed's response to the liquidity crisis in financial markets in March 2008 can best be understood in the context of its growing authority and independence over the course of its history. As discussed in the Introduction, the Fed was founded primarily in reaction to the banking panics that plagued preindustrial America. It was created to step in as lender of last resort when banks would no longer lend to each other. In inhibiting panics, it was expected to create more orderly relations between the market and society, maintaining the social order by reducing market volatility and stabilizing prices. This worked in theory until it was tested by the banking crisis of the Great Depression, where it failed miserably.[62] According to Milton Friedman and Anna Schwartz, it was the Fed's failure to provide liquidity to banks that was to blame for the depth of that devastating contraction. As Ben Bernanke showed in his early research that built on Friedman and Schwartz, it was the cascading bank failures resulting from the Fed's reluctance to supply liquidity that was the most critical contributor to the depth of the Great Depression.[63] More recently, Allan Meltzer has specified that the Fed's ineptness is explained by an interpretive failure: the widespread acceptance of the idea that the banks that had made loans used in the excessive financial speculation of the 1920s needed to be purged by letting them go bankrupt.[64] In the context of this purging culture, Bagehot's Dictum was literally unthinkable.

The Banking Act of 1935 broadened the Fed's power. Policymaking authority was concentrated in a Board of Governors that served on a new monetary policy committee, the FOMC. In 1951, the Treasury–Federal Reserve Accord took the Fed out from under the wing of the executive branch and made it "independent within the government." By 1979, the Fed was sufficiently autonomous that the FOMC could use monetary policy to attack inflation despite the fact that it precipitated a steep recession in an election year. Under the chairmanships of Paul Volcker and Alan Greenspan, the Fed's power and independence grew. Monetary policymakers gained a reputation for controlling inflation and maintaining growth even as fiscal policy, requiring congressional action, became more politically difficult. Ben Bernanke inherited a central bank with credibility, autonomy, and authority.

The Fed offered dramatic displays of its authority when it used section 13(3) to create the Term Securities Lending Facility, and by advancing $13 billion to Bear Stearns and then $30 billion to JPMorgan to buy Bear Stearns. It used its authority again the same weekend to create the Primary Dealer Credit Facility with a first installment of $200 billion cash. These first uses of section 13(3) since 1936 made clear the Fed's intention and ability to take action in a crisis and to effectively use its prerogative. As FOMC members expected, the Fed was attacked for rescuing those banks most implicated in high-risk behavior, but as Tim Geithner said, not to use the authority out of fear of criticism was not a strong argument.

The consensus within the FOMC about the use of its authority to intervene in the liquidity crisis in financial markets did not extend to the discussion of monetary policy and the management of the wider economy a week later. Several members shared Milton Friedman's contention about the limited scope of monetary policy. During the March 18 meeting, Charles Plosser quoted from Friedman's presidential address to the American Economic Association: "We are in danger of assigning to monetary policy a larger role than it can perform, in danger of asking it to accomplish tasks that it cannot achieve, and, as a result, in danger of preventing it from making the contribution that it is capable of making."[65] Jeffrey Lacker called into question the Fed's capacity to inhibit the recession and recommended, as Friedman had, that they focus on inflation:

We cannot prevent this recession, and it's doubtful to me that we could have or should have even if we had had perfect foresight. We are unlikely, as I said, to have much effect on the ultimate magnitude of mortgage losses at this point, and I don't think we can do much to accelerate the resolution of uncertainty about those losses. We cannot resolve uncertainty about the fundamentals underlying the creditworthiness of financial market counterparties, and we cannot enhance the liquidity of any financial instrument without altering its relative price. What can we do? We can control inflation, and we can limit the extent to which uncertainty about our inflation intentions adds to market volatility.[66]

This statement reinforces the conclusion that organizational capacity is not just a matter of resources and authority, but reflects an interpretive capacity. The FOMC members are part of an academic debate within the professional logic of economics. In Friedman's version, that logic dismissed monetary policy's capacity to intervene effectively in the situation. Economic logic is not uniform, but rather a cluster of rationales for organizing action. Members use these rationales selectively, like tools in a tool kit. Training, theoretical assumptions, and experience tell those members to reach for different tools. Those who favored a more activist approach countered the idea of limited capacity. Like their opponents, who were opposed to further intervention, they did not offer evidence of the efficacy of their ideas. Instead, they posed a counterfactual.

> FREDERIC MISHKIN: I wasn't going to discuss this, but I just really can't not react to the comments that you made, President Fisher. There's a view out there in the media that monetary policy has been ineffective. This was the statement that I think you made, and I think it is just plain wrong. . . . My view is that monetary policy has been very effective because things would be much, much worse if we hadn't eased. On the other hand, we just had an incredibly nasty set of shocks as a result of what you described were the problems in these sectors.[67]

> BEN BERNANKE: I would just agree with Governor Mishkin about the efficacy of our policy. I think that it has had an effect and it has been beneficial. We obviously affect short-term rates, including commercial paper rates and the like, which have implications for financing and for borrowing. . . . Where would we be if we had not lowered rates? I think that lower rates have both lowered safe rates and offset to some extent

the rising concerns about solvency, which have caused the credit spreads to widen.[68]

The activists were worried about the shocks and insolvency and used a state logic of order maintenance to justify the Fed's easing interest rates. But even the activists seemed aware that the monetary policy and lender-of-last-resort tools would not be enough. It was increasingly clear that fiscal measures, infusions of money from the US Treasury into the economy, would be necessary, extending the state logic still further. But, argued the activists, the Fed's action should not be based on fiscal measures the Congress might take.

TIM GEITHNER: Even though it would be nice if we had a consensus in the United States about a set of fiscal measures that we think would be good on the merits, we can't make monetary policy in a framework where we condition our actions on actions by the Congress. In an environment like this, it is not possible. If we do the right thing, does that mean it takes the pressure off them? Maybe, but probably not so much. But it can't constrain us from doing what is appropriate now.[69]

BEN BERNANKE: We are getting to the point where the Federal Reserve's tools, both its liquidity tools and its interest rate tools, are not by themselves sufficient to resolve our troubles. More help, more activity, from the Congress and the Administration to address housing issues, for example, would be desirable. We are certainly working on those issues here at the Board, and I will be talking to people in Washington about what might be done to try to address more fundamentally these issues of the housing market and the financial markets.[70]

This chapter suggests that much of the interpretive capacity of the Fed in March was based on various forms of economic logic about the efficacy and role of the Fed. The interpretive capacity of the Fed in March was embedded in the economic ideas that shaped its members' thinking. The FOMC members were not stuck in one idea or role. As good improvisers in the midst of crisis, they adopted Bagehot's Dictum as their dominant theme and guiding principle. The handling of the liquidity crisis showed that the punitive "purge" theories of the 1930s had been delegitimated by the work of Friedman and Schwartz, Bernanke, and others on the causes of the Great Depression. The Fed was now generally blamed for failure to supply liquidity when needed by the banks. As Ben Bernanke told Milton Friedman and the audience at a celebration of Friedman's ninetieth birthday in 2002, when he was still a new governor at the Fed, "Regarding the Great Depression. You're right. We're very sorry. But thanks to you, we won't do it again."[71] Bagehot's Dictum, requiring bold state action, was accepted as the favored treatment for a banking panic.

In the current crisis there was a different set of economic ideas that were in dispute. Much of the discussion of monetary policy at the March 18 meeting was dominated by the assumption that there was a tradeoff between inflation and recession. Most members acknowledged that they were compelled to choose between the risk of one or the other. The idea of a tradeoff was a given, though ideas about the capacities and responsibilities of the Fed to deal with it were different. As it turned out, the real risk of inflation was nonexistent.[72] Finally, competing ideas about the efficacy of monetary policy in a liquidity crisis, once again based on the work of Milton Friedman, shaped members willingness to lower the fed funds rate by three-quarters of a percentage point. These ideas all involved theoretical rationales about the capacity of the market and the state to cope with the crisis. The intersecting logics of academic economics, the market, and the state guided both understanding and action.

The performance of the Fed in the March 2008 liquidity crisis offers an impressive display of its own organizational, and especially interpretive, capacity. Technocrats accustomed to the routine of monetary policy made sense of the liquidity crisis and improvised action to mitigate its consequences. Emergency infusions of cash were supplied for the short-term lending market, the purchase of Bear Stearns, and the Fed's primary dealers. All of this far surpassed the Fed's weak reaction at the onset of the Great Depression. But this interpretive capacity did not extend to recognition of the weakness of the wider system of banking and credit. This system, like its riskiest component, Bear Stearns, was still too interconnected to fail. The system remained fragile and threatened by toxic assets that the banks themselves had created. Several banks were not far removed from Bear's vulnerable condition. This catastrophic potential remained beyond the group's interpretive capacity.

5

Contested Frames / Competing Logics

APRIL—AUGUST 2008

Crises often generate a contest of retrospective framing moves, interpretations of actions taken and not taken. On April 3, 2008, the Senate Committee on Banking, Housing, and Urban Affairs held a hearing to examine the collapse of Bear Stearns and the loan of nearly $30 billion of public funds by the Fed to facilitate JPMorgan's purchase of the failed firm. Chairman Ben Bernanke and President Timothy Geithner were called to testify before the Senate committee. Perhaps the most provocative question came from Senator Jim Bunning of Kentucky who wondered why the Fed had intervened in Bear's bankruptcy at all.

> I am very troubled by the failure of Bear Stearns, and I do not like the idea of the Fed getting involved in a bailout of that company. But before making a final judgment, I want to hear from our witnesses why they thought it was necessary to stop the invisible hand of the market from delivering discipline. That is socialism. At least that is what I was taught. And I would imagine everybody at that table was taught the same thing. It must not happen again.[1]

Although no other senator accused the central bankers of practicing socialism, there was a clear note of skepticism in many other remarks and clear patterns in the ways in which the senators framed the Fed's action. Unsurprisingly, the senators adopted the language already widely used in the media and public discussion. They referred to the Fed's action as a bailout. This term had unmistakable negative connotations when used in the context of Wall Street firms. In the hearing, the term "bailout" had two major interpretations, both of them expressing the senators' doubt about the Fed's policy. The first was a "fairness" frame. Why are millions of homeowners being left to lose their homes while Wall Street is rescued? This framing shifts discussion of Fed policy from the technical issues of liquidity and solvency that preoccupied the Fed's technocrats to the more overtly political questions of who benefits from government action. As Senator Chris Dodd, chair of the Senate committee put it, "Was this a justified rescue to prevent a systemic collapse of financial markets or a $30 billion taxpayer bailout, as some have called it, for a Wall Street firm while people on Main Street struggle to pay their mortgages."[2] It is noteworthy that it was exclusively Democratic senators who raised the question of fairness, suggesting that their framing of policy solutions is not only a political act, but that congressional framing, like the Fed's, draws from a set of generic story lines that justify ongoing policy positions.

CHARLES SCHUMER: Everyone agrees that Bear Stearns was staring into the abyss. What about homeowners who are also staring into the abyss? It is true that a large institution creates systemic risk problems. An individual homeowner does not. . . . And I worry that as quickly as the Federal Government moved to save Bear Stearns from complete failure, it has moved at a snail's pace, if at all, to save homeowners from foreclosures.[3]

ROBERT MENENDEZ: What are the consequences of sticking taxpayers with a $29 billion loan that could fail? And . . . how do we continue to look struggling homeowners in the eye when we pull out all the stops to help a sinking ship on Wall Street but homeowners are still adrift at sea, drowning in foreclosure?[4]

An equally critical framing of "bailout," mostly from the Republican side, was the "authority" frame, questioning the Fed's legitimacy in intervening in Bear's failure and, as Senator Bunning put it, stopping the invisible hand. As Senator Richard Shelby explained, "The Fed's recent actions may have been warranted. Nonetheless, the Committee here today needs to address whether the Fed or any set of policymakers should have such broad emergency authority going forward."[5] The concern here is with the power of government to intrude in the marketplace and, once again, the appropriate use of taxpayer funds. It echoes the concerns about authority expressed within the Federal Open Market Committee (FOMC) itself. Senator Robert Bennett gets to the heart of the authority frame, referring to the Fed's power based on section 13(3) of the Federal Reserve Act: "You used a phrase in the Federal Reserve Act, Chairman Bernanke and President Geithner, that says you can do this 'in unusual and exigent circumstances.' . . . But that is clearly not what the framers of the Federal Reserve Act had in mind in 1913."[6] Of course, the Federal Reserve was created in 1913 as a lender of last resort in panics and the extension of this role in section 13(3) was added in 1932 during the Great Depression. The framers of the law could not have foreseen the changes in financial markets over nearly a century. But the lender-of-last-resort role played by the Fed was always in conflict with free market advocates. The questioning was along predictable lines, but was nonetheless threatening.

As one might expect given the critical tone of the senators, Bernanke and Geithner were somewhat defensive and technocratic in their responses. They were being asked questions about who benefits from Wall Street bailouts and the intentions of Progressive Era legislators. They sidestepped these questions but responded directly to the questioning of the legitimacy of their action. As technicians of the financial regulatory system, they were focused on maintaining that system, rather than considering the political and distributional consequences of their action. Certainly, their discussions in the regular meetings we have examined so far in this book reveal few political or distributional concerns.[7] The identity expressed here has been that of technical experts focused on stability. The gist of the justification for their action in the Bear Stearns collapse came from a "systemic risk" frame. Responding to Senator Bennett's concern with their use of section 13(3), Bernanke said:

> Senator, . . . this is twice in 75 years that we have used this, that we have applied this power. . . . If the financial markets had been in a robust and healthy condition, we might have taken a very different view of the situation. But given the weakness and the fragility of many markets, we thought the combination was indeed unusual and exigent. We will certainly be very diligent in resisting calls to use this power in other less exigent situations.[8]

The systemic risk frame runs counter to the assumption, made by Senator Bunning, that market discipline should have been left to work. It assumes that "weakness" and "fragility" in the markets inhibit the restorative power of the invisible hand and that the interconnectedness of financial institutions makes contagion potentially catastrophic. As Bernanke put it, conditions were "indeed" unusual and exigent. Even though the Fed's action was in keeping with Bernanke's own academic work, he was careful to reassure the senators that the Fed would be diligent in resisting calls for the use of its authority in less threatening situations.

Tim Geithner used the systemic risk frame to emphasize that the Fed's authority was used to protect the wider economy. The loan to JPMorgan that facilitated its purchase of Bear was described as preventive medicine.

> In our judgment, an abrupt and disorderly unwinding of Bear Stearns would have posed systemic risks to the financial system and magnified the downside risk to economic growth in the United States. A failure to act would have added to the risk that Americans would face lower incomes, lower home values, higher borrowing costs for housing, education, other living expenses, lower retirement savings, and rising unemployment. We acted to avert that risk in the classic tradition of lenders of last resort, with the authority provided by the Congress. We chose the best option available in the unique circumstances that prevailed at that time. . . . The risk in this arrangement—and there are risks in this arrangement—are modest in comparison to the substantial losses to the economy that could have accompanied Bear's insolvency.[9]

Geithner's last sentence is noteworthy in light of the Fed's response to the insolvency of Lehman Brothers six months later. It suggests that Geithner knew what to expect from the failure of a large, interconnected investment bank. The April hearing may be understood, then, as a preliminary set of framing moves in the interpretive contest over the Fed's response to the financial crisis. The Democrats' framing represented the interests of homeowners facing foreclosure. The Republican framing represented the interests of businesses concerned with circumscribing government intrusion. The Fed's framing represented its own organizational interest in maintaining its claim as the legitimate regulator of the market for money and credit and guardian of economic stability.

This hearing highlights a point that analysis of the transcripts alone could not. Fed discourse, the language of technocrats, depoliticizes their action. The FOMC's language of upside and downside risk obscures the issue of fairness. The risk being discussed by Geithner and Bernanke is to an abstraction called "the economy," rather than people or classes of people. Of course, it was Tim Geithner who pointed out to the senators that it was average Americans who would suffer deeply from a system failure as, in the course of events, they did through unemployment, delayed careers, and lost equity in homes and other assets. But within the FOMC, the discourse among members remained clinical, like weather forecasters discussing a storm or surgeons a series of MRI scans. Nevertheless, FOMC discourse was not totally depoliticized. As we have seen, the Fed was concerned with the politics of its own credibility and legitimacy and debated its use of section 13(3) to bring liquidity to the markets. This was not about distributional politics but rather the mission-focused organizational interests of the agency itself. Those interests were based in returning to the relative stability that existed before the crisis.[10]

Framing is an indisputably political act.[11] It is action designed to influence the interpretation of policy.[12] But the frames offered by the participants were not spontaneous creations of the moment. Rather, they were part of the available tool kit of policy justifications that guide action in practical situations. The frames themselves—bailout, authority, and systemic risk—were grounded in the institutional logic of the state and reflected the ongoing controversy over the role of intervention in the marketplace. This tool kit of ideas is the seedbed for interpretive moves by the participants.[13] In this chapter, we explore how these ideas and their interplay guide the evolving sensemaking efforts of the members of the FOMC during a highly ambiguous transitional moment in the crisis.

Turning the Corner? April and June 2008

FREDERIC MISHKIN: When I look at where I was at the last FOMC meeting, there has really been a big change for me. I re-read the transcripts, because you always want to see what things sounded like, and I sounded so depressed then, as though I might take out a gun and blow my head off. . . . But my sunny, optimistic disposition is coming back [*laughter*]. I think it is very possible that we will look back and say, particularly after the Bear Stearns episode, that we have turned the corner in terms of the financial disruption that we have just experienced. . . . But I think there is a very strong possibility that the worst is over.[14]

The FOMC meetings in April and June were characterized by cautious optimism. The dominant narrative was "improvement," first in regard to financial conditions, but later extending to the real economy. Regarding the financial turmoil, one can almost hear an audible sigh of relief. As Eric Rosengren explained in April, "Many financial indicators have improved since the last meeting, as was highlighted in Bill Dudley's report. The stock market has moved up. Many credit spreads have narrowed. Treasury securities and repurchase agreements are trading in more-normal ranges, and credit default swaps for many financial firms have improved."[15] Both Geithner and Bernanke glossed this improvement narrative by attributing the improvement to the series of actions the Fed had taken to improve liquidity. As Geithner put it, "The markets reflect increased confidence that policy will be effective in mitigating the risks both of a systemic financial crisis and of a very deep, protracted recession."[16] Ben Bernanke was even more sanguine:

> Let me first say that I think we ought to at least modestly congratulate ourselves that we have made some progress. Our policy actions, including both rate cuts and the liquidity measures, have seemed to have had some benefit. I think the fear has moderated. The markets have improved somewhat. As I said yesterday, I am cautious about this. There's a good chance that we will see further problems and further relapses, but we have made progress in reducing some of the uncertainties in the current environment.[17]

At the June meeting, the improvement narrative expanded to include expectations for real growth in the economy. As Gary Stern commented, "Like some others—maybe many others—I, too, have raised my forecast for growth for this year, basically just extending what's happening in the first half of the year, and I've raised my projection for growth next year marginally as well."[18] Kevin Warsh described the economy as "more resilient and more dynamic than consensus had anticipated."[19] There was increasing confidence that Fed policy had improved prospects for the economy.

But this positive interpretation of the cues was not uniform within the FOMC. During the April and June meetings the members debated the risks coming from financial markets versus the risks posed by inflation. Inflation concerns had increased because of rising prices for food and energy. Most of the inflation hawks, including Charles Plosser, Richard Fisher, Charles Evans, James Bullard, and Thomas Hoenig, now saw these risks as balanced or weighted toward rising inflation. Hoenig expressed the prevailing sentiment in this group:

> I believe that we are entering a dangerous period, if I can use that word, in which inflation expectations are beginning to move higher and inflation

psychology is becoming more prominent in business decisions. . . . I am concerned that maintaining a highly accommodative policy stance for an extended period would greatly increase the likelihood that inflation exceeds our long-run objectives.[20]

A more provocative position was taken by Bullard, who said, "The fragile credibility of the Committee is being eroded as we speak, and we will do well to take steps to reassert inflation-fighting resolve at this meeting."[21] The inflation hawks repeatedly referred back to the Great Inflation of the 1970s, but several of their colleagues on the FOMC pointedly rejected this comparison.

FREDERIC MISHKIN: So it's very important to emphasize that this is not the 1970s, and I really get disturbed when people point to that as a problem. We do have to worry about inflation expectations possibly going up, but it's not a situation that, if we make a mistake, they go up a whole lot. They could go up, and it might be costly to get them down, but it would not be a disaster.[22]

JANET YELLEN: I don't think we have become more tolerant of inflation in the long run, and I did see today's reading on the employment cost index as further confirmation that at this point nothing is built into labor markets that suggests that we are developing a wage-price spiral of the type that was of such concern and really propelling the problems in the 1970s.[23]

Although the debate on inflation risks took up much of the time in the April and June meetings, it reflected a divided group rather than a consensus that inflation was the primary problem. When the 2008 transcript was first released in 2014, a reporter at the *Financial Times* did a word count on the use of the term "inflation" in the June meeting and found that it far exceeded the use of "recession" and "crisis." On a closer reading we can see that this is an artifact of a serious debate in which the inflation doves felt they had to counter the inordinate alarm of the hawks. In fact, there was little consensus on the significance of inflation. At the April meeting, Chairman Bernanke offered a conciliatory tone on the increase in inflation expectations, saying, "I do think it's an important issue, and I do think that there is benefit to pushing against the perceptions. In this business, perceptions have an element of reality to them, and we understand that. That's an important part of central banking, and I fully appreciate that point."[24] By June he was siding unreservedly with the doves.

I would like to say just a couple of words about the 1970s because they keep coming up and I do think that these comparisons are a bit misleading. First, in the current episode, commodity prices—particularly oil prices—are basically most or almost all the inflation that we're seeing. That was not the case in the '70s. . . . There was already a serious inflation problem before the oil price shocks came. Hence, credibility was already damaged at the time of the oil price shocks. That is not the case here.[25]

It was in the June meeting that a few members began to reprise a narrative from the Bear Stearns liquidity crisis that was dissonant with the sense that they had turned the corner on the financial turmoil. It raised again the specter of "systemic risk." Such risk comes from an event to which the market mechanism cannot effectively adjust. As Bernanke warned, "I do not yet rule out the possibility of a systemic event. We saw in the intermeeting period that we have considerable concerns about Lehman Brothers, for example. We watched with some concern the consummation of the Bank of America–Countrywide merger. . . . So I'm not yet persuaded that the tail risks are gone."[26] Tim Geithner elaborated on this systemic risk narrative, adding to it the role that the Fed itself might play in causing such an event.

The improvement in financial markets that many of you spoke of is not as significant as we think or hope; we have had a lot of false dawns over this period. A lot of what you see as improvement is the simple result of the existence of our facilities in the implied sense that people infer from our actions that we are going to protect people from a level of distress that we probably have no desire, will, or ability to actually do.[27]

One might expect that the competing improvement, inflation, and systemic risk narratives would make the negotiation over the appropriate matching policy action more difficult. Instead, the uncertainty attached to the competing narratives in April and June yielded an agreement on the need for a pause in the dramatic easing of monetary policy. The negotiation was over timing. There was some debate between those who wanted an immediate pause and those who still wanted a little more stimulus to offset the housing decline and the financial turmoil. The inflation hawks cited the need to reassert inflation-fighting resolve by signaling an intention to move toward tightening. But even those like Chairman Bernanke, wanting more stimulus, understood that it might be a good idea to signal the Fed's "willingness to sit, watch, and listen for a time."[28] Most believed they were approaching a long-awaited transitional moment. Bernanke explained the delicate nature of that moment:

> We are at an important transition point in our communication strategy. One of the risks that we took when we made the very rapid cuts in interest rates earlier this year was the problem of coming to this exact point, when we would have to communicate to the markets that we were done, that we were going to flatten out, and that we were going to a mode of waiting. It was always difficult to figure out how that was going to work in a smooth way.[29]

At the end of the June meeting, the FOMC members voted to hold the fed funds rate steady at 2 percent, signaling a pause and maybe an end to the Fed's easing of monetary policy. But rather than adjourn, the FOMC remained in session. The second part of the meeting was devoted to discussion of a staff report on the monitoring of primary dealers who had access to the Primary Dealer Credit Facility (PDCF) created in March. The goals of the monitoring program were to gather information on the liquidity and capital positions of those firms and encourage the primary dealers to manage their risks more conservatively. By late March, the monitoring program had learned that none of the four largest remaining investment banks could withstand the kind of bank run experienced by Bear Stearns.[30] At the time of the June meeting, they were still negotiating with the Securities and Exchange Commission (SEC), the primary regulator of investment banks, to coordinate on obtaining information on the financial condition of these firms and setting expectations for their risk management.[31]

After a report from the staff, the FOMC members had a freewheeling discussion venting their frustrations about the precariousness of the position in which the Fed found itself because of the weakened state of the banking system. The dominant frustration concerned a perceived "regulatory gap." The Fed, which had no regulatory oversight of investment banks, was concerned about putting its money and reputation on the line while having to rely on the SEC as the primary regulator of the investment banks that used the PDCF. Compounding this concern, neither the SEC nor the Fed had kept up with the dramatic changes in the financial markets and institutions. Dennis Lockhart, Don Kohn, and Frederic Mishkin voiced these frustrations.

DENNIS LOCKHART: I see the touchstone of all of this to be our perceived accountability for systemic risk and financial stability. . . . I think that we are largely perceived as the most accountable party. I have to ask myself,

Do we have a system today that is aligned with the reality of the financial markets? Or, put in more vernacular terms, do we have the right stuff to do what we need to do to take responsibility as best we can for financial stability? My answer to that is "no." I don't think we have the right stuff.[32]

DON KOHN: I think that we have learned something about the financial system in the process, and we have learned that the regulatory structure and the liquidity provision structure were not sufficient to give the economy the protection it needed from the new style of financial system. That is really the background of why we are here, not just because we made the loan or we set up the facilities because we thought we needed to do so to protect the system under the circumstances.[33]

FREDERIC MISHKIN: Although we got here under exigent circumstances, in a financial disruption, we might have gotten here anyway. The reality is that there was a fundamental change in the way the financial system works. When banks are not so dominant, the distinction between investment banks and commercial banks in terms of the way the financial system works is really much less. It would be nice to think that we could limit the kinds of lending facilities that we have so that we didn't have to worry about regulating or supervising other institutions, but I don't think that is realistic.[34]

There is a sense of resignation in all these statements. The financial system had transformed in recent decades. It had developed new structures, new instruments, and new levels of risk. The existence of a shadow market for money and credit residing in investment banks and hedge funds was well established. It was now clear that the financial system was too laden with risk and the concomitant instability. Regulation had not kept up. The distinction between the firms the Fed regulated and those they didn't would not protect them or their agency's legitimacy. Darkest of all was the fear, as Dennis Lockhart put it, that they might not have "the right stuff" to protect the financial system.

A Fragile Situation: August 2008

By the August 5 meeting, James Bullard was the only remaining proponent of the improvement narrative.

It now appears that the worst quarter associated with the current episode of financial turmoil was probably the fourth quarter of 2007, when the economy abruptly stalled. The slow- or no-growth period was through the winter, with the economy gradually regaining footing through the spring and summer. If there were no further shocks, I would expect the economy to grow at a more rapid rate in the second half of this year.[35]

Most members of the FOMC saw the economy weakening, prospects for growth declining, and financial instability intensifying. As Tim Geithner explained, "Downside risks to growth remain substantial, in my view, and have probably increased relative to what we thought in June. Risks on the inflation front remain weighted to the upside, perhaps somewhat less than in June, but this is hard to know with confidence."[36] Even the inflation hawks described growth as "weak" and "anemic" (Fisher), although others still saw the economy "skirting" (Plosser) recession and "rebounding" (Lacker) in 2009.[37] The recognition of increased financial instability was marked by the reemergence of the crisis narrative as a prominent part of the discussion. The crisis narrative was given new life by events in July that revealed increasing concern about the viability of Fannie Mae and Freddie Mac, the government-sponsored entities (GSEs) that held more than $45 trillion in mortgage debt and funded 75 percent of all new mortgages.

Fannie and Freddie were established as public companies by federal leg-islation to encourage home ownership. They borrowed money at very low rates because lenders assumed that the government would stand behind their obligations. The GSEs then used that money to buy mortgages and mortgage-backed securities. As increasing numbers of those instruments either de-faulted or lost value during the housing crisis, Fannie and Freddie's solvency was called into question. This had negative consequences for the stockholders of Fannie and Freddie, the mortgage-backed securities market, the rate of home foreclosures, and the already rapidly declining price of homes. In mid-July, Henry Paulson, the Secretary of the Treasury, had asked Congress for unlimited authority to invest in Fannie and Freddie and even the power to take them over, if necessary. Explaining his unusually far-reaching request, Paulson memorably told the Senate Banking Committee, "If you've got a squirt gun in your pocket, you may have to take it out. If you've got a ba-zooka, and people know you've got it, you may not have to take it out. By having something that is unspecified, it will increase confidence, and by increasing confidence it will greatly reduce the likelihood it will ever be used."[38] Paulson, had, in effect, asked for a blank check to bail out Fannie and Freddie. Congress granted it on July 26.

The troubles at Fannie and Freddie, especially the talk of their possible insolvency, had shaken the markets. Now that the Treasury Department had guaranteed their solvency, it was the liquidity and solvency of major banks that raised the most immediate concerns at the August meeting. Since the failure of Bear Stearns in March, the Fed had been urging the banks to add capital and take other actions to reduce their risk. Members of the FOMC expressed doubt that this risk reduction was occurring. They made the fragility of financial institutions the focus of the renewed crisis narrative.

KEVIN WARSH: I think management credibility among financial institutions is at least as suspect as it has ever been during this period. Even new management teams that have come in have in some ways used up a lot of their credibility. It would be nice to believe that they have taken all actions necessary to protect their franchises and their businesses, but most stakeholders are skeptical that they've taken significant or sufficient action.[39]

RANDALL KROSZNER: I continue to see that the situation is quite brittle and that small pressures potentially can lead to large and rapid responses. The "severe financial stress" alternative simulation in the Greenbook is certainly not my central tendency one, but I think that we can't dismiss it too easily because there still could be another—what I have now taken to calling, since I chair the supervision and regulation committee—flare-up with one of my problem children.[40]

FREDERIC MISHKIN: We are now a year into this. Bank balance sheets do not look very good, for all the reasons that we have been discussing. In fact, they look pretty grim. We have had some failures, and we are concerned about other failures. So we have a very different environment. In that situation, if a shoe drops—and we have had big shoes dropping; we had Bear Stearns, we had the GSEs, and we had smaller cases like IndyMac—and if financial systems are in a very weakened state, really bad things could happen. I think that there really is a serious danger here.[41]

Although the improvement narrative was in eclipse at the August meeting as the crisis narrative reemerged, the inflation narrative remained prominent. Charles Evans described oil prices as "coming off the boil . . . but still scalding."[42] Richard Fisher quoted the CEO of Walmart as telling him, "My biggest concern is inflation. This month we had an experience that Walmart has never ever had before, which is that a major supplier told us we need a 9 percent increase or we will not supply you at all."[43] Even those who were not generally inflation hawks expressed growing concern.

> KEVIN WARSH: Turning finally to inflation, my view is that inflation risks are very real, and I believe that these risks are higher than growth risks. I don't take that much comfort from the move in commodity prices since we last met. If that trend continues, then that would certainly be good news; but I must say I don't feel as though inflation risks have moved down noticeably since we last had this discussion.[44]

> RANDALL KROSZNER: We have to be very careful about inflation expectations. I think we have mixed evidence on inflation expectations and inflation, although I am heartened that things do not seem to have become unanchored. Some of both the market-based measures and the survey-based measures have come down a bit, although I think, as Governor Kohn said, that the situation is much more fragile.[45]

Chairman Bernanke admitted that "like everyone else," he had concerns about inflation, but he tempered the significance of these concerns saying, "I think that containing inflation is enormously important, and I think it is our first responsibility. We need to watch this very carefully. I think there will be continued pressures even if commodity prices don't rise, but I do think there is also a chance that we will see a moderation of this problem going forward."[46]

This growing concern with inflation had a strong influence on the effort to identify an appropriate policy to match the narratives. The FOMC discussed only two policy options. In the first, the fed funds rate would hold steady at 2 percent, but language would be added to the public statement indicating increased concern with inflation. In the second option, the rate would be raised to explicitly address the increased concerns with inflation. There was more conflict in the discussion than usual. The inflation hawks saw the existing fed funds rate as overly stimulative and wanted it raised. They were careful about the semantics of their strategy.

> THOMAS HOENIG: I appreciate the fact that reasonable people may differ, and I do differ. In saying that, I am not advocating a tight monetary policy. I am advocating a less accommodative monetary policy. . . . We introduced the policy that we have, as I think others mentioned, as an insurance policy early on, when we were more in an immediate crisis. . . . The subpar growth is not going to go away soon, so we are delaying removing the insurance

policy. I worry about that. I think in the long run that does increase the risk of an inflationary problem of a sizable magnitude later on.[47]

Charles Plosser also used the "less accommodative" phrasing to avoid the implication of tightening in the midst of a crisis, but he went further than Hoenig in echoing what had become a growing public sentiment after the congressional legislation to provide "bailout" funds for Fannie Mae and Freddie Mac.

CHARLES PLOSSER: To be sure, shifting policy to a less accommodative stance will be a difficult decision to make, given the continued volatility in financial markets and the projected near-term weakness in employment and output growth. However, what has been referred to as the tail risk of a very negative growth outcome has decreased since the start of the year, whereas inflation risks have increased. I think the enhancements we have made to our liquidity facilities should be sufficient to address any remaining dysfunctions in the financial markets, but they will not address the credit or insolvency issues. . . . The markets will have to do that admittedly heavy lifting.[48]

Plosser expressed the belief that he anticipated bank failures, but he favored leaving them to the market adjustment mechanism. The banks would have to take care of themselves.

Most other members of the FOMC believed that the risks of inflation and recession remained balanced. The most passionate proponents of continuing the pause in interest rate movement anticipated bank failures but they had a very different reaction than Charles Plosser. Janet Yellen characterized the growing crisis among financial institutions as a "credit crunch" with significant consequences for the real economy and put far greater weight on the financial crisis than on inflation.

We are in the midst of a serious credit crunch that has, again, worsened during the intermeeting period, as exemplified by the developments at Freddie and Fannie and the other things that many of you have pointed to in our last round. We are likely seeing only the start of what will be a series of bank failures that could make matters much worse. Given these financial headwinds, it is not clear to me that we are accommodative at all. . . . I see no case for jolting expectations in such a way as to, in effect, tighten policy now. I feel especially strongly about this in view of the major downside risks to the economy from an intensifying credit crunch.[49]

Most members focused on their belief that the data on inflation did not yet support a tightening. Ben Bernanke, as chairman, welcomed the discussion of inflation but rejected the inflation hawks' premise that there was adequate evidence to suggest raising the fed funds rate.

> It would be extraordinary if we were to begin raising rates without an immediate inflation problem with the economy still in a declining or extremely weakened situation. If inflation does in fact become the problem that many around the table think it is, particularly if commodity prices begin to go up again or if the dollar begins to weaken, then I will be the first here to support responding to that. . . . So I welcome the ongoing discussion we should have about the pace of withdrawal of accommodation.[50]

Just before the taking the vote, Bernanke struck an even more conciliatory tone, saying, "I want to thank everyone for your comments today. I know we don't have agreement around the table, but as somebody once said, if everybody agrees, then everybody except one is redundant" [*laughter*].[51] In the end, the formal vote did not alert Fed watchers to the degree of disagreement in the group. The only vote in opposition to continuing to hold the fed funds rate at 2 percent was cast by Richard Fisher. The other inflation hawks were presidents of the regional Reserve Banks who were not voting members in 2008.[52]

Competing Logics

The framing moves in the FOMC became increasingly contentious in the period from April to August 2008. Efforts to justify policy action reflected clear differences in the guiding principles being applied to the situation. The clash between those guided by a profound confidence in the resilience of markets and the rationality of bankers, on the one hand, and those responding to the threat of market failure and the increasing attribution of contagion and crisis, on the other, was the most striking aspect of the FOMC members' deliberations.

This conflict can be seen most clearly in two frames that were used to warrant Fed policy on the emerging crisis: the market adjustment frame and the systemic risk frame. The market adjustment frame was based on the theory-driven expectation that rationality and the self-interest of firms would supersede the risky behavior being observed and restore equilibrium. James

Bullard, who had just joined the FOMC in April, forcefully advocated the strong form of this frame.

> My sense is that the level of systemic risk associated with financial tur-
> moil has fallen dramatically. For this reason, I think the FOMC should
> begin to de-emphasize systemic risk worries. . . . My sense is that, because
> the turmoil has been ongoing for some time, all of the major players have
> made adjustments as best they can to contain the fallout from the failure
> of another firm in the industry. They have done this not out of benevo-
> lence but out of their own instincts for self-preservation. . . . The period of
> substantial systemic risk has passed.[53]

Charles Evans suggested a similar position. Again, there is an assumption that given the time elapsed since the Bear Stearns failure, financial firms
would adjust their risk. According to Evans, "Institutions have had time to
cope with bad portfolios, much as President Bullard mentioned. They have
made significant progress in raising capital and have increased provisions
against losses. I think our lending facilities have helped financial institutions gain time to facilitate the adjustment process."[54] This rationale is quite
similar to former Fed chairman Alan Greenspan's surprising admission to
a congressional hearing investigating the financial crisis just two months
later, when he said, "I made a mistake in presuming that the self-interest of
organizations, specifically banks and others, were such that they were best
capable of protecting their own shareholders and their equity in the firms."[55]

The logic in these statements is based on an idealization of economic behavior found in classical and neoclassical versions of economic theory. This
faith in theory is reflected in Jeffrey Lacker's critique of the systemic risk frame:

> I want to commend President Bullard's discussion of systemic risk. . . . In
> popular usage, it seems to mean an episode in which one bad thing hap-
> pens followed by a lot of other seemingly related bad things happening,
> and as such, it's a purely empirical notion without any content or useful-
> ness by itself as a guide to policy. It doesn't say whether those other bad
> things are efficient—things that ought to happen—or inefficient and pre-
> ventable by suitable policy intervention. To invoke the notion of systemic
> risk to support a particular policy course requires theory . . . I haven't seen
> a convincing case for the existence of policy-relevant market failures in the
> financial markets in which we've intervened, apart from the usual distor-
> tions owing to the federal financial safety net.[56]

As Lacker points out, the systemic risk frame assumes a social process in which "one bad thing happens" followed by another. This is, of course, the basis of the contagion narrative and the related systemic risk policy frame that Ben Bernanke, Tim Geithner, and Janet Yellen, among others, promoted in their strongest form. Bernanke, whose research in the area of systemic risk was well known in the room, took some offense at the claim that it was not a sufficient theory on which to base policy.

> President Lacker and I have, I hope, respect—I respect him, and I hope he respects me. . . . I take his criticism to be that it works in practice, but can it work in theory? Systemic risk is an old phenomenon. There are literally dozens and dozens of historical episodes that are suggestive of that phenomenon. There is also an enormous theoretical literature. Maybe it is not entirely satisfactory, but certainly many people have thought about that issue. I, myself, have obviously worked in this area. Clearly, it is not something that we can tightly explain in all aspects, but I do think it is a concern. We need to remain concerned about it.[57]

Despite Bernanke's modesty, it is clear that he found the historical record a persuasive source for inferring a pattern. These empirical patterns were enough to overcome adherence to an efficient market theory in which actors always make the right adjustments. Several members were skeptical of the notion that bankers would necessarily protect their self-interest given the time since the threat first became clear. Frederic Mishkin used a historical example to refute this claim.

> I have to disagree very strenuously with the view that, because you have been in a "financial stress" situation for a period of time, there is no potential for systemic risk. In fact, I would argue that the opposite can be the case. Just as a reminder, remember that in the Great Depression, when—I can't use the expression because it would be in the transcripts, but you know what I'm thinking—something hit the fan [*laughter*], it actually occurred close to a year after the initial negative shock.[58]

These tense framing moves reflect the deeper conflict of competing logics. The logic of the state suggests active intervention when the economic system is threatened. The market logic discourages it, assuming that there will be a natural adjustment, a return to equilibrium with which the state should not interfere. There is an ongoing tension here. Central banks, as we saw earlier, sit at the intersection of the market and the state. This tension is built into the institution of central banking as a latent conflict that is awaiting pressing events. On the one hand, market logic is based on competition and efficiency. State logic, on the other, is about regulated stability and order. The illusion of free market thinking is that these things are necessarily in opposition. Central banks are an instance where they are complementary social arrangements for the achievement of societal goals. As John Commons explained:

> Competition is not Nature's "struggle for existence" but is an artificial arrangement supported by the moral, economic, and physical sanctions of collective action. The theory of free competition developed by economists is not a natural tendency towards equilibrium of forces but is an ideal of public purpose adopted by the courts, to be attained by restraints upon the natural struggle for existence.[59]

Although the framing moves of individual members are competing for influence, at the institutional level of the central bank, the market and the state are interdependent. It is somehow both appropriate and ironic that central bankers, the managers of this system for regulating the market for money and credit, should be arguing over its fundamental logic. The debate over intervention in the "free market" remains a core negotiation within the logic of the state, yet at the same time, central bankers are hired to administer this "artificial" system of control based on legislative mandates about growth, price stability, and banking safety.[60] As we have seen in this chapter, even the strongest market adjustment proponents would administer tighter money to choke off inflation. The market and state logics are not opposites. Rather, the structure of the Fed was created so that the market for money and credit might operate without massive disruption. The FOMC members are enacting the tensions inherent in the institution and reproducing frames and logics that have been in contention since its founding in 1913.

It would be tempting to infer the economic interests that underlie the competing frames found at the FOMC, but interests do not align clearly with members' choices. The market adjustment advocates (who overlap with the inflation hawks) are most likely to be found among the regional bank presidents, and one might infer that they are representing the commercial interests, especially banking, of those who appointed them. But this cannot explain why just as many regional bank presidents seem to be on the other side of the debates over inflation and market adjustment, seeing the threat to economic growth from the financial crisis as the bigger risk.[61] Since the August 2007 meeting, the event that began this book, the systemic risk frame has gained support over the market adjustment/efficient market frame as the importance of risk management became more pressing. This suggests that perceived changes in the situation and the influence of colleagues can shape the outcome of the framing contest.

But the interpretive flow of the FOMC members was not purely situational. The consistent pattern in frame usage among certain members suggests that they identify more or less strongly with a frame and the logic behind it. This identification is likely to be associated with economic training, political socialization, and professional experience in banking, government, or the academy. It is in these experiences that the tool kit of frames and logics is acquired. Frame usage is embedded in the resulting identities.[62] The framing moves exhibited by members of the FOMC are triggered by the interaction of these identities with concrete situations and the framing moves of their colleagues.[63]

Although the competition between market adjustment and systemic risk is a debate between technical experts, it is dealing with political questions in a high-stakes context. The Fed's power to intervene in the market puts it at the center of controversy. Its founding involved a contest over how much power would be concentrated in the Board of Governors in Washington. The result was that twelve regional banks were established across the country. Episodic attacks on the power of the Fed were launched from both the left and the right over the course of its history. The left was generally more vocal during periods of tightening economic policy when interest rates rose and credit became expensive. The right was equally vocal when the Fed was seen to be too accommodative. This was reflected again in the controversy over "bailouts" discussed at the beginning of the chapter. Does the Fed have the legitimate authority to loan $29 billion to a Wall Street bank? Should it rescue the next big bank that is threatened? Significant sentiment existed on both ends of the political spectrum that it does not and should not. We will explore this clash of politics and central banking in greater depth in Chapter 6, with particular attention to its impact on the flow of sensemaking at the FOMC.

6

Accounting for a Legitimacy Crisis

SEPTEMBER 2008

> For market discipline to be effective, it is imperative that market
> participants not have the expectation that lending from the Fed,
> or any other government support, is readily available.... For
> market discipline to constrain risk effectively, financial
> institutions must be allowed to fail.
>
> —HENRY PAULSON, JULY 2008, QUOTED IN BRUCE FEIRSTEIN,
> "100 TO BLAME"

This short chapter is a digression from our unfolding of the sensemaking process at the FOMC. It is a digression made necessary by the pivotal event of the financial crisis and its influence on subsequent sensemaking at the Fed. Understanding the events of Lehman weekend, a major shock to the financial system, is integral to the analysis of the evolving contest over frames and logics that shaped ensuing policy. Our analysis to this point has suggested that Ben Bernanke and Tim Geithner, who assumed the roles of crisis managers as they had on Bear Stearns weekend, were strong adherents of the logic in which the state intervenes to reduce systemic risk. Yet the outcome of Lehman weekend suggests that market logic, in which firms must be allowed to fail in order to maintain market discipline and limit risk-taking by other firms, effectively won the policy contest. Lehman was allowed to fail. This chapter argues that it was not that the crisis managers changed their minds; rather, the economic stability concerns of the systemic risk frame were trumped by a deeper, more immediate concern about the legitimacy of the Federal Reserve in the context of the political and cultural moment.

Lehman Weekend

Lehman weekend began with the CEOs of the major Wall Street banks being summoned to the New York Fed on Friday evening, September 12. Henry Paulson, former CEO of Goldman Sachs and, at the time, Secretary of the Treasury under President George W. Bush, opened the meeting by emphasizing that there would be no government money for the rescue of Lehman Brothers. Said Paulson, "You're going to have to figure this out."[1] Tim Geithner organized the bankers into three teams. The first team was to plan for financial assistance to a buyer for Lehman; the second would seek a consortium of banks to buy Lehman, much as a consortium in the 1990s bought the toxic assets of Long-Term Capital Management; and the third would develop a plan to minimize the fallout from a Lehman bankruptcy if the other options failed.

The bankers knew that two banks, Barclays and Bank of America, had shown interest in buying Lehman Brothers and were negotiating upstairs at the New York Fed. They also knew that Lehman's stock price had fallen to $3.31 per share on Friday, a loss of 93 percent since January 31; that Lehman had virtually no cash left; and that Dick Fuld, CEO of Lehman, had been unable to complete deals with the Korean Development Bank, MetLife, two Middle Eastern sovereign wealth funds, and China's CITIC Securities.[2] All of this was common knowledge in their world. They did not know that Geithner had spoken to Fuld "some fifty times between March and September urging him to raise new capital and find a buyer willing to take a large stake in Lehman."[3] In the days prior to Lehman weekend, Henry Paulson had encouraged Ken Lewis, CEO of Bank of America, to consider the purchase. Lewis sent a team to review Lehman's books but made clear that he expected the government to guarantee $40 billion in losses on Lehman's assets.[4]

When the bankers reconvened at the New York Fed on Saturday morning, the options had narrowed. Bank of America was not interested in any deal that did not include a government guarantee for $70 billion of Lehman's toxic assets. At the same time, Bank of America had quietly begun negotiations to buy Merrill Lynch, the nation's third biggest investment bank. Merrill's leadership, increasingly convinced that the government would not rescue Lehman, realized that they were highly vulnerable in a Lehman default. Meanwhile, the team of bank CEOs working on assembling a consortium to buy Lehman reported that the size of the toxic assets was too big for the banks to absorb given their own situations, and the bankruptcy team reported that such an outcome would undoubtedly lead to frozen markets and a cascade of further bankruptcies—a panic.

The sole remaining option was the assisted purchase of Lehman by another bank. Any buyer would undoubtedly require a loan similar to the one given to JPMorgan to buy Bear Stearns. This assistance could only come from the government or other banks. The Barclays representatives were still at the Fed negotiating to buy Lehman on Saturday night. The bankers who had given up on a consortium to buy Lehman's assets continued to work on a plan to assist in a purchase by Barclays.

Sunday brought crushing news to the crisis managers. That morning, Callum McCarthy, the chief regulator of financial markets in the United Kingdom, informed Tim Geithner that he did not believe Barclays had adequate capital to do the deal and even if Barclays had the capacity for such a deal, it would take at least thirty days to obtain the required shareholder approval. Geithner got off the phone with McCarthy, walked into Paulson's temporary office at the New York Fed, and said, "We're fucked."[5]

Paulson immediately called Alistair Darling, Chancellor of the Exchequer, to see if the requirement for a shareholder vote could be waived. Darling, who was skeptical about Lehman, wanted to know what financial involvement the US government would have in the deal. "What are you offering?" he asked, knowing that the government had assisted in the purchase of Bear Stearns and the rescue only days earlier of Fannie Mae and Freddie Mac.[6] Paulson, who had been emphatically against government involvement in the deal, said that he hoped for a consortium of banks. The conversation turned to plans for a Lehman bankruptcy.

Geithner recognized that his options were narrowing. After this call, he said to Paulson, "Okay, let's go to Plan B."[7] Plan B referred to preparations for a Lehman bankruptcy on Monday. Geithner and Paulson entered the conference room where the full group of bankers was making progress on funding a Barclays deal. Paulson delivered the news. "But we have the money," said Jamie Dimon of JPMorgan. Paulson replied that there was no buyer left.[8] The bankers left the building to prepare for the inevitable panic on Monday. Lehman's board was directed to declare bankruptcy before the markets opened in Japan early Monday morning. Panic selling ensued shortly thereafter in financial markets and the economy descended into the Great Recession.[9]

Given the magnitude of the resulting panic, and the fact that Lehman was the only major investment bank that did not receive government money in the crisis, the $40 billion initially requested from the Fed by Ken Lewis, CEO of Bank of America, to avert the Lehman failure would have been a bargain. Guaranteeing Lehman's assets until Barclays shareholders voted would also have been a bargain. So why then, before and throughout the "Lehman weekend," had the crisis managers signaled all parties that no government money would be used to save Lehman, thereby discouraging Bank of America and the British regulators and dooming negotiations?

Accounting for Lehman Weekend

The explanation for the Fed's behavior on Lehman weekend continues to be debated. Alternative accounts reveal competing framings of the crisis. The Fed's earliest explanation for its behavior on Lehman weekend reflects a medical metaphor in which the market's self-healing power was exceeded by its dysfunction.[10] This account was presented to the Congressional Joint Economic Committee by Ben Bernanke on September 24, 2008, a little more than a week after Lehman weekend. Bernanke addressed the Fed's response to the failure of Lehman in the midst of the resulting market panic:

> In the case of Lehman Brothers, a major investment bank, the Federal Reserve and the Treasury declined to commit public funds to support the institution. The failure of Lehman posed risks. But the troubles at Lehman had been well known for some time, and investors clearly recognized—as evidenced, for example, by the high cost of insuring Lehman's debt in the market for credit default swaps—that the failure of the firm was a significant possibility. Thus, we judged that investors and counterparties had had time to take precautionary measures.[11]

This explanation sounds like a market adjustment framing of the Fed's action. Bernanke argued that the Fed expected that firms had already taken protective measures and adjusted to the fallout from Lehman's likely demise. In colloquial terms, the explanation says, "We thought the market could handle it." This claim, which sounded reasonable in the immediate aftermath of Lehman weekend, is at odds with the evidence in Chapter 5 that shows Chairman Bernanke strongly defending the systemic risk frame against the market adjustment advocates, based on his own research. It also seems surprising given the widespread expectation that the Fed would rescue Lehman and the prescient expectation by the crisis managers and bankers of a market panic resulting from a Lehman bankruptcy. The argument that Bear Stearns had been "too interconnected to fail" proved at least as true for the significantly larger Lehman Brothers. Bernanke later withdrew this explanation, which he referred to as "deliberately vague." Although it doesn't seem vague in the context of its resonance with the market adjustment frame, the explanation does suggest that the failure to commit public funds was the result of a misjudgment. He later criticized the statement for promoting "the mistaken view that we could have saved Lehman."[12]

This brings us to the second account of Lehman weekend, promoted in both Bernanke's and Geithner's memoirs of the crisis. In this account, "crisis" is not a medical metaphor but an engineering one, in which the actors return to the argument that Lehman was too interconnected to be allowed to fail. The justification in this account is that in such a case, the system regulator must intervene and adjust the system to stabilize it. This account is in agreement with what we know Bernanke and Geithner were saying at the August 2008 meeting about the potential for systemic risk. In their memoirs of the crisis, both men provide similar explanations for failing to steer Lehman through the crisis. Their explanations are constructed from the authority frame that was advanced when section 13(3) of the Federal Reserve Act was first applied back in March 2008 to create liquidity at the time of the Bear Stearns crisis. It says, in effect, that "we would have intervened if we could, but we just didn't have the authority." As Tim Geithner explained, "We didn't believe we had the legal authority to guarantee Lehman's trading liabilities . . . And we didn't believe we could legally lend them the scale of resources they would need to continue to operate, because we didn't believe they had anything close to the ability to repay us."[13] Bernanke echoes this account: "Lehman's insolvency made it impossible to save with Fed lending alone. Even invoking 13(3) emergency authority we were required to lend against adequate collateral. The Fed had no authority to inject capital or (what is more or less the same thing) make a loan that we were not really sure could be fully repaid."[14]

This rationale, using the authority frame, would seem to be exculpatory. The crisis managers lacked the legal authority to make the loan. This explanation relieved the Fed of its responsibility for maintaining stability in the crisis but is ultimately an unsatisfying account of the events. In 2011, the report of the Financial Crisis Inquiry Commission found no evidence that the Fed had produced a thorough analysis of Lehman's collateral at the time.[15] In July 2016, economist Laurence Ball produced the only extent analysis of Lehman's collateral for the National Bureau of Economic Research.[16] Ball's report, over two hundred pages, shows that Lehman was solvent, that it had significant collateral, and that a loan from the Fed offered three possibilities. First, it might have allowed Lehman to survive. Second, it might have allowed it to be acquired by another firm such as Barclays. Third, it might have allowed it to wind down, selling off assets in a way less disruptive to the financial markets. The Fed's account claims that it didn't have the authority to do any of these things. Ball's report suggests three reasons to doubt the Fed's authority account for its performance on Lehman weekend.

Evidence of Collateral

First, Ball concludes that there is no evidence that the Fed had examined the adequacy of Lehman's collateral. He demonstrates that in the summer of 2008, Fed officials were exploring how they might use the Primary Dealer Credit Facility (PDCF), created after Bear weekend, for loans to Lehman. They showed little concern with Lehman's collateral during this time. Ball shows that even during the week before the Lehman bankruptcy, the Fed was developing a plan for liquidity support.[17] But on Lehman weekend, the New York Fed refused Lehman's requests for such support. The crisis managers later argued that the Fed could not have legally rescued Lehman because of inadequate collateral. But the Financial Crisis Inquiry Commission (FCIC) could not find any documents discussing adequate collateral. The FCIC made repeated requests to see the calculations that the Fed had used to reach this conclusion, but never received a response.[18] One of the CEOs involved in the strategy sessions at the New York Fed on Lehman weekend, John Thain of Merrill Lynch, told the FCIC, "There was never discussion to the best of my recollection that they couldn't (bail out Lehman). It was only that they wouldn't."[19]

Legal Authority

Second, Ball argues that section 13(3), which had been used on Bear Stearns weekend, provided the authority needed to assist Lehman. It required that the situation be unusual and exigent and that the lender exhausted all other sources of financing. These conditions were met and the Fed had become the lender of last resort. What Ball refers to as "the tricky part" is the requirement of deciding what constitutes "satisfactory security" for a loan, meaning that the collateral is likely to reimburse the lender in the case of a default.[20] Ball cites internal legal memos from 2008 stating that the Fed's discretion in defining satisfactory security was extremely broad, meaning that the Fed could count the assets it chose to count.[21] On September 14, 2014, the *New York Times* reported interviews with six Fed insiders revealing that they believed at the time that the Fed had the authority to rescue Lehman. As one informant explained, "We had lawyers joined at the hip. . . . They never said we couldn't do it." As another put it, "It was a policy decision and political decision, not a legal decision."[22]

Adequate Collateral

Third, Ball closely examined the balance sheet provided by Lehman's bankruptcy. He notes that the firm's assets were approximately equal to its liabilities, each about $570 billion. Thus, the firm was solvent. More important, its liabilities included $115 billion in long-term unsecured debt that was not due for twelve months or more. As Ball states, this suggests "that Lehman had enough collateral for any liquidity support it might have needed."[23] The firm also had equity of $28 billion as of August 31, 2008, so Ball calculates a total of $143 billion available collateral.[24] It is highly unlikely that all short-term liabilities would come due at once, so Ball then estimates Lehman's real liquidity needs assuming a bank run on Lehman. He considers a four-week horizon that would have given Lehman time to find a buyer, most likely Barclays, or wind down its businesses without causing the kind of corrosive panic that occurred. He estimates that Lehman would have needed to borrow $88 billion from the Fed. Examining Lehman's existing collateral, Ball finds that it had ample assets and that it could have survived if the Fed had not restricted its access to the PDCF.

A Third Account

The contradictions and gaps in the Fed's own accounts of its action provide reason to consider an alternative explanation of events. There is a third way to account for Lehman weekend, one that reframes the issue of authority. In this interpretation of events, the inadequacy of the first account is taken for granted. Neither the crisis managers at the Fed nor the major firms on Wall Street expected the market to efficiently adjust to a Lehman failure. A catastrophe was expected based on the understanding that Lehman was "too interconnected to fail." The Fed's emergency powers, especially since the Great Depression, were created to maintain order in the face of "unusual and exigent" circumstances in the markets. But, the crisis was not solely in the markets. It was a mutual failure of the market and the state. The legitimacy of the existing regulatory arrangements was called into question and appropriate action was paralyzed. In this account of the crisis, the failure was in the interdependent relationship of two social institutions.

A legitimacy crisis occurred when the application of existing regulatory arrangements was widely and vehemently disparaged.[25] These public attacks revealed a glaring discrepancy between the Fed's emergency powers and the expectations of a hostile political and cultural environment. As we saw in the rescue of Bear Stearns, Fed action to save a Wall Street firm was dubbed a "bailout." The term became ubiquitous in the week before Lehman weekend as the government placed Fannie Mae and Freddie Mac in conservatorship, pledging to provide whatever funds would be necessary to guarantee the firms' obligations. Bernanke notes in his memoir that both media and political views were against any "extraordinary measure to prevent Lehman's failure."[26] Numerous media outlets sniped that Treasury Secretary Hank Paulson had saved Fannie and Freddie with the bazooka that he had claimed would stay in his pocket. In his memoir, Bernanke describes the days before Lehman weekend:

> The media piled on. London's respected *Financial Times* noted the government takeover two weeks earlier of Fannie Mae and Freddie Mac, adding "Further such rescues should be avoided like the plague." The *Wall Street Journal* opined, "If the feds step in to save Lehman after Bear and Fannie Mae, we will no longer have exceptions forged in a crisis. We will have a new de facto federal policy of underwriting Wall Street that will encourage even more reckless risk-taking.[27]

On September 9, the *Wall Street Journal* carried an opinion piece by John McCain and Sarah Palin, the Republican nominees for president and vice president, titled "We'll Protect You from More Bailouts." On September 12, the *Washington Post* ran a front-page article that began with a summary of the cultural tropes being applied to the developing Lehman situation.

Self-reliance. Individual responsibility. A faith in free markets and a belief that people should have the opportunity to fail or succeed on the basis of their hard work and ingenuity. These are the qualities that have been as central to the national identity as they have been to the American economic model.

Which is why it is so extraordinary that the government now finds itself hip-deep in the direct management of the financial system.... This unprecedented intrusion of government is coming in the waning days of the administration of a Republican president who made privatization, deregulation, and faith in free markets the centerpiece of his economic policies and of his political agenda.[28]

Other media outlets commented on the irony of a potential bailout for Lehman using classic versions of market logic. The *Christian Science Monitor* wrote on its front page:

Has the US entered a new era of government bailouts for business? First, Uncle Sam intervened to rescue investment bank Bear Stearns. Then last week the government took over failing mortgage giants Fannie Mae and Freddie Mac. Now Lehman Brothers is tottering—raising the prospect of another US salvage operation . . . the bailouts have occurred under a supposedly pro-free market administration.[29]

The *St. Louis Post-Dispatch* was less ironic and more pointed on the first page of its business section:

The words "federal" and "bailout" are appearing together much too frequently these days. Even with a president who professes his belief in free markets, we seem to have entered an era in which Uncle Sam's deep pockets are seen as the solution to every problem. . . . Unfortunately, instead of treating bailouts as something to be avoided, our society is increasingly looking to government as a lender of first resort.[30]

The *Wall Street Journal* ran an editorial saying, "At least in the Bear case there was a legitimate fear of systemic risk."[31]

This widespread media critique implied that a bailout of Lehman threatened America's cultural traditions.[32] A potent and very public narrative had emerged in the media that combined the sacred value of individual responsibility with the anathema of government bailouts. This narrative captured a wide spectrum of American values at a moment when Wall Street was at a low ebb in its popularity. The media were tapping into a fundamental vain of anger and frustration.

After the bailouts of Fannie Mae and Freddie Mac, the political atmosphere was highly charged. It is not surprising that there was little political interest in being seen to support a bailout given the media hostility. The critique was omnipresent, with journalists noting the irony of free market politicians using public funds to bail out Lehman. Both candidates for president, John McCain *and* Barack Obama, opposed a taxpayer bailout of Lehman.[33] Geithner wrote in his memoir that Senator Obama had put out the word that he didn't want a taxpayer-financed rescue of Lehman. "This was also the emphatic consensus of both parties in Congress."[34] Geithner wrote further that Hank Paulson's aides "were pressing him (Paulson) to draw a line in the sand against bailouts."[35] By the end of the week, a Lehman bailout had become politically untenable. According to Andrew Sorkin's investigative reporting, Paulson told the bankers assembled at the Fed on the first night of Lehman weekend, "There's no consensus for government to get involved, there is no will to do this in Congress." He talked about how Nancy Pelosi had been "all over him" opposing a bailout.[36] The political support for administrative action had contracted at the very time it needed to expand.[37]

The impending failure of Lehman had become a kind of allegorical social drama. Even on Wall Street, Lehman was seen as a reckless corporate citizen, assuming irresponsible levels of risk.[38] Lehman's CEO, Dick Fuld, was being mocked by his peers on Lehman weekend.[39] In the rising financial chaos, Lehman was a public symbol of all that was wrong with Wall Street, and its potential rescue was portrayed as both unfair and a bad example for other firms. Allowing Lehman to fail represented partial amends for Wall Street's risk-laden excess and a momentary corrective for the government's perceived overindulgence in bailouts. The political culture and its elites called for redress.

So, how did the crisis managers at the Fed and Treasury deal with this political and media environment? What were the consequences of this environment for their behavior? By the Wednesday before Lehman weekend, Ben Bernanke was telling Jamie Dimon, CEO of JPMorgan, referring to Hank Paulson, "The negative publicity is really getting to him."[40] The fallout from the bailout of Fannie Mae and Freddie Mac was still very fresh. Tim Geithner reports that on the next day, Thursday, Paulson told him that after his instrumental role in the rescue of Fannie and Freddie, "I can't be

Mr. Bailout." He instructed Geithner that the message to the Wall Street bankers must be very clear: "No government money." According to Geithner, sensing that this would severely limit any bank's interest in playing the role that JPMorgan had played in the purchase of Bear Stearns, "I told Hank this was a huge mistake . . . This was one of the few times there was any distance between Hank and me."[41] As Geithner explains, "Whatever the merits of no-public-money as a bargaining position, I didn't think it made sense as actual public policy."[42] At the Friday meeting at the New York Fed, Geithner did indeed tell the bankers that "there is no political will in Washington for a bailout."[43] In fact, the message had already been leaked to the press by Michele Davis, Paulson's head of communications, that Paulson was "adamant."[44]

Paulson, both overtly in the meetings with bank CEOs at the New York Fed and covertly through leaks to the media, asserted his preeminence as crisis manager. Yet it was the Fed that had the emergency lending authority in this instance and the decision to use section 13(3) rested with its leadership. Although the Fed is an independent agency and had separated from Treasury influence in 1951, the Secretary of the Treasury meets weekly with the Chair of the Federal Reserve. In 1987, after the stock market crash, the Treasury Department established the President's Working Group on Financial Markets to handle crises. It included the Treasury Secretary and the chairs of the Federal Reserve and the Securities and Exchange Commission. Paulson added the president of the New York Fed, Tim Geithner, when he became secretary in 2006.

Paulson's opposition probably doomed any rescue effort. On Friday, when the bankers gathered at the New York Fed, Geithner, Bernanke, and Paulson all still hoped a deal could be made in which another bank would buy Lehman. But Geithner believed that public money would still be needed to close the deal and that failure to close the deal would result in panic in the financial markets. "I didn't mind no-bailouts as a negotiating stance, as long as we understood that ultimately, private money wasn't going to defuse a global panic on its own."[45] Geithner told Paulson, "The amount of public money you're going to have to spend is going up, more than you would otherwise. Your statement is way out of line."[46] But Paulson's insistence on "no government money" undoubtedly discouraged potential buyers of Lehman. According to reporting by Andrew Ross Sorkin, the statement made to the bankers assembled at the New York Fed that there would be no government money "seemed ridiculous to many in the room. Without Fed help, this wasn't going to happen."[47] By the time Paulson told Alistair Darling in England that no government money would be used in a deal with Barclays, the rescue effort was dead.

The Dynamics of Legitimacy

The fervid rhetoric about "bailouts" in the media expressed the idea that the prevailing system of norms and values (e.g., faith in free markets and belief in the opportunity to fail and succeed) was being challenged by the potential rescue of Lehman Brothers. The journalists invoked a widely used version of the American national identity, one that had been dominant at least since Ronald Reagan was president. There was a presumption that Lehman should be allowed to fail. This left little or no room for political or administrative dialogue. Hank Paulson's adamant protest that "I cannot be Mr. Bailout" was a recognition that there was no legitimate space for the technocratic/ administrative solution. It was a capitulation to a political culture in which the rational state-based solution was held in contempt. There was a political and cultural clash between the experts and their public.[48]

Formally, the Fed is not part of the executive branch and not beholden to it. It is, in fact, a quasi-governmental institution chartered by Congress. Legally, the decision to use section 13(3) was in the hands of the Federal Reserve Board. In theory, a powerful institution such as the Fed could defy the dominant media and political discourse. But, was that likely to happen when these actors understood that they were in direct opposition to the political and cultural zeitgeist? In this sense, the Lehman weekend was a legitimacy crisis for the Fed, a questioning of the appropriateness and acceptability of an organization's actions by its stakeholders.[49] Thus, the financial crisis was also a political and administrative crisis. A bailout of Lehman, imperative to avoid a severe financial panic, threatened the withdrawal of public and political legitimacy from the Fed. Any arrangement for a rescue of Lehman was widely disparaged. In this context, the Fed had no clear source of support. It had been undermined by the bailout of Fannie Mae and Freddie Mac, after which government intervention had been demonized beyond the crisis managers' ability to justify action. The Fed's typical behind-the-scenes policymaking had become front-page news focused on the claim that it was about to violate fundamental principles of both the market and the political culture.

This account argues that by Lehman weekend, Federal Reserve assistance in a purchase of Lehman had little chance of happening, thereby ensuring Lehman's failure and its devastating consequences for financial markets and the wider economy. The expert stakeholders, the Fed and the Wall Street bankers, expected these consequences. They worked all weekend to improvise a solution similar to the one used for Bear Stearns. But Hank Paulson had already disavowed such a solution on Thursday night. Any doubt about his intentions melted away over the course of the weekend. There would be no government money. By the following Tuesday, at a meeting of the Federal Open Market Committee (FOMC), Eric Rosengren summarized the outcome as follows: "I think it's too soon to know whether what we did with Lehman is right. Given that the Treasury didn't want to put money in, what happened was that we had no choice. . . . We did what we had to do, but I hope we will find a way to not get into this position again."[50]

An Improvisation Interrupted

In the Bear Stearns crisis in March, the Fed performed an improvisation, creating lending facilities, the Term Securities Lending Facility and the Primary Dealer Credit Facility, and brokering a deal with JPMorgan to buy Bear Stearns with a $29 billion loan from the New York Fed. This improvisation was based on Bagehot's Dictum that the central bank must lend boldly in a panic. Six months later the same crisis managers faced an even bigger crisis. Once again, it was a liquidity crisis in an investment bank. This time the improvisation was more elaborate. They brought Wall Street bankers together at the New York Fed to work simultaneously on three scenarios, two reflecting alternative financing strategies for preventing a bankruptcy that would tip markets into panic and the third for mitigating the consequences of such a panic. At the same time, in the same building, Fed officials cajoled Bank of America and Barclays to play the role played by JPMorgan in March. But these improvisational efforts to interpret the Lehman situation and match it to a Bear-like solution were doomed. The improvisers did not have the same freedom to improvise, to reorder the "unusual and exigent" circumstances.

So, it was not that the Fed's crisis managers thought that the market would adjust to the failure. They successfully mobilized themselves and the Wall Street bankers to interpret the situation and find a solution. They were improvising on the same lender-of-last-resort theme as in the Bear Stearns crisis. The cues were similar; the causal narrative, a run on short-term funding, was similar; and the attempted matching solution, based on Bagehot's Dictum, was the same. Tim Geithner expected the Fed to play the same sort of role. As crisis managers, the Fed felt once again empowered to go outside the routine to interpret the circumstances. But this time, the media and political environment provided different cues and a competing narrative. The power of the "no more bailouts" narrative restrained Hank Paulson and disrupted the Fed's improvisation.

Accounting for Failure

The first two accounts of Lehman weekend described efforts by the Fed crisis managers to make sense of these events for others, to create a workable interpretation for the media, politicians, and the general public. These accounts salvaged the legitimacy of the Fed and assigned normatively appropriate justifications, the first drawn from market logic and the second from state logic. These alternative interpretations reflected the unresolved contest between market and state logics that is at the heart of central banking in crisis. The events of this weekend were ominous and signified a threat to the reputations of the agency and the actors. The third account offers a broader interpretation of the events. It suggests that the Fed's improvisatory efforts to intervene in a way similar to its action on Bear Stearns weekend were overwhelmed by a legitimacy crisis that afforded a temporary advantage for the culturally endorsed market logic. In Chapter 7 we will see how the consequences of Lehman weekend created a systemic threat that reduced political and cultural resistance to a state-based solution, shifted the narrative further toward contagion and systemic risk, reenergized the improvisatory skills at the Fed, and facilitated renewed learning and innovation.

7

Learning after Lehman

SEPTEMBER–DECEMBER 2008

One of the best indicators of the health of an organization is its ability to learn in the midst of a crisis. Members must share an awareness of the threat posed by the crisis and overcome patterns of behavior that favor routine. The more severe the crisis, the more crisis managers must reach outside their traditional practices and knowledge if they are to identify effective solutions. To do so they make sense of disorienting cues that are in continuous flux, develop a shared narrative about what is occurring, and recognize and agree on an appropriate set of actions. The ability of the Federal Open Market Committee (FOMC) to accomplish these tasks was in question in the weeks and months after Lehman weekend. This chapter argues that despite the limitations of retrospective data and the inertia of existing practice, it became clear that standard procedures were inadequate to the severity of conditions. The obsolescence of traditional monetary policy after Lehman weekend and a redefinition of appropriate practice created the conditions for transformational organizational learning.

September 16, 2008: "Wait and See"

The September FOMC meeting was scheduled for the Tuesday after Lehman weekend; thus there was little time to make sense of the situation. American stock markets dropped about 4.5 percent on Monday. Financial markets around the world had declined significantly and were continuing to drop during the meeting. Financial firms with a direct trading relationship to Lehman were particularly vulnerable. At the start of the meeting, Bill Dudley from the New York Fed reviewed the actions that had already been taken. On Monday, the Fed had broadened access to the Primary Dealer Credit Facility that it had created in March by extending the types of collateral it would accept from borrowers. It also offered two auctions of $35 billion each at its Term Securities Lending Facility (TSLF) that provided banks with Treasury securities in exchange for their risker and less liquid assets. This action would, as Dudley put it, "get quite a bit of TSLF liquidity into the market this week."[1] Early in the meeting, Chairman Ben Bernanke requested that the FOMC delegate to its foreign currency subcommittee "unspecified authority, in terms of amount" for arranging swaps of US dollars for foreign currency to major central banks as needed. The Committee approved the request unanimously. This lending reflected the international nature of the contagion. The Fed became the world's lender of last resort.

Though the Fed had opened the spigots of liquidity to financial markets, staff economist David Stockton was ambivalent about predicting the long-term fallout from the Lehman collapse:

> I don't really have anything useful to say about the economic consequences of the financial developments of the past few days. I must say I'm not feeling very well about it at the present, but I'm not sure whether that reflects rational economic analysis or the fact that I've had too many meals out of the vending machines downstairs in the last few days [*laughter*]. But in any event, we're obviously going to need to wait a bit to see how the dust settles here.[2]

The cues coming from financial markets since the announcement of Lehman's bankruptcy on Sunday seemed ominous. There were two narratives about the long-term effects of these cues. One predicted significant impact, the other argued that it was "hard to say." Part of the disagreement in narratives was surely explained by the immediacy of events. Another part was tied to the fact that the growth forecasts that members brought to the meeting had been projected before the events of the prior weekend. As David Stockton said, "I don't think we've seen a significant change in the basic outlook, and certainly the story behind our forecast is very similar to the one that we had last time, which is that we're still expecting a very gradual pickup in GDP [gross domestic product] growth over the next year and a little more rapid pickup in 2010."[3]

The "significant impact" narrative reflected the FOMC members' concern that the credit markets were freezing up and that lending to businesses, investors, and consumers would come to a halt. This speculative prediction was based on very recent extreme events whose intensity elicited strong reactions. Elizabeth Duke expressed the anguished anticipation of the "significant impact" narrative. "The markets are fragile to dead," she said. "So what are they going to do? The only thing they can do is contract the balance sheet and not lend. . . . So what are they doing in terms of credit? Any heavy uses of credit or predominant uses of credit are just not being done."[4] This narrative was, in a sense, an extension of the contagion narrative, elaborating its expected effects. These speculations were pessimistic but accurate.

ERIC ROSENGREN: The failure of a major investment bank, the forced merger of another, the largest thrift and insurer teetering, and the failure of Freddie and Fannie are likely to have a significant impact on the real economy. Individuals and firms will become risk averse, with reluctance to consume or to invest. Even if firms were inclined to invest, credit spreads are rising, and the cost and availability of financing is becoming more difficult. Many securitization vehicles are frozen. The degree of financial distress has risen markedly.[5]

GARY STERN: Well, even before the events of the last several days, I thought that this was the most severe financial crisis, certainly, that I have seen in my career. . . . So I think it is fair to say that the headwinds confronting the economy have intensified even further. It is difficult to comment on the degree or the duration, but I think we know the direction.[6]

The majority of members were more reticent in projecting the effects of the unfolding financial situation. These members, like Charles Evans, were disinclined to say what the effects might be. "In one or two weeks, we may know better that either the economy will somehow muddle through or we're likely to be facing the mother of all credit crunches," he said. "I think that the first outcome would be quite an accomplishment under the circumstances, but at the moment it's very *hard to say* how this will turn out."[7] It was particularly unclear which financial firms and how many of them would be endangered, as Lehman was, by the withdrawal of investors and trading partners.

The markets were in a volatile moment. As Kevin Warsh explained, "I think the question before us today that's hard to judge is whether financial markets are now to the point at which they are acting indiscriminately, testing all financial institutions regardless of capital structure or business model. I'd say that the evidence of the past twenty-four or forty-eight hours is still unclear."[8] Ben Bernanke tried to encapsulate this reticent narrative.

> Financial markets received a lot of attention around the table. . . . Almost all major financial institutions are facing significant stress, particularly difficulties in raising capital, and credit quality is problematic. . . . However, the medium-term implications of the recent increases in financial stress for the economy are difficult to assess. We may have to wait for some time to get greater clarity on the implications of the last week or so.[9]

The members had undoubtedly prepared for the Tuesday meeting in the prior week and the statistics on which they based their preparations bore no trace of the Lehman failure. Despite the negative cues coming from conditions in the financial markets and the existence of competing narratives, there was general consensus among the FOMC members about appropriate policy. They agreed that they should wait for more data before providing further accommodation to the economy by lowering the fed funds rate. Besides, the Fed was extending access to its 13(3) liquidity facilities and had approved fortified foreign currency swaps with other central banks to liquefy markets in Europe and Asia. Janet Yellen explained the rationale: "With respect to policy, I would be inclined to keep the funds rate target at 2 percent today. For now, it seems to me that the additional liquidity measures that have been put in place are an appropriate response to the turmoil."[10] Most members shared a desire to wait and see how the turmoil influenced the larger economy. Charles Plosser reminded his colleagues the policy must focus on the "real economy" rather than financial markets:

> While a lot of attention in the short run is being paid to financial markets' turmoil, our decision today must look beyond today's financial markets to the real economy and its prospects in the future. In this regard, things have not changed very much, at least not yet. . . . I agree that the recent financial turmoil may ultimately affect the outlook in a significant way, but that is far from obvious at this point.[11]

The fragility in financial markets meant that the policy statement released by the FOMC after the meeting would be parsed even more closely than usual. This was reflected in the cautious wordsmithing by the members. They took great pains to convey that even though they were holding the fed funds rate steady, they were alert to the situation.

KEVIN WARSH: I think the sentiment we are trying to suggest is watchful waiting. We are not indifferent, we are not clueless, we are paying attention, but we are not predisposed.

DON KOHN: My suggestion was to substitute "carefully" for "closely." I agree that "monitor closely" had this other connotation, but I think we should be seen as paying more attention than usual.

BEN BERNANKE: We don't want the world to feel that we are not awake, that we are not paying attention. We know that very unusual things are going on in the financial markets; and we are prepared, maybe not through monetary policy but through whatever mechanism is necessary, to address that. . . . The semiotics class will begin as soon as the—[*laughter*]. All right. "Carefully"—is that okay? I'm seeing nodding.[12]

Beneath the humor and agreement to wait for further developments lay a latent tension over the appropriate role of the Fed in responding to the deepening crisis. Those least comfortable with state intervention in the markets praised the decision not to rescue Lehman Brothers. James Bullard linked the Lehman decision to holding the funds rate at 2 percent. "By denying funding to Lehman suitors, the Fed has begun to reestablish the idea that markets should not expect help at each difficult juncture," he said. "Changing rates today would confuse that important signal and take out much of the positive part out of the previous decision."[13] Thomas Hoenig feared that markets were behaving strategically in anticipation of intervention: "I think what we did with Lehman was the right thing because we did have a market beginning to play the Treasury and us, and that has some pretty negative consequences as well, which we are now coming to grips with."[14] Jeffrey Lacker argued that it was important to signal a willingness on the part of the Fed to let major firms fail as markets adjust themselves, weeding out the weak actors, saying, "What we did with Lehman I obviously think is good. . . . I don't want to be sanguine about it, but the silver lining to all the disruption that's ahead of us is that it will enhance the credibility of any commitment that we make in the future to be willing to let an institution fail and to risk such disruption again."[15]

As discussed in Chapter 6, the Fed's crisis management team, led by Bernanke and Geithner, worked well into the weekend to improvise a sale of

Lehman rather than a bankruptcy.[16] Bernanke and Geithner were concerned about the systemic risk created by the interconnectedness of Lehman to many other banks. In that light, Jeffrey Lacker's comment about the Fed's willingness to let an institution fail provoked the following exchange about the role of the Fed versus the role of Congress and the limits to intervention in the market.

> BEN BERNANKE: President Lacker, I have a question. I really would like your advice on this. . . . Do you think that we should remain very tough until such time as it becomes inevitable that fiscal intervention is needed?

> JEFFREY LACKER: We have a legislated program of fiscal intervention— deposit insurance—and the boundaries around that are very clear. . . . That's what the Congress has enacted, and it's not clear to me whether we should go beyond that.[17]

Later in the meeting, the Bernanke came back to the issue. His statement below reflects inner turmoil. His remarks suggest that he and probably other policymakers were groping their way toward an interpretation of their situation. He questions the scope of their responsibility for reducing systemic risk and how far-reaching interventions should be. More knowledge was needed and the learning process for both individual members and the policy group as a whole had only begun.

> I have been grappling with the question I raised for President Lacker. . . . We have found ourselves . . . in this episode in a situation in which events are happening quickly, and we don't have those things in place. We don't have a set of criteria, we don't have fiscal backstops, and we don't have clear congressional intent. So in each event, in each instance, even though there is this sort of unavoidable ad hoc character to it, we are trying to make a judgment about the costs—from a fiscal perspective, from a moral hazard perspective, and so on—of taking action versus the real possibility in some cases that you might have very severe consequences for the financial system and, therefore, for the economy of not taking action. Frankly, I am decidedly confused and very muddled about this.[18]

The final vote was unanimous in favor of holding the interest rate steady and "carefully" monitoring the situation. It is noteworthy that Bernanke stated in his 2015 memoir that not moving the fed funds rate at the September meeting was a mistake.[19] It was a mistake driven by the limits of the

FOMC to make sense of a recent and dynamic situation and conflicting ideas about the FOMC's appropriate role in crisis management.

October 7, 2018, Conference Call: Growing Concern

Three weeks after the September meeting, the chairman arranged a conference call to get the FOMC's approval for a half percentage point reduction in the fed funds rate, from 2.0 percent to 1.5. The move was to be coordinated with five other central banks and had been negotiated in response to the spreading contagion and credit crunch that had been anticipated at the September meeting.

BEN BERNANKE: The only agenda item for this meeting is the discussion of a proposed coordinated action with five other major central banks. It will be a six-bank coordinated action. Besides ourselves, the other banks involved are the European Central Bank, the Bank of England, and the Bank of Canada, and since I spoke to you, the Swiss National Bank and the Bank of Sweden have joined in this collective action. . . . The plan, conditional on our approval, would be for all six major central banks to cut policy rates by 50 basis points jointly and announce tomorrow at 7:00 a.m. Eastern time before the U.S. markets open.[20]

Bernanke turned to Bill Dudley, manager of open market operations. Dudley presented cues that suggested that the Fed's escalation of auctions of Treasury securities and foreign currency swaps had not been enough to stabilize markets.

First, market participants continue to pull back in their willingness to engage with one another. . . . Second, financial conditions continue to tighten, and in recent weeks, the tightening has been substantial. . . . On the equity market side, for example, the S&P 500 index has fallen about 18 percent since the September 16 FOMC meeting. . . . .The third aspect of the market that I think warrants noting is that the U.S. financial sector in particular remains under pressure, especially with respect to share prices and banks' ability to obtain funding, especially term funding. . . . I am struck by the feeble market response to the substantial escalations implemented over the past ten days.[21]

In the ensuing discussion, the members constructed a "growing concern" narrative. This narrative assessed the situation in a range from "quite worrisome" to "dangerous." Bernanke admitted that he thought that 2 percent would be the bottom for the fed funds rate, saying, "I very much expected that we could stay at 2 percent for a long time, and then when the economy began to recover, we could begin to normalize interest rates. But clearly things have gone off in a direction that is quite worrisome."[22] Don Kohn suggested that expectations for the major statistical indicators of the economy should be reconsidered: "I think the incoming data and the events of the last month or so suggest a major downward revision to expected income and a substantial revision to expected inflation. . . . This is a credit crunch. . . . I think there's a real risk of a very sharp downturn in the economy here."[23] Kevin Warsh pushed the reconsideration of expectations even further, saying, "I think the best way to view financial markets is to say that what's fundamentally going on is a reassessment of the value of every asset everywhere in the world, and what might have been triggered by housing has certainly gone beyond that."[24]

The dramatic cues in the financial markets and the revised expectations for the economy made the members willing to support the coordinated action that Bernanke had negotiated with the other central banks. But most members were skeptical that the move would have any significant impact. The ongoing turmoil in the markets was having immediate effects on credit whereas rate cuts were typically felt in the economy with a six-month lag. Members saw the cuts as largely symbolic. As Charles Plosser said, "They may provide some solace to the markets. I hope they will."[25] Justifications for the cuts were most often tied to the signal it might send to the markets about the central banks' engagement and willingness to intervene. Bernanke, sensitive to the skepticism about the efficacy of the rate cuts, repeatedly framed the action as a bridge to other policy responses, in particular, a fiscal response from Congress.

> I want to say once again that I don't think that monetary policy is going to solve this problem. I don't think liquidity policy is going to solve this problem. I think the only way out of this is fiscal and perhaps some regulatory and other related policies. But we don't have that yet. We're working toward that. We are in a very serious situation. So it seems to me that there is a case for moving now in an attempt to provide some reassurance—it may or may not do so—but in any case, to try to do what we can to make a bridge toward the broader approach to the crisis.[26]

October 28–29, 2008: Sensing Implosion

BEN BERNANKE: I don't think this is going to be a self-correcting thing anytime soon.[27]

In the three weeks between the conference call and the next regularly scheduled meeting, the contagion in financial markets spiraled downward and the Fed used its 13(3) authority to respond with substantial extensions of liquidity to markets, banks, and investment firms. At the beginning of the meeting, Bill Dudley once again recounted some of the efforts:

> The Federal Reserve dramatically expanded its programs of liquidity support. The size of each TAF [term auction facility] auction has been raised to $150 billion—the same size as the entire TAF program just six weeks ago. Fixed-rate tender dollar auctions were implemented by the BoE, the BoJ, the ECB, and the SNB. The asset-backed commercial paper money market mutual fund liquidity facility (AMLF) and the commercial paper funding facility (CPFF) were implemented, and plans for a money market investor funding facility (MMIFF) were announced. The Federal Reserve and other central banks stepped forward to engage in transactions with a broad range of bank and, in the case of the Fed, nonbank counterparties.[28]

In the ensuing discussion, the members constructed an implosion narrative, a sense that a dramatic collapse was occurring. Richard Fisher, with his usual linguistic flair, captured the mood of the implosion narrative and provided its label: "We have had an implosion of economic activity. . . . The situation is dire. There is no question about that. We are in dire straits. . . . The risks are to the downside on economic growth."[29] Ben Bernanke described the precipitant for the implosion as follows: "The investment banks essentially faced runs. We did our best to stabilize them, but I think that it was that run, that panic, and then the impact the panic had on these major institutions that was the source of the intensification of financial crisis."[30] Tim Geithner added scope to the causal dynamic and specified its consequences, saying, "The outlook has been deteriorating ahead of the policy response. . . . The magnitude and speed of the tightening financial conditions, the erosion in business and consumer confidence, the fall in actual spending, and the shift in inflation risk together present very grave risks to growth and to the financial system."[31]

Several members remarked on the timing of the implosion, placing it in the wake of Lehman weekend. As Jeffrey Lacker explained, "A discrete shift in outlook seems to have occurred. It seems to me to have originated during the week of September 15 or shortly thereafter."[32] Charles Evans, making a Halloween reference, described the psychological effect of the event: "An abrupt change occurred in September. People are spooked—sorry—[*laughter*] and it is showing through to spending."[33] The members of the FOMC adopted the language of panic, a social/emotional process that included loss of confidence, anxiety, and irrational economic behavior. The natural imagery of the self-correcting system had been replaced by recognition of human behavioral dynamics, escaping the confines of an equilibrium-based model.

Both the staff and the members were highly uncertain when predicting the consequences of the implosion. The staff projections offered a range of possible outcomes. As it had been throughout the financial crisis, forecasting the implications was a matter of professional judgment rather than using the results from statistical models. Sandra Pianalto reiterated the inadequacy of the data and models in this situation, saying, "Like the Greenbook projection, my projection is heavily influenced by judgments that we are bringing to the projection from forces that are not captured by our models. The magnitude of the judgmental adjustment has become strikingly large."[34] Despite long experience at the Fed, Don Kohn could not offer a confident judgment. "Critically, the downside risks around activity forecasts are huge and tilted to the downside," he said. "I think they're huge because we've never seen a situation like this before, certainly not in my experience dating all the way back to 1970, and have only the vaguest notion of how it will play out in financial markets and spending."[35]

When the FOMC members turned to the discussion of policy options, the group was divided. Most members, responding to the conditions that generated the implosion narrative, felt that the "downside risk" was sufficiently high that more dramatic action was justified. They believed that another half percent decrease in the fed funds rate, from 1.5 to 1.0, was needed. As Eric Rosengren explained, "We are facing problems of historic proportions, both here and abroad. A 50 basis point easing . . . is both necessary and appropriate. . . . To avoid a severe and prolonged recession, we will very likely need further monetary easing and a significant fiscal package, even after this 50 basis point reduction in the federal funds rate."[36] Sandra Pianalto expressed the sense of urgency that many felt and that matched the implosion narrative. "I know that some prefer a more measured response, especially as we move closer to the zero bound," she said, "but the lesson I take from history is that more and sooner is better than taking smaller steps over time."[37] Janet Yellen echoed this sense of urgency, rejecting any argument for hesitation:

> Frankly, it is time for all-hands-on-deck when it comes to our policy tools, and the fed funds rate should be no exception. . . . We need to do much more and the sooner, the better. One might argue against such a policy move in favor of a wait-and-see approach to better gauge if the recent flurry of policy initiatives will turn things around. In normal times, I would have some sympathy for this argument, but these are about as far from normal times as we can get. We are in the midst of a global economic and financial freefall.[38]

The minority position also reflected the implosion narrative but saw the appropriate response as a pause in the action. As Thomas Hoenig put it, "Right now, we're subject to waiting and seeing. There's been a lot done, and attitudes are a critical part of this now, and we just have to wait to see how those change over the next quarter or two."[39] There was a sense that if the implosion in financial markets was a panic, then it needed time to calm down. Charles Plosser explained that it was the Fed's job not to feed the panic by overreacting. "I think it's a mistake to overreact to volatile data . . . the economy is better served if monetary policy is a steadying hand, taking appropriate action when the intermediate-term view dictates, but not overreacting to fluctuations in the market with an inappropriate tool."[40] As Plosser was suggesting, some members believed that a lower fed funds rate would not solve the liquidity problems in financial markets. There were other "tools," such as the 13(3) liquidity facilities and congressionally approved fiscal policy that they believed could be more targeted, providing a better match between the problem and the solution. James Bullard stated this position clearly:

> My preference based on this would be to leave rates alone and say, "Let's use fiscal policy." I don't think what we have now is an interest rate problem. What we have now are problems in credit markets, and I think they are being fairly well addressed by the most recent fiscal actions, including capital injections into the banking sector. So that would be my preference at this point.[41]

Once again, as in previous meetings, there were deeper issues that underlay the negotiation. The first issue was that by lowering the funds rate to

1.0 percent, the FOMC was approaching the zero lower bound of its key policy tool. What form and scope would policy take once that boundary was reached? As Richard Fisher framed the zero bound problem, "The real question is, 'What do we do about it, and what's the cognitive road map from here?'"[42] Jeffrey Lacker reminded the FOMC members that they had approached the zero bound in 2003 and discussed policy options. His observation prompted an interruption and reply by the chair.

> JEFFREY LACKER: I wasn't a member of the Committee five years ago. My understanding, though, is that much thought was given to how we would conduct monetary policy if we needed to reduce the nominal federal funds rate to zero or its effective equivalent.

> BEN BERNANKE: May I? . . . [L]et me just make a suggestion, which is that there were a number of memos and studies done in 2003. I think we ought to look at them, update them, and circulate them fairly soon.[43]

The concerns expressed by Fisher and Lacker about the zero bound were related to the foundational logic of state intervention at the Fed. Several members argued that interventions by the Fed were themselves creating instability and preventing markets from restoring themselves. Reaching the zero bound implied that the Fed was likely to experiment with even more far-reaching nontraditional forms of policy. This prospect distressed the FOMC's staunchest defenders of the logic of the market and its recuperative powers. Jeffrey Lacker argued that these interventions interfered with restorative action by market actors. "A sequence of policy actions and statements has spread an inchoate fear," Lacker said. "In response to that, a wide variety of economic agents have delayed outlays. The breathtaking credit market interventions that we have undertaken in the last several weeks are going to make it hard to judge whether those markets are stabilized."[44] Richard Fisher explained that the market's recuperative powers were dependent on knowing how far the state would intervene in rescuing failing firms and injecting capital: "You cannot have a functioning capitalist system if you have total uncertainty. These are the issues that I believe President Plosser, President Hoenig, earlier President Lacker, and others were referring to."[45] Some members, like Charles Plosser, felt the Fed may have already gone too far. "I think we have dug ourselves a very deep hole in terms of the breadth and depth of our lending to the private sector. We seem, at times, to be the lender of first resort as well as the lender of last resort."[46]

Tim Geithner and Ben Bernanke, who had been on the frontlines of crisis management at least since Bear Stearns weekend, defended the logic of state action. Geithner's strong rebuttal to the critics reflected his personal investment in aggressive intervention and his perception of the systemic threat represented by the financial situation.

> I do not believe that this Chairman and this Committee have been irresponsibly experimenting at the cost of predictability and confidence going forward. What we have done is a relatively well designed series of escalations in monetary policy and liquidity intended to be preemptive against what we knew was substantial risk of a very adverse economic and financial outcome. The risks were not broadly shared, not just in this room but outside.[47]

Bernanke stated the case for aggressive action and experimentation in less defensive tones but was definitive in rejecting the idea that the market might restore itself without further intervention.

> I do think that one lesson of both Japan and the 1930s as well as other experiences is that passivity is not a good answer. We do have to continue to be aggressive. We have to continue to look for solutions. Some of them are not going to work. Some of them are going to add to uncertainty. I recognize that critique. I realize it's a valid critique. But I don't think that this is going to be a self-correcting thing anytime soon. I think we are going to have to continue to provide support of all kinds to the economy.[48]

The vote to lower the fed funds rate to 1 percent was unanimous. Of the minority who argued against the move, both voting members, Fisher and Plosser, joined in the unanimous approval. After the vote, Richard Fisher remarked that it was important to be "fully supportive" of the Fed's initiatives. Charles Plosser and Jeffrey Lacker, anticipating the December meeting, reiterated the request that the staff refresh the 2003 research on policy options beyond the zero bound.

December 15–16, 2008: A New Regime

BEN BERNANKE: Good afternoon, everybody. . . . As you know, under the extraordinary circumstances we added an extra day to the meeting. The purpose of the meeting taking place today is to discuss the zero lower bound and related policy and governance issues, and I hope that the discussion today will set up our policy decision for tomorrow.[49]

The point at which the FOMC could no longer lower the fed funds rate offered a juxtaposition of order and disorder to the policymakers at the Fed.[50] The FOMC's practice of monetary policy was primarily anchored in the orderly raising and lowering of its target interest rate. Reaching the lower boundary of that rate not only disrupted the conventions of standard monetary policy, but as Richard Fisher pointed out in the October meeting, it left them without a map, thereby prompting a threat of disorder and an exploration for alternatives. In response to members' requests at the October meeting to revisit the 2003 discussions of policy options, the staff prepared twenty-one notes on various issues and options. Chairman Bernanke arranged for the FOMC to gather ahead of the usual December meeting for a broad-ranging discussion of options and approaches. As staff economist Steve Meyer explained the problem, "With the target federal funds rate at 1 percent and the effective rate significantly lower, the Committee has little scope for using conventional monetary policy to stimulate the economy. . . . Whether or not the Committee chooses to cut its target rate to zero, policymakers may find it helpful to expand the use of nonstandard monetary tools."[51]

The arrival at the zero bound, concurrent with the accelerating implosion of the economy, focused attention on the ambiguity of future policy options and created the context for a moment of transformational learning. At such a moment, the conventional reproductive process of learning discussed in Chapter 3 is no longer effective. Continued incremental movement of the fed funds rate was no longer possible. This was a moment of normlessness for the policy group. There was little precedent and an unclear understanding of effective operating procedures. The following account of the first day of the December meeting will examine the process of group learning in this transformational moment.

Recognizing the Moment

The first step toward transformational group learning was building a consensus that the situation required novel action. As Jeffrey Lacker put it, "Mr. Chairman, this is a critical moment for the Fed and the economy. Whatever we do and say at this meeting is going to mark a discrete change in the way we have conducted policy and communicated about it to the public in recent years."[52] Not only was the moment marked as distinct, but it was understood that the action to be taken would be seen as unorthodox and controversial. Sandra Pianalto explained, "I do think it is time and it would be helpful to begin focusing the public's attention on the unconventional approach to monetary policy."[53] Across the spectrum of policy activism on the FOMC there was agreement that this was the moment and that there was some urgency in signaling that the Fed was not without ideas and resources for coping with it. Many seemed to realize that the zero bound posed a threat to the Fed's image. As Charles Plosser stated, "I think it's time that we publicly convey that we have entered a new monetary policy regime. To do otherwise perpetuates the view that we are no longer in control of monetary policy."[54]

Embracing Exploration

BEN BERNANKE: With respect to monetary policy, we are at this point moving away from the standard interest rate targeting approach and, of necessity, moving toward new approaches. Obviously, these are very deep and difficult issues that we are going to have to address collectively today and tomorrow. I want to say that, although we are certainly moving in a new direction and the outlines of that new direction are not yet clear, this is a work in progress. The discussion we're having today is a beginning.[55]

The recognition of the moment was a necessary but not sufficient condition for transformational learning at the FOMC. The group also exhibited an openness, even urge, to explore a variety of new practices. There was considerable trepidation but also enthusiasm for the learning process they were undertaking. As Sandra Pianalto described it, "While I certainly wish we were not in this circumstance, I do think that this is a critical conversation for us to be having at this meeting, . . . I think that we are going to be learning a lot in the process of implementing policies into ever more uncharted waters."[56] The willingness to explore was purposeful. As Richard Fisher explained, once more using the imagery of a cognitive map, the object of the meeting was to begin to construct an agreed-upon set of principles for the new regime: "I welcome the discussion and welcome the papers so that we can not only have a cognitive road map for ourselves but also figure out how we're going to clearly articulate a deliberate change in regimes to the public."[57]

The willingness to explore was not without apprehension. Members were very conscious that the exploration came with risks. Many of the members compared their situation to the accommodative policies that had been applied in earlier years in Japan and Sweden, with Japan having been relatively unsuccessful in its efforts. Few felt that these countries offered appropriate models. As Randall Kroszner put it:

> We can use analogies from Japan. We can use analogies from other parts of history or from Sweden, but there are a lot of parts that are unique, and a lot of what we're doing is, as I think President Bullard said, outside where some of the data have been in the past. So we do have to come at this with a little humility.[58]

Christine Cummings, standing in for Tim Geithner at the meeting, said, "We are in uncharted waters but we are groping our way forward."[59] Once again, Richard Fisher provided the most vivid description of the mixture of apprehension and enthusiasm for learning in the transformational moment. His comment highlights the pragmatic nature of such learning.

> In addition to reading the 21 papers that were sent out and the Bluebook, this last week I read a novel called *World without End* written by Ken Follett. . . . One of the interesting lessons from reading that book is that the monks in that period, who dominated society, reverted to the old orthodoxy learned from the Greeks. They were the best educated. They were the Oxford-educated intelligentsia. But by reverting to the old orthodoxy, they did not learn what the nuns learned, which is what you learn from practice. The reason I mention this, Mr. Chairman, is that I think there is great value, as we try to figure out and articulate the new regime, to have these shared discussions at the table. . . . All of us have different levels of experience and backgrounds, and we learn from those different levels of experience and backgrounds.[60]

Negotiating the Scope

BRIAN MADIGAN: Ten days ago, we sent you 21 notes covering lessons from the U.S. and Japanese experiences in disinflationary or deflationary environments; the possible costs to financial markets and institutions of very low interest rates; the potential benefits of further rate reductions; and the advantages and disadvantages of nonstandard approaches to providing macroeconomic stimulus that could be employed when the federal funds rate cannot be reduced further.[61]

Part of embracing exploration is a negotiation of the scope of transformation being contemplated. Agreeing on the extent of transformation called for shared understanding of its dimensions and mutual adjustment to differences among members.[62] If the zero bound elicited monetary policy by other means, then what means, how unconventional, and of what magnitude remained unclear. The Fed would need to make significant adjustments to its balance sheet rather than depending on low interest rates as the basis of its monetary policy. Such nontraditional policy was already known as quantitative easing (QE), the large-scale purchase of government or other securities to lower interest rates and increase the money supply. Bernanke opened the discussion of quantitative easing by telling the group that the Fed's 13(3) liquidity-providing facilities had already moved the Fed into a rapid expansion of its balance sheet. He emphasized the experimental nature of these innovations and said that the experiments should continue.

> In some respects our policies are similar to the quantitative easing of the Japanese, but I would argue that, when you look at it more carefully, what we're doing is fundamentally different from the Japanese approach. . . . In particular, we have adopted a series of programs, all of which involve some type of lending or asset purchase, which has brought onto our balance sheet securities other than the typical Treasuries that we usually transact in. . . . I think we ought to think about it as a portfolio of assets, a combination of things that we are doing on the asset side of our balance sheet, that have specific purposes and that may or may not be effective; but we can look at them individually.[63]

After Bernanke's statement, members began to negotiate about which risky instruments, such as mortgage-backed securities (MBS), the Fed should be willing to buy from financial intermediaries. This negotiation was the means by which the group would learn what quantitative easing would mean to it, defining the direction of the "new regime." The point in question was that they would be accepting financial instruments that carried greater risk than those they had accepted previously. Some FOMC members were wary but willing to accept the debt of government agencies that were deeply overextended, such as Fannie Mae and Freddie Mac.

KEVIN WARSH: In a different regime, I would have been uncomfortable about agencies. But my view is that they are wards of the state at this time. The U.S. government has said so. To the extent that we can provide our fire power to both the Treasury market and the agency market, it is probably worthwhile to do both.[64]

At the end of this discussion, the chairman attempted to summarize and consolidate what might fit under this emerging definition of quantitative easing. A number of FOMC members had said that asset purchases by the Open Market Desk at the New York Fed as well as the 13(3) liquidity-providing facilities fit within their definition of appropriate practice under the current crisis conditions. Bernanke said, "I think that the great majority of the Committee is comfortable with MBS and Treasury purchases. . . . What I take from this is that these asset-side programs, the credit facilities as well as the MBS and other programs, are part of our new regime, that most people view them as part of our new regime."[65]

Power Dynamics

Transformational moments are, by their nature, a threat to the status quo of organizational arrangements. Traditional roles and the distribution of power among those roles are shaken up. This can create confusion, resentment, and conflict. If the Fed were to hold the funds rate at or near zero for an extended period, then the central function of the FOMC, interest rate setting, would become mostly anachronistic. At least some of the regional bank presidents on the Committee were concerned that the function of the FOMC would be eclipsed by the Board of Governors, which had authority under section 13(3) of the Federal Reserve Act to oversee the creation and extension of the liquidity facilities.

Chairman Bernanke addressed this apparent power shift by noting the continuing functions of the FOMC. It was still the FOMC's outlook for the economy that would appear in Fed communications. It would be the FOMC that would decide the length of the commitment to holding the fed funds rate at the zero bound. Finally, he reiterated his vision of cooperation between the Board of Governors and the regional presidents. This commitment to cooperation was echoed by other governors, including Don Kohn.

It is not so much about legalities as it is about how to reach the best decisions and how best to explain those decisions to the world at large. We have always worked in a collaborative and cooperative way, and I think we need to continue to do that. Crisis management strains the normal collaborative and deliberative mode of Federal Reserve operations. Decisions get made on short notice, often over a weekend, but as you said, Mr. Chairman, we can work at improving our collaboration.[66]

Bernanke offered a compromise in which the public statement would indicate that the FOMC had "indicated its approval" of extensions of the liquidity facilities. "That may not be entirely satisfactory," he said, "but it would certainly indicate to the public that the FOMC has reviewed it from a monetary policy perspective, and it would appear in the directive, the minutes, and so on. I put that out as just a possible compromise on that issue."[67] But the presidents were not so easily placated. Jeffrey Lacker expressed the clearest sense of resentment. He seemed to feel that FOMC functions, such as foreign exchange swaps with other central banks, were extensively discussed in the Committee, whereas they were simply informed about the development of liquidity facilities, such as the Term Asset-backed Securities Loan Facility (TALF).

I can appreciate the strict constructionist governance view of who gets to approve them (liquidity programs); it is not important that we vote on them. But I have been thinking about this in terms of the ideal—the vision you portrayed and described for us yesterday of a cohesive consensus-building decision making process. . . . We were basically informed about the TALF rather than consulted in any meaningful sense.[68]

Other presidents made it clear that the governance issue was not resolved. As Charles Plosser asserted:

I agree with the Chairman that we need to maintain and embrace the collaborative process between the Board of Governors and the FOMC, which has been our method of moving forward during this crisis. But I remain convinced that in these times of uncertainty we need to be explicit and to communicate that monetary policy remains under the purview of the FOMC.[69]

Richard Fisher reinforced that the governance issue was not resolved. "I do think that President Plosser has raised good issues on the governance matter," he said. "I hope that we will continue to discuss this . . . so that we have to get at least our lines of understanding clear as we go through time."[70] A more complete agreement on shared governance during the crisis would require further adjustment.

Signaling to the Markets

As the discussion of governance indicates, the FOMC members were concerned about how the new regime would be perceived by those in the marketplace. As they adopted unconventional procedures, members were aware of the potential for misunderstanding and even a loss of confidence in the Fed's efficacy. According to Randall Kroszner:

> We basically have a lot of explaining to do, and one of the key things to explain is that we have not gotten to the end of our tether, that there's still a lot more that we can do, even though a lot of the world thinks that, once we have "given up" on interest rates or gotten down to our lower bound, we can't be that effective. We have to be very effective in arguing that, no, that's not the case.[71]

Much of the members' concern was stated in terms of "selling" the new regime. As Richard Fisher put it, "I think it's very important, whether we have press conferences or whether you give speeches, that we need to hammer the theme of the new regime that we are about to embrace over and over and over again."[72] James Bullard was even more instrumental in his signaling strategy, saying, "So to get the intended effect in the minds of the private sector, you eliminate references to the federal funds target and force them to rethink their views of monetary policy and rethink what we are doing."[73]

Getting the intended effect—that is, a return to lending, spending, and investing—called for a signaling strategy that already had a name and a theory behind it: forward guidance. The idea was that setting clear expectations about Fed policy would enhance the rationality of market participants' actions. Traditional monetary policy did not specify a time commitment for any announced policy. Ben Bernanke suggested a sentence that he wanted to add to the public statement: "The Committee anticipates that weak economic conditions are likely to warrant federal funds rates near zero for some time."[74] Members generally supported such signaling to control expectations and reduce uncertainty in the markets. As Don Kohn explained, "I do think it would be useful to tell people the conditions under which we expect to keep rates low and the conditions under which we would be prepared to raise interest rates. I think we can tell them if we think it is going to be soon or if it is going to take some time."[75]

More controversial was a negotiation over whether to offer forward guidance on the FOMC's goal for inflation as the crisis evolved. Ben Bernanke had long advocated for inflation targeting and saw this moment when inflation was not a threat as an opportunity to accomplish this goal. Some members, like Jeffrey Lacker, were prepared to announce an inflation target in the hopes that it would discourage deflation. "I think it makes eminent sense to be very explicit very soon about our numerical objective for inflation," Lacker said. "Monetary policy at the zero bound is all about discouraging expectations of deflation. If we haven't tried first announcing an explicit objective for inflation, we don't have any excuses if we fail to prevent a fall into a deflationary equilibrium."[76] Most others were more concerned about the threat of inflation from extensive quantitative easing. They were unprepared to declare what level of inflation would be tolerated while they introduced policies to add liquidity to markets and reinvigorate the economy. The meaning and interpretation of inflation targeting was not yet shared within the FOMC, and the members were not ready to experiment with it. Learning was not uniform across issues. It was an ongoing negotiated process.

The Second Day: "All Available Tools"

On the second day of the December meeting, the Committee returned to its customary sensemaking process. The fed funds rate still stood at 1 percent. The FOMC was faced with important decisions about whether it was prepared to reach the lower bound and what to signal about its intentions going forward. The staff presentations contained a litany of bleak cues from the economy. The emerging narrative constructed by the members described a continuing implosion triggered by the financial crisis. The dynamics that intensified after Lehman weekend were becoming substantially worse. As Don Kohn explained, "The economy is in a steep decline. There was a break in confidence somewhere in September that took what had been a gradual decline in employment, production, and output and made it much, much, much, much steeper. The feedback loop between the financial markets and the real economy just intensified—turned up many, many notches at that time."[77] Richard Fisher added a behavioral component to the narrative: "As one of my CEO contacts outside my region said, we are basically all, in his words, 'chasing the anvil down the stairs,' and that is that the behavioral responses of both businesses and consumers are driving us into a slow-growth cul-de-sac and a deflationary trap."[78]

A second narrative, related to the continuing implosion narrative, involved predicting the magnitude and length of the deepening recession in the economy. FOMC members were pessimistic, expecting that the data would get increasingly adverse. As Janet Yellen put it, "In my view, cumulative recessionary dynamics are deeply entrenched, with mounting job losses leading to weaker consumer spending, tighter credit, more job losses, and so on; and this nasty set of economic linkages is gaining momentum. Like the Greenbook, I anticipate a long period of decline."[79] Ben Bernanke extended this narrative, interpreting the probable duration and depth of the recession as being a result of the stunning decline in financial markets.

> A number of previous recessions have had financial headwinds of one type or another. . . . But overall, the financial aspects of this episode are, I think, much more serious than in previous cases. . . . So, as I said, there are a number of reasons to think that this is going to be a very severe episode and that we are far from being at the turning point.[80]

When the FOMC members turned to the policy decision, there was a consensus that it was time to reach the zero bound of the fed funds rate. The appropriate response to continuing implosion and troubling predictions seemed clear. As Eric Rosengren asserted, "The bleak outlook calls for aggressive action. With the effective federal funds rate already well below our target, there is a logic to moving to the floor at this meeting and redirecting attention to nontraditional policies."[81] Janet Yellen specified what such aggressive action should be. "I think we should go as low as we can as fast as we can without harming the functioning of money markets, so keeping the funds rate trading in the 0 to .25 range is desirable."[82] The predominant justification for moving to the zero bound at this meeting was a fear of being reticent in the face of crisis. The action was characterized as trauma management by Sandra Pianalto, who said, "We are now more in a situation of treating mass trauma. Perhaps some of our actions will later be judged as having gone too far. But in my view, right now it clearly is better to ensure that the treatment is large enough rather than risk falling short."[83] The concern, expressed by a number of members, was that they might replicate the experience of the Japanese bankers who moved more slowly to the zero bound and found themselves unable to stimulate recovery in the 1990s. As Thomas Hoenig explained, "When you don't go in and try to drive it back quickly, you get the Japanese outcome of prolonging it."[84]

The vote to reduce the fed funds rate to its lower bound was unanimous, though there was disagreement whether to state the fed funds rate target or not. The public statement issued after the meeting included all the major elements of the new regime:

> The Federal Open Market Committee decided today to establish a target range for the federal funds rate of 0 to ¼ percent. . . . The Federal Reserve will employ all available tools to promote the resumption of sustainable economic growth and to preserve price stability. In particular, the Committee anticipates that weak economic conditions are likely to warrant exceptionally low levels of the federal funds rate for some time.
>
> The focus of the Committee's policy going forward will be to support the functioning of financial markets and stimulate the economy through open market operations and other measures that sustain the size of the Federal Reserve's balance sheet at a high level. As previously announced, over the next few quarters the Federal Reserve will purchase large quantities of agency debt and mortgage-backed securities to provide support to the mortgage and housing markets, and it stands ready to expand its purchases of agency debt and mortgage-backed securities as conditions warrant.[85]

By the end of the December meeting the FOMC had decisively shifted its role from system maintenance to system rescue. There was a clear recognition that the market was not going to be self-correcting on a time line that was acceptable. As Ben Bernanke had promised Milton Friedman at his ninetieth birthday party, the Fed was not going to allow the financial system to collapse as it did at the start of the Great Depression. The logic of the state was now in full control of the Fed's interpretive process. The definition of appropriate policy had been reimagined. The Fed's role in the state's search for stability was being elaborated and amplified. The Fed's policymakers would experiment, explore, and learn to defend the system.

Epilogue

The new regime mapped out in December 2008 was implemented over the next six years. The Fed grew its balance sheet from $800 million to $4.5

trillion, purchasing Treasury, agency, and mortgage-backed securities. The effect was to lower interest rates on a variety of financial instruments and increase the money available for credit and spending. There is a consensus that the first round of quantitative easing was successful in reducing systemic risk in financial markets and supporting economic activity. The second and third rounds of quantitative easing were more controversial. Some observers questioned their effectiveness and others worried about the consequences when the Fed tried to sell its assets back into the market, but most economists saw quantitative easing as a positive stimulus that did not increase inflation.

The Fed did not take a loss on the assets it purchased from troubled banks. In fact, it returned its gains to the Treasury, almost $100 billion in 2014 alone. By the time quantitative easing purchases ended, unemployment was down to 5.7 percent, inflation remained below the Fed's 2.0 percent target, and output was 8 percent higher than before the recession. Although this recovery cannot be attributed to Fed policy alone, there is little doubt that the Fed's "new regime" contributed significantly. Though other countries made use of quantitative easing, the efforts initiated by the Fed were widely seen as the most effective in a developed economy. When Janet Yellen succeeded Ben Bernanke as chair of the Fed, the policy of low interest rates was extended and economic growth continued.

Unfortunately, there can be no unqualified happy ending for this saga. It is the story of one central bank's efforts to cope with a national and international economic disaster. The learning and innovations of the Fed could not prevent the consequences of the Great Recession for those millions of people who endured long unemployment and loss of income. It could not allay the suffering involved in loss of homes, the delay of careers, and the stressors associated with them. The benefits of the subsequent economic growth were unevenly distributed. This was exacerbated by technological change and the effects of globalization on the distribution of jobs in the economy. Finally, the transformational learning at the Fed could not forestall the erosion of confidence in both state and market institutions that resulted from the financial crisis and the Great Recession. The effects of that erosion are enduring.

8

The Pathos and Irony of Technocratic Control

The ideas of economists and political philosophers, both when
they are right and they are wrong, are more powerful than is
commonly understood.

—JOHN MAYNARD KEYNES, *THE GENERAL THEORY OF EMPLOYMENT,
INTEREST, AND MONEY*

In self-image and reputation, the Federal Reserve stands for technocratic control: the application of scientific thought to the resolution of administrative problems. No other institution in the United States so fully frames its policymaking in terms of economic models. No other institution places these decisions in the hands of a committee of economists who meet on schedule to analyze the latest data and fine-tune policy. None employs such large economic research departments, even publishing their own prestigious journals. And in no other institution are the governors of that institution portrayed by the media as technical wizards and masters of an arcane knowledge that produces a public good.[1] All of this might suggest that central banking has become fully scientific, thereby eliminating the social and political elements historically associated with controlling the supply of money and credit in the United States. This book has demonstrated that this is not so.

Early in the writing of this book I presented a draft of the first chapter in a seminar series at another university. A distinguished political scientist at the seminar asked me, "Why are you so hard on these policymakers?" Taken aback, I replied that having analyzed more than a hundred meeting transcripts, I had great respect for them. I saw them as serious, resourceful, and deeply knowledgeable. My colleague did not seem to be satisfied with that answer. Neither was I. I have thought a lot about that question since then. I realized that I hold two positions that might seem contradictory to others. On the one hand, the members of the Federal Open Market Committee (FOMC) are dedicated public servants who make extensive and sincere efforts to interpret data and arrive at reasoned conclusions. They undertake these efforts in support of an institutional mission: the stability of the economy. On the other hand, these experts failed to anticipate the financial shocks from toxic assets, were slow to adjust their narrative to the changing situation, and lost control over the crisis on Lehman weekend. The two positions are not contradictory, but they do suggest a tension that I have come to think of as the pathos of technocratic control.

The most prevalent source of this tension lies in the limits of scientific knowledge as the basis for administration. Most of the analysis in this book expresses an implicit sympathy for the Fed policymakers. I find a poignancy in the visibility and difficulty of their task, given the cognitive, informational, and conceptual limits that manifest as fluctuating textures of doubt in their deliberations. Despite these limits, on Bear Stearns weekend and after the Lehman failure, they produced improvisatory and innovative actions that facilitated the stabilization of the financial system. On the other hand, I am less sympathetic to ideological stringency. Through much of the crisis, policymakers clung to an undying faith that financial markets would adjust to the spreading contagion. The enduring and unwarranted confidence of these policymakers in the belief that the self-interest of bankers would lead them to anticipate the Lehman failure and prepare for its consequences seems only explicable as conceptual rigidity and a collapse of critical thinking. This enduring confidence testifies, once again, to the power of economic ideas—"when they are right and when they are wrong," as Keynes put it.

But individual experts are human and the fallibility of economics should come as no surprise. The deeper problem lies in the institutional limits of technocratic action. Although the Fed is formally independent, it is accountable to Congress and the executive branch. With the Lehman failure, the policymakers were caught in a situation in which fundamental societal values were being called into question by their anticipated action. In the end, to paraphrase Eric Rosengren, they had no choices. The choices were quashed by the actions of Secretary of the Treasury Henry Paulson and the pressure from both politicians and the media. Thus, there is another tension in the story I have told, a kind of moral pathos engendered by the technocrats' power and momentary powerlessness. They were given great power because of their expertise. But that expertise was not sufficient to prevail over complex events or the deus ex machina in their political and cultural environment. Expert interpretation and technical rationality were no match for political power. The limits of technocratic control are not only cognitive, informational, and conceptual, they are political.

The irony of technocratic control at the FOMC flows directly from its human, scientific, and institutional limits. The irony is that FOMC practice does not fit with usual expectations for scientific practice. As we have seen throughout our analysis of the transcripts, the FOMC members depend on a sensemaking process. That process begins with the identification of cues. Some of these cues are standardized, but they are supplemented by situationally relevant cues that seem "idiosyncratic" to the Fed's critics and by anecdotes that are inherently unsystematic and subjective.[2] The largest part of the transcripts, and therefore the meetings, is taken up by narrative construction, the creation of plausible stories that capture the evolving consensus interpretation of the members. Finally, they arrive at a shared policy solution that is based less on a calculation of its consequence than on a sense that it is an appropriate match with the consensus narrative. Once a crisis has been recognized, the confidence usually reserved for agreed-upon facts is dominated by doubt. This doubt is critical for provoking the sensemaking process into exploration and innovation. Such are the elements of technocratic control.

The Limits of Scientific Knowledge

Modern central banking may be understood as a natural experiment in technocracy: administration by technical experts. The financial crisis was a severe test of the hypothesis that technical experts can manage the system of money and credit effectively. The preceding chapters have explored how technical expertise works in this context. Members of the FOMC relied on conflicting cues whose implications were, at times, unclear and statistical models that excluded critical financial variables. This made them prone to predictive failure in a financial crisis. In this context, the "facts" themselves were not seen as definitive but as open to interpretation. The narrative interpretations were plausible products woven in the process of the group's discussion. These narratives were often in competition with each other, and every narrative was shaped by the bias of competing theoretical perspectives.

All this suggests that the oracular image of performance at the Fed portrayed in the media, especially during the Greenspan era, is misplaced. Technocratic control at the Fed is a constantly emerging social process and we should expect both doubt and error.

These limits of scientific knowledge are intrinsic to economic policymaking but become especially critical during a crisis, a time in which typical patterns are broken. There is a tendency to believe in the resilience of a system that is resilient most of the time. In the case of the Fed, the technical experts manage a cycle of expansion and contraction in which the oscillations are mostly moderate and economies are expanding most of the time. They are focused on mandated goals and familiar risks and are disinclined to anticipate the rare emergence of crisis-level systemic risk. Additionally, the complexity of the economy makes it extremely difficult to detect all the destructive interactions between its components. As we saw, the Fed's highly complex predictive models did not include the financial variables that would capture these interactions and the risks to the wider economy.

It cannot be argued that the Fed was ignoring signals that were widely understood elsewhere. Systemic risk to the economy from subprime mortgages and derivatives was not a major topic of conversation in either the business or economics communities. The Fed staff gathered and aggregated information from a wide variety of sources between the FOMC meetings. Business leaders did not foresee a crisis. In fact, they depended on the Fed for major predictions. Before the crisis, macroeconomists were discussing what was called the Great Moderation, a welcome period of relative economic stability. It was after the crisis that the fragility of the system and the attendant systemic risk began to receive the attention they deserve.[3]

The analysis of the Fed's sensemaking found in the preceding chapters should not be read as a Luddite argument against technical expertise. It is appropriate to depend on technical experts for the regulation of complex systems. Managing the money supply and financial stability are intricate and esoteric skills requiring a depth of knowledge. Despite limits to rationality and the ongoing legitimacy threats, the technical experts at the Fed used improvisation and innovation to help rescue the economy from potentially worse consequences wrought by mortgage-backed securities, related derivative instruments, and the firms that promoted them. The Fed's handling of the financial crisis, from Bear Stearns weekend to quantitative easing, confirms that the damage from such system failures can be diminished by the skilled action of experts. The financial crisis is, in some ways, the very definition of the kind of situation in which technical expertise is vital but not sufficient to outweigh political and legitimacy demands.

Technocracy and Politics

The analysis of the transcripts in the previous chapters would seem to suggest that FOMC sensemaking was largely independent of political influence. There was little discussion of the executive branch or Congress, outside of referring to the legislative mandate for stable prices and maximum possible employment or wondering when fiscal stimulus might assist them in crisis management.[4] The Senate hearing after Bear Stearns weekend suggested orthogonal framings of the crisis management issues. Rather, if sensemaking was "captured" by some entity, it was the policymakers' own discipline that shaped their thinking most significantly. The technocratic frame of macroeconomic analysis was only supplanted by politics on Lehman weekend, and the FOMC members seemed uncertain in the September meeting following the bankruptcy about the economic meaning of those events.

But, at another level, the implementation of US monetary policy has been a question of political values and interests since Alexander Hamilton proposed the First Bank of the United States and Andrew Jackson removed all federal assets from the Second Bank. The money supply and its management was, perhaps, the most important political issue at the end of the nineteenth century in America. Fluctuations in the money supply were at the heart of political conflict in what was known as the Populist movement. William Jennings Bryan, the Democratic candidate for president in 1896, ran on a "free silver" platform. Farmers, mostly in the South and West, wanted to supplement the gold standard with silver in the hope that it would increase the price they received for the commodities they produced. They were opposed by Eastern bankers and merchants who feared resulting inflation. Despite Bryan's famous and grandiloquent "Cross of Gold" speech at the Democratic convention, he lost to the Republican, William McKinley. It was during this period, plagued by high price volatility and occasional bank panics, that reform-minded bankers, looking to stabilize the money supply rather than expand it, initiated the legislation that eventually became the Federal Reserve Act of 1913.

Politics is at the core of the Fed's history and practice. It is found when the Fed's dual mandate, to maintain price stability while maximizing employment, gets interpreted as a tradeoff between inflation and growth. It is found in the conflicting narratives that reflected a belief in either market self-correction or state intervention among policymakers. And it is seen in the institutional norms that maintain and defend the status quo in the banking community. Technocratic control may be premised on the application of scientific rationality, but power and politics are deeply implicated in its practice.

The conflict between inflation hawks and inflation doves, the heated debate over market adjustment and systemic risk, and the decision not to use government money to prevent the panic that followed the Lehman bankruptcy all have a political component. Certainly, these issues can be and were argued using technical economic language. Experts are inclined to believe that their expertise supplants politics. But the line between unresolved economic or legal questions and political beliefs is murky. Technocracy is not value neutral and the values employed are bound to shape analysis. Whether those values are the product of political socialization, professional training, or theoretical reasoning is impossible to infer from the data analyzed here. But the contests over narrative construction and policy framing were not only matters of economic analysis, they often reflected thinly veiled political values, emblematic of core beliefs about the efficiency of the market and the efficacy of the state. These core beliefs exceeded established science.[5]

The depoliticization of discourse is innate to technical experts at the FOMC. The economic training of the FOMC members offers an apolitical language for debating such political trade-offs as inflation control versus economic growth. This is the same trade-off that occupied the electoral politics of the last part of the nineteenth century in the conflicts between bankers and farmers. At that time, it was an overt contest over class interests at a transitional moment in American economic development. In fact, the institution that arose out of these controversies, the Federal Reserve, was a compromise that enhanced the protection for price stability and bank centrality in the structure of economic relations.[6] The depoliticization is implied in what the FOMC discourse refers to as "natural" processes. Discussion of natural rates of unemployment and equilibrium real interest rates suggests that economic outcomes are part of a natural system. The political content of the policymaking is masked, even as the FOMC's actions show that members understand their role in these outcomes.

Advances in the field of monetary policy have, to some degree, calmed the tumultuous political debates over money that characterized nineteenth-century America. They have helped to reduce the volatility of the money supply and, as a result, lowered the political conflict over its management. Fed policymaking has become a mysterious and somewhat obscure part of government for most citizens. It has been largely removed from public view and understanding. This is an inevitable consequence of technocracy. The complexity and ambiguity of managing the money supply has been delegated to technical experts in an agency outside the executive, legislative, and judicial functions. Only under the extreme conditions preceding the Lehman bankruptcy was Fed policy pushed to the front of public consciousness.

The delegation of monetary policy to technical experts with advanced training in macroeconomics could plausibly reduce concern that the Fed is captured by Congress, the president, or even the banks.[7] Rather, the analysis in this book suggests that the delegation to academic experts has accomplished a more subtle and unobtrusive capture of monetary policy by academic models and their underlying assumptions as seen in our identification of narratives, logics, and frames. The conceptual tool kit provided by academic training both enables and inhibits the thinking of policymakers at the FOMC at every meeting.

This brings us back to the limits of technocratic control and suggests its contradictions as a democratic form of governance. The technocrats at the Fed make highly consequential decisions, but for all their expertise and control, democratic norms deny them the power to reform the system they oversee. Such reform requires legislative action. The financial crisis of 2008 did not result in a restructuring of mortgage-backed securities and derivatives trading to make them more transparent. It did not result in a significant reduction of risk-taking in these markets. This outcome was largely because Wall Street firms had the power to resist legislative and regulatory reform. As a result, financial instability and crisis seem likely to recur. The kind of outcome displayed on Lehman weekend, where the efforts of the Fed crisis managers were superseded by Henry Paulson and the political and cultural pressures facing the Fed, seems likely to happen again. In this context, it is elected officials, Congress and the president, who are most politically accountable. They are apt to intervene in future legitimacy crises. Democratic accountability often demands such intervention. There is a point in severe economic crises at which technocrats' authority is likely to be withdrawn and transferred to the political realm. That point remains ill-defined.[8]

Technocratic control poses a dilemma for democracy. It suggests that some complex systems, financial or otherwise, are put under the control of scientists because of their expertise and the impenetrability of the system to nonexperts. When a crisis in the system occurs, it is these experts who are most mostly likely to understand the causes of the crisis and its resolution. As in the Lehman case, the technocrat's solutions may not be popular and the democratically accountable solution may get it wrong.[9] But, democratic theory and practice suggest that elected officials are better able to represent the popular will. Democratic accountability, and the legitimate authority of those who are responsible for it, trump technocratic expertise. In an era of man-made systems with catastrophic potential, these democratic values are likely to be increasingly tested.

This raises the subsidiary question of trust. Technical experts have spent years, often long careers, learning things that most citizens and politicians either do not understand or cannot evaluate until the consequences of failure are obvious. The experts cite abstract indicators and favored theories as the basis for their authority. But citizens are often skeptical of such sources of authority. It is this very problem of trust that inclines marginal groups to call for an end to the Fed and/or a return to the gold standard where human discretion is eliminated from monetary policy.[10] This mistrust ironically obscures the poor if not tragic record of the gold standard as a source of stability. This mistrust makes it all the more important that we understand how technical experts, like those at the Fed, make sense of their policy environment. This calls for better tools to explore how policymaking groups of experts make sense of rare but potentially catastrophic events.

The Sensemaking Perspective

The analysis in this book emerged out of a close examination of policy discussions between August 2007 and December 2008. Systematic coding of the FOMC's verbatim transcripts revealed the policymakers' engagement in an elaborate sensemaking process at each meeting (see Appendix B for a discussion of coding). This sensemaking process is in contrast to the imagery of the classical decision model. The process does not involve deduction of an optimal solution from the component parts of a problem. As Gary Klein points out, the component parts in the classical model tend to be decontextualized "facts."[11] These facts are extracted from a highly complex environment. They tend to be conveniently calculable. But the dynamic nature of the policy context at the Fed often engenders ambiguity. Early in my analysis of the transcripts it became clear that the hours of discussion in which FOMC members engaged, the inductive narrative construction process, were all about adding context back into the conventional cues in order to weave a satisfying narrative that captured one or more causal stories that plausibly fit the situation that faced the policymakers. This process was adaptive to the vagaries of the unfamiliar environment that faced policymakers in successive meetings, providing them with flexibility and responsiveness.

This interpretative process seems likely to be favored in complex and ambiguous situations, like policymaking, where the decision makers are faced with limited or contested explanations. These conditions make it difficult to decompose the situation into its component parts and to calculate consequences. Any decomposition seems arbitrary, incomplete, and therefore unsatisfying to the decision makers. The facts are too diverse and their interdependencies too daunting. The situation itself runs the risk of being distorted by the decomposition. Policymakers have learned that statistics have limited utility for predicting the future, especially in rapidly changing situations. Instead, they treat the situation as open to interpretation, creating narratives about it and matching those narratives with patterns familiar from prior experience. They draw from a small group of existing solutions based on what seems appropriate to the situation. Group policymaking becomes a shared process of cue identification, narrative construction, and action generation, a classic example of sensemaking: the process by which actors explore ambiguous situations and construct explanations.[12]

Sensemaking in a technocratic context is likely to begin with attention to cues that the scientifically trained policymakers understand as empirical facts. In a crisis, which is a breach in the fabric of what is taken for granted, such facts are more likely to be called into question. It is not the cue itself, such as the price of a crucial commodity, but rather its meaning. Multiple causal stories related to the cue result in contested logics of action. For example, should policymakers respond to an apparent increase in the risk of inflation or is that risk outweighed by other events, such as the financial turmoil? This is where empirical facts become interwoven with interpretive narrative.[13] These narratives are rhetorical tools of persuasion, with cues being used by participants to constrain narratives and the narratives used to interpret cues. This rhetorical contest is one sense in which sensemaking is a social process.[14]

Another aspect of the social nature of sensemaking at the FOMC is illustrated by the information gathering of its members. Skilled policymakers do not rely solely on their own limited knowledge. They attend to the knowledge of a community of experts. At the FOMC, members rely on the work of regional bank economists, the staff economists in Washington who create volumes of data and analysis for each meeting, analysis done by private-sector economists, contacts in the business community, and not least, on the lengthy discussions with their FOMC colleagues. It is in the process of sensemaking that these pools of knowledge are winnowed into a coherent shared interpretation.

The sensemaking process at the Fed crosses and links levels of analysis. Sensemaking is both an individual act of interpreting and a social process. It is social in that the policymakers interact and influence each other's sensemaking. It is social in that it uses cues, whose meanings are defined by custom or negotiation in the policy group. It is social in that the members have actively gathered other individuals' and organizations' interpretations of the situation. Finally, it is social because the institutional logics that underlie sensemaking at the Fed reflect the contested balance between unfettered competition and social stability in the profession of economics and in society more generally.

The previous chapters describe at least three distinct moments that correspond to three contexts of sensemaking. The first moment, though full of the blooming and buzzing confusion of cues and idiosyncratic indicators, is relatively routinized in the policymaking group. In earlier research analyzing over a hundred FOMC transcripts from the 1970s, 1980s, and 1990s, I learned that the process of constructing a narrative is a collaborative practice at most meetings, based on conventional cues and standard policy options.[15] In these moments, narrative construction produced a story line that tended to persist across meetings. Even with continuously changing cues, the process followed customary practices and favored the most available explanations. In the early chapters of this book, the growing financial turmoil was observed by the policymakers, and although some anguish was expressed, the standard sensemaking process continued. There were new cues to be understood as the financial turmoil increased, but the policymakers seemed relatively comfortable that they could use the familiar narratives and solutions of established monetary policy to make sense of ongoing events. Members were slow to abandon their traditional tools of sensemaking. As we saw, unusual circumstance wrought by mortgage-backed securities and derivatives eventually resulted in circumstances in which participants were confused, misled by inadequate theories, and eventually beset by an overheated political and cultural environment.

The second moment of sensemaking was characterized here as one that triggered improvisation. In this moment, the context was experienced as urgent and threatening. The two archetypal improvisatory moments were during the Bear Stearns and Lehman weekends. The failure of these firms threatened to set off an immediate panic that would risk the survival of other firms and the stability of the financial system. It was, in a sense, easier for the actors to recognize this context because of its urgency. Once they grasped the situation, the existence of Bagehot's Dictum, a policy maxim for central bankers about lending into a panic, allowed the policymakers to pragmatically improvise variations on that theme, marshaling the actors and resources needed for lending into a panic. The improvisation was not done by a large committee employing exhaustive narrative construction. It was more nearly impromptu action by a trio of policymakers along with key staff members in constant communication as new cues emerged and possible solutions broke down. The solution itself was not a standard policy option. It was more like a stab in the dark requiring courage and flexibility to enact.

The fluctuating textures of doubt that punctuated the fall of 2007 and the winter of 2008 made the improvisation possible. Policymakers' doubt about the sustaining beliefs that had dictated their previous understanding and action undermined their conventions and opened them to the improvisation. It also allowed some of them to glimpse the interconnectedness of the system and the risk it carried. When positivist faith in predictive models and statistical facts failed, when the usefulness of theories of self-correcting financial markets was exceeded, the policymakers were compelled to pragmatic spontaneous action, creating modern variations based on principles from a nineteenth-century thinker who had been famously ignored in the Great Depression but whose ideas were revived as a dictum in 2008.

A third moment of sensemaking during the crisis was characterized as one that triggered learning. Like improvisation, learning was also an exploratory response to urgent and threatening circumstances, but it emerged less spontaneously than improvisation over a period of months. In the period before Lehman weekend, graduated interest rate adjustment was still exploited and the expectation that the market would self-correct was still prevalent. Learning was incremental based on an unfolding interpretation. In the period immediately after the Lehman panic, there was confusion and hesitation among the policymakers. At the first post-Lehman FOMC meeting, they were using statistics gathered and prepared before the bankruptcy occurred. Three weeks later, in a conference call, they began to redefine prospects, sensing that things were likely to be worse than earlier forecasts. In three more weeks, the cues were dire and the narrative shifted to implosion.

It may be argued that these worsening conditions and redefinition of the situation were necessary but not sufficient for transformational learning. It was only upon reaching the zero-bound of the fed funds rate that the exploration was transformational. At that point, the orderly movement of an interest rate reached its limit and the FOMC was threatened with anomic disorder.[16] The result was a move from incremental, adaptive learning to a redefinition of FOMC practice. As Richard Fisher put it, they needed new cognitive maps.

Efforts at sensemaking do not always lead to policy action in a crisis. Failed sensemaking transpires when the policymakers, intent on action, are obstructed by political and cultural forces. In such a moment sensemaking stalls, action is inhibited, and accounts are constructed for public consumption. The sensemakers lose control of their narrative. Such a moment occurred with the failure of Lehman Brothers despite the Fed's efforts at improvisation. These moments seem particularly likely when a policy domain that has been placed under technocratic control threatens state legitimacy. When such a crisis threatens, political leaders are likely to wrest control from scientists/experts even as the scientists are left shaking their heads and, as Tim Geithner did, telling the political leaders that they are making a mistake. In this light, it seems unsurprising that unelected technocrats would have their sensemaking supplanted. Sensemaking, which depends on autonomy and discretion, is vulnerable to suppression by those with more power and public accountability.

Finally, it seems important to acknowledge that the interpretive process at the FOMC has been the topic of considerable criticism by academic monetary policy experts. It has been referred to as "ad hoc" and "seat of the pants."[17] Less critical treatments compare the FOMC's "discretionary" regime to a preferred "rules-based" regime in which monetary policy would be tied to a target, such as 2 percent inflation, leaving much less room for discretionary interpretation. Despite decades of advocacy for a rule-based regime in the monetary policy literature and increasing agreement on its advantages, the FOMC has not seen fit to adopt a rule-based regime.[18] This may reflect cultural habituation and inertia, but given the foregoing analysis of the "discretionary" regime it seems more likely that the high stakes and ambiguity of the situations facing the policymakers favor a sensemaking process that admits layers of contextual complexity and situational nuance that offers greater satisfaction, perhaps even comfort, to those responsible for the decisions. Crises are moments when such interpretive discretion is most useful and most consequential.

The Role of Culture in Sensemaking

The determination of what cues, narratives, or solutions seem appropriate for use in the interpretation of any situation is largely a matter of cultural availability. Experts have generally been found to recognize familiar patterns in new situations, substituting solutions from their training and professional practice for continued search.[19] FOMC members refer to simple operating principles of central banking and their knowledge from prior applications of those principles both historically and over the course of their careers. This is most notable in their central operating principle: countercyclical interest rate policy. They raise interest rates when they judge that the economy is expanding and lower them when they judge that it is contracting. At most times, this is taken-for-granted expert practice. They also rely on more general theory-based ideas. In the early chapters, most members expected self-correcting financial markets to adjust for the turmoil. By August 2008, the FOMC members were debating market adjustment versus systemic risk as guiding principles even as Fannie Mae and Freddie Mac were going under and Lehman weekend loomed on the horizon. Fed technocrats are embedded in an intellectual worldview, that of the profession of economics, that provides a tool kit for their understanding of their environment.[20]

An instructive example of this reliance on culturally available theoretical ideas is found in the unsettled years immediately following the financial crisis in the application of the concept called "forward guidance." In the wake of the financial crisis of 2007–2008, as part of its quantitative easing, the Federal Reserve bought over $2 trillion in bonds, an extraordinary intervention in the market. More than four years after the start of these purchases, in late May 2013, Ben Bernanke testified before Congress that if the Fed saw improvement in the economy it "could, in the next few meetings, take a step down in our pace of purchases."[21] A month later, on June 19, 2013, Bernanke became more explicit and transparent, saying that the central bank intended to scale down its purchases beginning later in the year and end these purchases when the unemployment rate had declined to 7 percent. As a result of these announcements of a change in policy, there was a global market sell-off, with stocks losing trillions of dollars in value. Bond and commodity prices fell as well with ten-year Treasury notes falling over 10 percent in just over a month. Markets in Asia, Europe, and Latin America fell even more sharply than US markets. It was a remarkable display of the Fed's influence. As one concerned British observer explained, "The Fed isn't just the US's central bank. It's the world's central bank."[22]

Observers of this international sell-off wondered why the Fed was telegraphing its intended policy so far in advance, especially when the recovery still remained so fragile. This level of transparency was the opposite of the opacity for which central bankers are justly famous. This seeming paradox offers another example of how theoretical ideas, part of the Fed's cultural tools, shape its interpretive work. In the late spring of 2013, Ben Bernanke and Fed economists were increasingly committed to an economic theory positing that forward guidance, heightened transparency about the Fed's intentions, would allow markets to operate more efficiently. At the same time, the Fed was experiencing internal doubts over the effectiveness of the latest round of bond purchases. Thus, under Bernanke's leadership, the Fed adopted increasing transparency at a critical moment of market uncertainty if not frailty. This is yet another example of economic ideas guiding Fed action and the truth of Keynes's aphorism quoted at the beginning of the chapter.

The Tension of Competing Logics

The contested logics at the Fed reflect the agency's embeddedness in two institutional orders: the market and the state. The market, especially the financial sector, is grounded in the logic of competition. This competition is inherently volatile, creating and destroying wealth in its course. The state is grounded in a logic of order, stabilizing economic and political relations to that end. The Fed was established to support the goals of both logics, competition and order, but there was never full recognition of their contradictory dynamics nor full agreement on the appropriate balance between them. The Fed, as an institution, embodies these contradictions. Its history, especially the management of the financial crisis studied here, reflects the contest over this balance. Before the Fed was established, this contest was the province of farmers who wanted easier money and bankers who wanted "sound" money. Today it takes place between experts with PhDs in economics. The positions they take are less about personal economic interests and more about the proper role of the state in the economy.

Those believing more in the efficacy of the market to resolve economic shocks are willing to let the market encroach on public welfare because these perturbations are part of what they consider to be the natural order. The disruption ensues from the aggregation of individual acts and reflects the innate operation of a self-regulating system. But for those more concerned with the duty of the state to its citizens, the sovereign power has the ultimate responsibility for order and system stability. The relevant laws are not natural but political. In favoring state action, the policymakers found themselves reaching for a language of systemic risk to explain a difficult condition for economic thinking: being beyond natural law.

On one level, the market and state logics appear to be incompatible. This is a false dichotomy that masks a systemic logic in which they are interdependent. The ability of policymakers to move between the logics is a source of resilience for the institution. The decision to bail out or not bail out is about economic consequences and who will pay for them. If you don't bail out Lehman, the taxpayers are, presumably, off the hook. But investors, borrowers, those looking for jobs, and those who have lost them bear massive consequences. Ultimately, the economic and the political are inseparable. The decision not to bail out Lehman was about the legitimacy of democratic capitalism. Politicians judged that a bailout of Lehman was widely unpopular, threatening the legitimacy of political institutions, like the Treasury and the Fed, and the economic institutions of Wall Street. In this situation, system legitimacy is likely to supplant the welfare of vulnerable groups, though it is a topic worthy of a more robust democratic debate and comprehensive policy.

As was evident in the aftermath of the financial crisis, the argument over the roles of the market and the state in the economy is even less resolved in the wider American society than it is at the organizational level of the Fed. The degree and manner of state intervention in the market remains highly contentious. This contest does not divide clearly along class or status lines as it did in the nineteenth century. Rather, it is mostly a political and cultural contest over the use of the state as a tool. In America, the parties to the contest are labeled conservative and liberal, with both sides including both working-class and wealthy Americans. It is a contest based less on interests and more on beliefs about the role of the state in a market economy and the trust associated with that role. This contest flourishes even as Progressive Era state institutions, like the Fed, predicated on taming the worst externalities of the market, pass their hundredth anniversary. The notion that the debate over these political values could be ended by technocracy is an illusion.

End or Reform the Fed?

At the margins of American politics there are people on the left and the right who oppose the existence of the Federal Reserve. Their opposition repoliticizes monetary policy, an area that had been depoliticized, to some extent, by technocratic control. This opposition reflects anxiety about who controls the supply of money. It is certainly true that immense power has been concentrated in the central bank, even more so when fiscal policy is frozen by congressional gridlock. But why eliminate an institution designed to stabilize a market system susceptible to business cycles and crises? Before such radical action, there are two areas in which we need to extend our knowledge of this mysterious institution. First, we must deepen our understanding of what shapes the policy process at the Fed so that we may attempt to compensate for policymakers' cognitive, informational, and theoretical limits. This book has been an effort at such demystification. Second, based on that knowledge, we must assess whether it is reasonable to expect that an institution like the Fed can keep up with the increasing complexity and interconnectedness of the system it was designed to stabilize. If the answer is no, as I suggest, then it is the financial system rather than its regulators that is most in need of reform.

The argument about system complexity has an additional implication. The story that unfolded in previous chapters suggests that Fed policymakers were mindful of and responsive to their legislated mandate throughout the crisis. Nevertheless, there will always be concern that technocrats may abuse their discretion. Recently, Paul Tucker, a former central banker at the Bank of England, has put forward "design precepts" (DP) for independent central banks. He finds that during the financial crisis such central banks were "stretching the bounds of acceptability" of his precepts.[23]

> Almost no central banks had articulated operating principles for its lender-of-last-resort policies or for how it would operate monetary policy at the effective (or "zero") lower bound for interest rates (DP3). Few had thought how to ensure political accountability for operations that would not be im-

mediately transparent without sparking panic, exposing the people to even greater risk and hardship (DP4). Perhaps most problematic of all, no jurisdiction had clear rules of the game for determining how central banks could come to the rescue in unforeseen circumstances or, put from another perspective, when they should stop (DP5). That alone proved not far short of explosive in the U.S. when a series of nonbanks were rescued (AIG) or allowed to fail (Lehman).[24]

Tucker's complaint goes to the heart of my sense of expert discretion in complex systems. In a financial system that was generating new versions of mortgage-backed securities, collateralized debt obligations, and a wide variety of other derivative instruments whose credit ratings were questionable and where banks across the world were deeply interconnected as counterparties, the details of these situations were not so easily assessed by policymakers in a crisis. In such situations, technocrats will be given increasing discretion until the point at which the political system intervenes, correctly or incorrectly.

Like many economists, Tucker hopes to enhance the legitimacy of central banks by introducing clear, transparent rules that bind the banks in a way consistent with increased legitimacy.[25] I am sympathetic to his motivation but believe it would be difficult if not impossible to create a framework for the use of lender-of-last-resort power that would capture the contingencies of a major real-world crisis in financial markets. For example, one of Tucker's principles is "No lending to fundamentally insolvent firms."[26] But as we saw in Chapter 7, the claim that Lehman Brothers was insolvent on Lehman weekend remains an empirical question. Laurence Ball's analysis, done nearly a decade after the fact, suggests Lehman was not insolvent. How much more difficult might such a determination be on a fraught weekend in the midst of crisis? Tucker's faith in precepts does not do justice to the complexity and ambiguity of such situations.

When a system's catastrophic potential is too complex and ambiguous to reliably prevent the occasional catastrophe, the most obvious solution is to simplify the system.[27] In the case of the financial system, simplification includes the segregation of extreme risk-taking from institutions that are too interconnected to fail. That, of course, did not happen in the Dodd-Frank reforms after the financial crisis. Congress, given campaign spending and lobbying by Wall Street, was unlikely to threaten existing organizational arrangements and those most invested in them. A less drastic reform would involve increasing transparency. Requiring that derivative instruments, like collateralized debt obligations, be traded on exchanges would make it easier for a regulator to monitor the markets. Making the content of mortgage-backed securities and the basis for their credit rating transparent would help as well. Acceptance of systems with catastrophic potential is a political choice and requires political solutions.

Taming the Market

In the wake of the financial crisis, considerable analytical effort was made to identify its immediate causes. Among the favored culprits were the housing bubble, the defaults in the subprime mortgage market, the resulting risk associated with mortgage-backed securities and their related derivatives, the negligence of credit rating agencies, and the excessive levels of risk carried by America's largest financial institutions.[28] All of these factors and others that made the financial system fragile were related to the unrestrained pursuit of profit in a lax regulatory environment.[29] There was little attention to these factors or their connections in FOMC discussions. Perhaps this was because these factors were already knit into the fabric of the financial turmoil or because the FOMC's attention was on an abstract market mechanism that was subject to restorative dynamics. These factors were treated as trees in one part of the forest as the policymakers attempted to execute their mandate to achieve price stability and maximum employment.

In this book, rather than focusing on various vivid examples of speculative excess, our attention has been on the performance of the state's most visible hand and lender of last resort—its central bank. This is not because the speculative excess was not causally related to the crisis and often full of deception and malfeasance, but because only the state has the responsibility for protection and maintenance of the system. The Fed manages this responsibility through technocratic control. This study, then, may be understood as a cautionary tale about the limits of information, interpretive capacity, conceptual knowledge, and power in technocratic control.

Our examination of sensemaking at the FOMC suggests that it is not designed for crisis recognition or the exploration of its causes. It is designed for adaptive incremental learning about conditions in the "real" economy. It is embedded in a professional culture that assumes the continuous slight adjustment of the market. It is embedded in an organizational structure that favors analysis of discrete categories like housing, banking, and consumer goods rather than interconnections in the system. This division of labor allows specialization and the sharing of expert knowledge. But when subsystems are deeply interconnected, like the financial system, the estimation of systemic risk requires a level of complexity in policymakers' sensemaking that runs counter to this specialization and exceeds both individual and group capacity as well as the capacity of the Fed's best predictive models. As a result, errors were made. But in the midst of crisis, sensemaking triggered learning and improvisation as well. It was the policymakers' sensemaking, their variety of epistemologies and their fluctuating textures of doubt, that challenged conventional practice and opened them to improvisation and innovation. This analysis suggests that making sense of crisis calls for openness, humility, imagination, and collaboration among experts. Future crises will demand even more.

APPENDIX A

MEMBERS OF THE FEDERAL
OPEN MARKET COMMITTEE,
AUGUST 2007–DECEMBER 2008

Federal Reserve Governors

Ben Bernanke (Chair, Board of Governors; PhD, Massachusetts Institute of Technology)

Ben Bernanke became chair of the Board of Governors of the Federal Reserve in 2006. Before that he was chair of President George W. Bush's Council of Economic Advisers, a governor of the Federal Reserve, and professor and chair in the Princeton University Department of Economics.

Elizabeth Duke (Governor; MBA, Old Dominion University)

Elizabeth Duke was appointed to the Board of Governors in June 2008, filling a vacant position. Duke started her career in banking at the Bank of Virginia Beach. She was CEO of the Bank of Tidewater and vice president at SouthTrust after Tidewater's acquisition. She served as chair of the American Banking Association during 2005–2006.

Donald Kohn (Governor; PhD, University of Michigan)

Donald Kohn joined the Board of Governors of the Federal Reserve in 2002. He had already worked for the Fed for over forty years. Governor Kohn began his career as a financial economist at the Federal Reserve Bank of Kansas City. He served the Fed in Washington as chief of capital markets, as director of the Division of Monetary Affairs, and as secretary to the Federal Open Market Committee, among other positions.

Randall Kroszner (Governor; PhD, Harvard University)

Randall Kroszner joined the Board of Governors in 2006. He has been a professor of economics at the University of Chicago since 1990. He served on the President's Council of Economic Advisers from 2001 to 2003.

Frederic Mishkin (Governor; PhD, Massachusetts Institute of Technology)

Frederic Mishkin was a member of the Board of Governors from 2006 to 2008. He has been a full professor in the Graduate School of Business at Columbia University since 1983. He also taught at the University of Chicago and Northwestern University. He was director of research at the Federal Reserve Bank of New York from 1994 to 1997.

Kevin Warsh (Governor; JD, Harvard University)

Kevin Warsh was appointed to the Board of Governors in 2006. At thirty-five, he was the youngest appointment to the Board in its history. Immediately preceding his appointment, he was special assistant to the president for economic policy. Before that he worked at Morgan Stanley, an investment bank in New York City.

Presidents, Regional Reserve Banks

James Bullard (President, St. Louis FRB; PhD, Indiana University)

James Bullard became president of the St. Louis Federal Reserve Bank on April 1, 2008, when he succeeded William Poole. He first joined the bank in 1990 as an economist in the research division and served in a variety of positions, including deputy director of research for monetary analysis.

Charles Evans (President, Chicago FRB; PhD, Carnegie-Mellon University)

Charles Evans became president of the Chicago Federal Reserve Bank in 2007. Before that he had been director of research and the senior economist in the macroeconomics research group at the Chicago Fed. He taught at the University of Chicago and the University of Michigan.

Richard Fisher (President, Dallas FRB; MBA, Stanford University)

Richard Fisher became president of the Reserve Bank of Dallas in 2005. He started his career at Brown Brothers Harriman, an investment bank. He worked at the US Department of the Treasury in the 1970s before returning to Brown Brothers Harriman. He also served as deputy US trade representative in the administration of President Bill Clinton.

Tim Geithner (President, New York FRB; MA, Johns Hopkins University)

Timothy Geithner was president of the Federal Reserve Bank of New York from 2003 to 2009. He worked at the US Department of the Treasury from 1988 to 2001. Just before joining the New York Fed he was a senior fellow at the Council on Foreign Relations from 2001 to 2003. He left the Fed to become secretary of the treasury under President Barack Obama. His MA is in international economics.

Thomas Hoenig (President, Kansas City FRB; PhD, Iowa State University)

Thomas Hoenig was president of the Kansas City Federal Reserve Bank from 1991 to 2011. He first joined the bank as an economist in 1973 and served for thirty-eight years in a variety of positions.

Jeffrey Lacker (President, Richmond FRB; PhD, University of Wisconsin)

Jeffery Lacker was president of the Federal Reserve Bank of Richmond from 2004 to 2017. He joined the Richmond Fed as an economist in 1989 and served as research officer and director of research before becoming president.

Dennis Lockhart (President, Atlanta FRB; MA, Johns Hopkins University)

Dennis Lockhart became president of the Atlanta Federal Reserve Bank in 2007. He worked for Citibank in a variety of domestic and international positions from 1971 to 1988. He then worked at Heller Financial until 2001, when he moved to Zephyr Financial, a private equity firm, and later to Small Enterprise Assistance Funds, a manager of venture capital funds. His MA is in international economics.

Michael Moskow (President, Chicago FRB; PhD, University of Pennsylvania)

Michael Moskow served as president of the Chicago Federal Reserve Bank from 1994 to 2007. He began his career teaching economics at Temple University, Lafayette College, and Drexel University. He then served as deputy secretary of labor, director of the Council on Wage and Price Stability, senior staff economist with the Council of Economic Advisers, and deputy US trade representative under President George H. W. Bush.

Sandra Pianalto (President, Cleveland FRB; MA, George Washington University)

Sandra Pianalto served as president of the Cleveland Federal Reserve Bank from 2003 to 2014. She joined the bank as an economist in the Research Department in 1983, after working at the Board of Governors and as a staff member on the Budget Committee of the US Senate. She served in a variety of positions at the Cleveland Fed before becoming its president. Her master's degree is in economics.

Charles Plosser (President, Philadelphia FRB; PhD, University of Chicago

Charles Plosser was president of the Philadelphia Federal Reserve Bank from 2006 to 2015. Before joining the Philadelphia Fed, Plosser was dean of the Graduate School of Business Administration at the University of Rochester. He also served as Distinguished Professor of Economics and Public Policy there. Plosser also was coeditor of the *Journal of Monetary Economics* for more than twenty years.

William Poole (President, St. Louis FRB; PhD, University of Chicago)

William Poole was president of the St. Louis Federal Reserve from 1998 to 2008. He started his career as an economist at the Board of Governors of the Federal Reserve System in 1964. He was a professor of economics at Brown University starting in 1974, eventually becoming Herbert Goldberger Professor of Economics until he joined the St. Louis Fed.

Eric Rosengren (President, Boston FRB; PhD, University of Wisconsin)

Eric Rosengren became president of the Boston Federal Reserve Bank in 2007. He joined the bank as an economist in 1985 in the Research Department. He served in a variety of positions at the Boston Fed, including as head of banking and monetary policy and as head of the supervision and regulation department.

Gary Stern (President, Minneapolis FRB; PhD, Rice University)

Gary Stern was president of the Federal Reserve Bank of Minneapolis from 1985 to 2009. He served on the faculties of Columbia University, Washington University, and New York University. He also worked at the New York Federal Reserve Bank for seven years.

Janet Yellen (President, San Francisco FRB; PhD, Yale University)

Janet Yellen was president of the San Francisco Federal Reserve Bank from 2004 to 2010. She taught economics at Harvard, the London School of Economics and Political Science, and the Haas School of Business at the University of California, Berkeley. She served on the Board of Governors of the Federal Reserve System from 1994 to 1997 and the President's Council of Economic Advisers from 1997 to 1999. She became chair of the Board of Governors of the Federal Reserve System in 2014.

APPENDIX B

A NOTE ON METHODS

Archival Ethnography

I was driving home from work one evening in 1998 listening to *Marketplace* on public radio. A story came on about a reporter who sued the Federal Reserve using the Freedom of Information Act (FOIA). I learned that five years earlier, in 1993, Congressman Henry Gonzalez had uncovered that the Fed had transcripts of the meetings of the Federal Open Market Committee (FOMC) going back to 1976.[1] The judge in the FOIA case ruled that the Fed would have to release the transcripts five years after the meetings. I found the report thought provoking, but then I was quickly distracted by the next story. When I arrived home, my wife Amy asked me if I had heard the story about the Fed transcripts. I told her that I had. She said, "You should call the Fed and get them." Several days later a stack of eight transcripts, one year's worth and about eight inches high, arrived in my mailbox.[2] They contained the FOMC's deliberations from 1981. I tell the story both to give due credit to Amy and to reprise the ancient methodological wisdom of the serendipity involved in research.

Once I had this first batch of transcripts I began hungrily reading random sections to see how these elite decision makers talked to each other behind closed doors. I saw that the transcripts provided an unprecedented real-time view of high-stakes policymaking. I immediately sent for more. My first impression was that the transcripts from the 1970s and 1980s were not calculative but discursive. Members of the FOMC did not base their discussion on a predetermined set of factors whose quantitative value would direct their policy. Rather, their discussion was, as economists Raymond Lombra and Michael Moran characterized it with some dismay, a "seat-of-the pants operation" full of "ad hoc theorizing and policy making."[3] The discussion was somewhat idiosyncratic depending on the situation and the current concerns of market participants. The process reflected the ambiguity, complexity, and fluidity of the environment. It also reflected the equivocal nature of the data they were receiving. From a sociological point of view, the discussion resembled a group of professionals working to construct meaning out of a complex and ambiguous environment.

My first inclination was to explore how the FOMC's policymaking process varied or didn't, according to the situation in the economy. I fell back on the analytic methods that I had applied in previous studies of trading floors in stocks, bonds, and commodities.[4] I began my systematic analysis by reading through a transcript in its entirety to get an impression of what was going on in the committee and their sense of the economy at that historical moment. Then I went back over the transcript assigning labels to sentences and bunches of sentences and creating definitions for those labels in the process. These labels were chosen to capture the meaning produced by the FOMC members. The labels became refined as coding proceeded through the transcript. Most labels were native codes—that is, they derived directly from the language of the FOMC members. Other labels derived from economic and sociological categories that emerged in the data. This is basically the open coding process described by Anselm Strauss and his colleagues.[5] As the codes mounted, they were refined into higher-order categories. I recoded and clustered the emerging categories until patterns (themes) began to emerge. These clusters revealed the foundation or source for much of the interpretive work of policymaking: the competing frames and logics in the policymakers' tool kits.[6] Early in the process I realized that the FOMC members were engaging in what Karl Weick referred to as "sensemaking" and that the transcripts offered a unique and detailed source of real-time sensemaking by elite organizational actors.[7] Subsequent coding yielded abstract categories leading to a model of the process of narrative construction at the FOMC.

I explored the nature of sensemaking at the Fed in a series of papers using transcripts from the 1970s to the 2000s.[8] I found no significant difference in the sensemaking in the committee before the members knew that the transcripts would be released and after. Although the members' presentations were more formal, the sensemaking processes of identification of cues and the construction of narratives were quite similar. A strong ongoing committee and academic culture determined preferred cues and narratives. The eventual public release of the transcripts didn't seem to make much difference in how these experts made sense of their environment. By the time the financial crisis arrived, I had developed my understanding of how FOMC members used cues to construct narratives that interpreted their situation. I was curious to see how crisis sensemaking would be different. For this book, I extended my analysis of sensemaking to its logical conclusion— policymaking. I found the kinds of pattern recognition among decision makers discussed in works by James March[9] and Gary Klein[10] reflected in my data. The practice of sensemaking was surprisingly consistent across decades and suggested a robust interpretive practice at the FOMC.

I had to wait five years from the beginning of the financial crisis for the release of the first transcripts from that time. When I began in 2012 to analyze the transcripts from 2007, the staff and the FOMC members' optimistic forecasts of a restoration of market function repeatedly reminded me that there was a tsunami approaching that the members could not see. This knowledge helped to highlight the strong assumptions that members made about the financial markets and how those markets worked. The assumptions were right there in the logic and language they used. These assumptions entered my codebook as cultural conventions and economic theories: conceptual lenses shaping what members see and don't see. I began to code the debate over these assumptions as a contest of fundamental institutional logics.[11] These logics became increasingly visible as the crisis unfolded.

The Transcripts as a Data Source

Two important studies using the transcripts appeared after I began my analysis of the crisis-era data.[12] The studies, published in 2013 and 2017, used versions of automated textual analysis (ATA) to explore the transcripts as data. In these computer-assisted methods the coding process described above is replaced by a program that makes the choices, searching for common words and phrases. As with human coding, different programs make different choices. By using ATA, years of coding transcripts can literally be condensed into seconds, mimicking the process I referred to previously as open coding. ATA is a useful tool for large data sets, such as the Fed transcripts, but ATA cannot yet capture the process of narrative construction, the competition between those narratives, and the contest of logics revealed here. Those analytic observations require a kind of theoretical abstraction from the data not available to the computer programs.

In her 2013 work, Cheryl Schonhardt-Bailey maps the changes in the form and content of the FOMC discussions between 1979 and 1999. She also examines critical events at the beginning and end of that period to assess the significance of the deliberative process: the role of economic ideas and argumentation in shaping decisions on monetary policy. She finds increasing use of an analytic perspective, which she refers to as the supply-demand/output gap/NAIRU[13] framework, thereby suggesting a reduction in the "seat of the pants" nature of the deliberations. Supporting this, Schonhardt-Bailey finds that deliberation is important in shaping policy over the entire period. Going further, she states that "Bernanke's FOMC appears to have evolved into a forum in which deliberation is less constrained . . . that is, a generally collegial committee but still one with a clear leader."[14] Her analysis shows that members employ strategies of persuasion, that the effect of this persuasion is especially evident across meetings, and that learning by individuals and the group is possible. The meetings are decidedly not pro forma. Deliberation matters. My work extends this finding through a close analysis of the interpretive process used in those deliberations.

In their 2017 work, Neil Fligstein, Jonah Stuart Brundage, and Michael Schultz use a form of automated textual analysis called topic modeling to identify the themes discussed at the seventy-two FOMC meetings between 2000 and 2008. They find that macroeconomic concepts structured the FOMC's reasoning during this period. They argue that the FOMC members failed to anticipate the risks involved in the financial crisis because this macroeconomic framing made it difficult to connect events into a story that would link problems in financial markets to the larger economy. They refer to "the new Keynesian synthesis" in macroeconomics as the framework that inhibited this recognition. These findings are similar to my own, suggesting that qualitative and quantitative analyses of the data reinforce and confirm each other. Nevertheless, qualitative analysis remains essential for capturing the contest and negotiation over the meaning of language that lies at the heart of interpretive policymaking. Quantitative analysis flattens out the conflictual nature of narrative construction in a policy group.

The work of both Schonhardt-Bailey and Fligstein, Brundage, and Schultz challenges the claim that the transcripts (at least since they were made public) are too formal for useful analysis.[15] Their analyses show that even as the presentation of views became more formal, with FOMC members often speaking from notes or text, the content was still laden with important indicators of the process and content of macroeconomic discourse at the FOMC.[16] The present work, using qualitative analytic methods, shares these authors' focus on process and content. It extends the study of process through its attention to the unfolding process of sensemaking and narrative construction. It shows further how sensemaking both inhibited and facilitated processes of learning, improvisation, and innovation at the FOMC. In sum, all three studies recognize the centrality of shared economic perspectives in the deliberation at the FOMC. Both Schonhardt-Bailey and Fligstein, Brundage, and Schultz lend support to my claim for the significance of the transcripts and the deliberations contained in them. There is much to be gained from careful analysis of these transcripts.

Unfortunately, there could be no verbatim transcript for the events of Lehman weekend discussed in Chapter 6. I used newspaper archives, investigative reporting on the crisis, published memoirs by the participants, and documents such as the 2011 Financial Crisis Inquiry Commission report and the 2016 National Bureau of Economic Research report by Laurence Ball. These sources suggested that there was reason to doubt the Fed's public account and provided the basis for the legitimacy account developed in Chapter 6. Bernanke's and Geithners' memoirs were unlikely to credit political pressures as an explanation for their authors' behavior and actors rarely justify their action based on social forces, such as a legitimacy crisis. But just as the Depression-era Fed believed that it had to allow the credit market to adjust to the widespread bank failures of that time, I argue that social, political, and economic forces came together that culminated in Henry Paulson's very public statement that no government money would be used. This explanation is a sociological extension of Andrew Sorkin's investigative reporting and Ball's economic analysis. I am convinced that political and cultural forces trumped technocratic control at this critical moment.

Admittedly, the analysis of Lehman weekend does not have the benefit of verbatim transcripts. No one followed Tim Geithner and Henry Paulson around with a recorder on that weekend. A great advantage of the transcripts is their face validity. They capture policymakers trying to persuade each other.[17] As a sociologist, I felt as though I had penetrated the inner sanctum of the temple. I hope the reader shares some of that excitement. Another advantage of the transcripts is that, like observational data, there is none of the retrospective interpretation that one inevitably gets in interviews with policymakers. The dialogue was occurring in real time. The policy negotiation itself was the behavior under study. My interest was in the sensemaking that the members did at the moment and how their discourse coalesced toward policy. A final advantage of verbatim transcripts became clear when it came to arriving at a decision at the end of each meeting. I was able to observe the members matching the narrative to what they perceived as a plausible policy option and debating the appropriateness of the match.

The transcripts are a great way to study the sensemaking process in organizations. At the same time, they seduce the reader into wanting to know about the actors and their motivations. As one reader of the manuscript asked, with real curiosity in her voice, "Who are these people?" Part of this is the mystification created by the arcane discourse of central bankers, but another part is that we are accustomed to attributing individual motives to action. The transcripts will not tell us individual motives for the positions these policymakers took, and even their votes do not allow us to infer their motivations, which were undoubtedly complex. The sensemaking perspective focuses instead on observable behavior: what the policy negotiations reveal about how members use existing frames and logics to influence each other and construct policy. This approach relies on the face validity of the members' strategic interaction and eschews inference at the level of individual preference or motivation.

I took this project on with some trepidation, given the arcane nature of monetary policy. I reassured myself with the knowledge that there is a long tradition of organizational sociologists studying complex areas of foreign policy, space shuttle launches, intelligence gathering, and nuclear accidents. The trading floors I studied previously had their own complexities. With some relief, I found intricate macroeconomic policy discussions amenable to sociological analysis. As with any group setting, and especially a policymaking group that had been meeting since the 1930s, the behavioral patterns that emerged in my coding were grounded in the culture of the group and the profession of its members. This book is not meant to be a history. It is meant to reveal essential elements of the practice of a group of people and thereby explain their behavior. My goal was to use this unique data set to capture the efforts of elite policymakers to make sense of a major disruption in their world and to explain how they learned and improvised in the midst of the unfolding crisis.

NOTES

Introduction

1. All transcripts used in this book can be found at the Federal Reserve's website, https://www.federalreserve.gov/monetarypolicy/fomc_historical .htm.
2. There is a burgeoning literature on sensemaking. The Ur texts of this literature are Weick (1979, 1995). I will cite other contributors to this literature throughout the book. For sensemaking's application to the Federal Reserve, see Abolafia (2004, 2005, 2010, 2012) and Abolafia and Hatmaker (2013).
3. These transcripts are released five years after the meetings, based on the decision in a Freedom of Information Act suit. (See Appendix B for further discussion of the transcripts.)
4. See Appendix B for a discussion of the quality of the data.
5. Schonhardt-Bailey (2013) establishes that significant persuasion occurs during the deliberations and that the influence of members on each other is clear from meeting to meeting. See Appendix B for further discussion.
6. See Swidler (1986) for a discussion of culture as a tool kit. Considerable literature has concerned itself with whether the Fed was "captured" by the president, Congress, or the banking industry. My research suggests that it is "captured" by the tool kit of economic concepts that it uses to make sense of its environment. Thus, it is captured by a professional culture that defines what is "thinkable."
7. For a discussion of institutional logics and their influence on behavior in organizations, see Friedland and Alford (1991) and Thornton, Ocasio, and Lounsbury (2012).

8. See Maitlis and Lawrence (2007) on the role of sensemaking in enabling further action.
9. This book is not intended as a history of the financial crisis. See Sorkin (2010), Blinder (2013), and Tooze (2018) for examples of this genre.
10. The transcripts include the sensemaking of all seven members of the Board of Governors and the twelve presidents of the regional Reserve Banks. Their discussion reflects not only individual thinking, but the definition of the situation that emerges over hours of deliberation.
11. See, for example, the compendium of reprinted articles in Persson and Tabellini (1995).
12. See Taylor (1999) for a collection of such studies.
13. Lombra and Moran 1980, 43.
14. Blinder 1998, 6.
15. Fligstein, Brundage, and Schultz 2017; Schonhardt-Bailey 2013.
16. Schonhardt-Bailey (2013) describes a similar finding in her analysis of transcripts.
17. Krugman 1994, 99.
18. Friedman and Schwartz 1963; Timberlake 1993.
19. Livingston 1986.
20. Friedman and Schwartz 1963; Meltzer 2003.
21. Friedman and Schwartz 1963.
22. Meltzer 2003.
23. This explanation received empirical support in the academic work of Ben Bernanke (2000).
24. Timberlake 1993, 324.
25. Brunner 1981.
26. Galbraith 1997, 27.
27. Marcussen 2009.
28. Insight into other areas of the Fed, such as banking regulation, would require a much bigger and different book.
29. The common educational experiences of members (advanced degrees in economics) and work histories (years spent at the Fed and at banks) suggest the basis for a common language and shared assumptions that will be revealed in subsequent chapters. See Appendix A for a short biography of each member.
30. The chair, knowing the range of opinion in the room, has already crafted a policy statement that the FOMC then debates and fine-tunes based on the prior discussion.
31. See Havrilesky and Gildea (1991); Chappell, McGregor, and Vermilyea (2005); and the papers collected in Mayer (1993) for examples.
32. My perspective on sensemaking and its role in policymaking starts from an assumption of limited but intended rationality, adding an interpretive component, elaborated on in Chapter 1, that derives from the work of Karl Weick, James March, and Clifford Geertz, among others.

33. See, for example, Lounsbury and Hirsch (2010), Sorkin (2010), Blinder (2013), and Tooze (2018).
34. See Conti-Brown (2016) and Jacobs and King (2016).

1. No Crystal Ball

1. Foreclosures would end the year up 75 percent from the previous year.
2. FOMC transcript, August 7, 2007, 6.
3. FOMC transcript, August 7, 2007, 115; emphasis added.
4. It should be noted that only a small number of economists *did* predict a crisis, and some its likely consequences from the problems in subprime mortgages and related instruments, among them Nobel Prize winners Robert Shiller and Paul Krugman. The same factors to be identified here influenced other experts who did not see the crisis coming. Unsurprisingly, it was unlikely anyone would predict the Lehman failure and its catastrophic fallout.
5. Weick 1995, 50.
6. FOMC transcript, August 7, 2007, 39.
7. FOMC transcript, August 7, 2007, 83.
8. FOMC transcript, August 7, 2007, 42.
9. FOMC transcript, August 7, 2007, 46.
10. FOMC transcript, August 7, 2007, 54.
11. FOMC transcript, August 7, 2007, 34.
12. FOMC transcript, August 7, 2007, 39.
13. FOMC transcript, August 7, 2007, 58.
14. Abolafia 2004, 2005.
15. It is noteworthy that the district bank presidents are less likely to elaborate on the contagion narrative than are the governors. The presidents are more focused on conditions in their districts. The real economy in their districts has not yet reflected the turmoil on Wall Street.
16. It is worth noting, though, that financial markets are often believed to be leading indicators of where the economy will be in six months.
17. See Abolafia (2010) for an elaboration of this idea.
18. FOMC transcript, August 7, 2007, 60; emphasis added.
19. It is the story of financial panics familiar from the nineteenth century and the Crash of 1929.
20. FOMC transcript, August 7, 2007, 39.
21. The concept of glossing on a narrative is borrowed from Boje (1991). It is the idea that narratives get fleshed out by successive speakers in a group who fill in the gaps, making the plot more coherent.
22. FOMC transcript, August 7, 2007, 67; emphasis added.
23. Although behavioral economists and economic historians acknowledge nonrational behavior, financial theory is still largely based on assumptions of rationality and efficient markets.

24. FOMC transcript, August 7, 2007, 31; emphasis added.
25. FOMC transcript, August 7, 2007, 53.
26. FOMC transcript, August 7, 2007, 83.
27. FOMC transcript, August 7, 2007, 84.
28. FOMC transcript, August 7, 2007, 80.
29. FOMC transcript, August 7, 2007, 74.
30. FOMC transcript, August 7, 2007, 67; emphasis added.
31. FOMC transcript, August 7, 2007, 77.
32. Expert judgment is often an intuitive, nearly automatic process. Causal analysis is an interruption of this intuitive process (Kahneman 2013, 97–99).
33. A 1977 amendment to the Federal Reserve Act clarified this mandate "to effectively promote the goals of maximum employment, stable prices, and moderate long-term interest rates" (Board of Governors of the Federal Reserve 2018). The Fed was criticized for focusing primarily on the "stable price" side of the mandate, thereby making inflation its primary concern.
34. I explicitly mean to say that there is nothing natural about economic trends. They are all social trends, the result of social behavior. The economy as a natural system metaphor is found again in members' use of the concept of "the natural rate of unemployment." This, too, is socially determined, having nothing to do with natural forces.
35. FOMC transcript, August 7, 2007, 64; emphasis added.
36. FOMC transcript, August 7, 2007, 39.
37. FOMC transcript, August 7, 2007, 79.
38. It is noteworthy that the mechanical and natural imagery underlying the restoration and growth narratives are very similar. The imagery underlying contagion, a disease metaphor, is far more sinister and frightening.
39. FOMC transcript, August 7, 2007, 83.
40. See March (1994, 11).
41. The staff does supply the FOMC with three policy options, but this analysis suggests that there is little comparison of these options and that the option that fits the dominant narrative is the one that gets discussed.
42. For discussion of matching or pattern recognition in organizational settings, see March (1994), Klein (1998), and Lipshitz et al. (2001).
43. This concept was developed by March and Olsen (1989) and March (1994).
44. FOMC transcript, August 7, 2007, 90; emphasis added.
45. There is a certain irony in Poole's use of the term "response rule" given the debate in the economic literature over discretion versus rules in the formation of economic policy. The Fed is famous for its use of discretion in choosing indicators and analyzing data. My use of the term "response rule" is meant to suggest that while policy formulation may not be guided by an explicit economic rule, it is guided by culturally available response rules that are validated as appropriate through discussion.
46. See March (1994) for a discussion of the role of identity in decisionmaking.
47. FOMC transcript, August 7, 2007, 89.
48. FOMC transcript, August 7, 2007, 85.

49. FOMC transcript, August 7, 2007, 51; emphasis added.
50. FOMC transcript, August 7, 2007, 63.
51. FOMC transcript, August 7, 2007, 32; emphasis added.
52. FOMC transcript, August 7, 2007, 50; emphasis added.
53. FOMC transcript, August 7, 2007, 91; emphasis added.
54. This moderation in inflation was contemporaneous with an increase in financial crises including the savings and loan crisis, Long-Term Capital Management, and the tech bubble, which seem like a prelude in retrospect.
55. This set of cultural tools is similar the rhetorical triad identified by McCloskey (1990) in her analysis of economic rhetoric.
56. The notion of culture as a tool kit first appears in Swidler (1986). Riles (2019, 23) makes a similar point about the nature of determinism in central banking culture, stating: "There is always plenty of room for agency, choice, and change in any community."
57. This conclusion is quite similar to the quantitative analysis of the transcripts found in Fligstein, Brundage, and Schultz (2017). As they summarize their argument, "We provide evidence that the Federal reserve's primary frame for making sense of the economy was macroeconomic theory. The content of macroeconomics made it difficult for the FOMC to connect events into a narrative reflecting the links between foreclosures in the housing market, the financial instruments used to package the mortgages into securities, and the threats to the larger economy" (2017, 879). Fligstein and I exchanged early drafts of this chapter and his paper and were delighted by the similar findings.
58. I do not assume here that markets have an intrinsic logic but, rather, that individuals, such as FOMC members, participate in a socially constructed view of market logic. This view changes with the fads and fashions of contemporary economics. The efficient markets hypothesis of Fama (1970) that has been popularized into a generally accepted principle is an example of the powerful role of economic ideas, although it is beyond the scope of this book. See also Bernstein (1992).
59. Although some argue that economics is an engine and not a camera for the economy, in this case it was an image of the economy in which the assumptions and predictions were both mistaken. See MacKenzie (2006).
60. A number of people claimed to have made such predictions, but when examined closely, their predictions were vague. Actual causation is far more specific. Famously, Brooksley Born, the chair of the Commodity Futures Trading Commission, warned Alan Greenspan, Arthur Levitt, and Robert Rubin at a meeting of the President's Working Group on Financial Markets in 1998 that new kinds of derivatives with no transparency threatened the financial markets. In the age of deregulation, her warning was ignored (Perrow 2010).
61. The high inflation of the 1970s left central bankers hypervigilant for signs of price instability, while the effective reduction in inflation reinforced the belief that monetary policy is the area in which they have, by far, the most influence. It is far harder to influence growth and employment.

62. See Bremner (2004, 5).
63. See Fisher's quote on page 24.
64. Thornton, Ocasio, and Lounsbury 2012.
65. FOMC transcript, August 7, 2007, 63.

2. Textures of Doubt

1. FOMC transcript, September 18, 2007, 20.
2. FOMC transcript, September 18, 2007, 52.
3. This weakness reflects the fact that such crises are extremely rare and that there is little data with which to estimate the models.
4. This distinction is borrowed from Weick (1995), 91–95.
5. FOMC transcript, September 18, 2007, 67.
6. FOMC transcript, September 18, 2007, 39.
7. For a discussion of this distinction see Weick (1995) and March (1994).
8. This is reminiscent of bank runs in the 1930s, when depositors were turned away at the door.
9. FOMC transcript, September 18, 2007, 54.
10. FOMC transcript, September 18, 2007, 47.
11. FOMC transcript, September 18, 2007, 73.
12. In the interpretive policy perspective developed here, framing is used to refer to the justifications that policymakers use to support their claims of appropriateness between the narratives and the policy. See Abolafia (2004) for an extended discussion of framing.
13. FOMC transcript, September 18, 2007, 56.
14. FOMC transcript, September 18, 2007, 72.
15. FOMC transcript, September 18, 2007, 109.
16. FOMC transcript, September 18, 2007, 118.
17. FOMC transcript, September 18, 2007, 102.
18. FOMC transcript, September 18, 2007, 43.
19. FOMC transcript, September 18, 2007, 111.
20. FOMC transcript, September 18, 2007, 118.
21. FOMC transcript, September 18, 2007, 110; emphasis added.
22. FOMC transcript, September 18, 2007, 112.
23. FOMC transcript, September 18, 2007, 86.
24. FOMC transcript, September 18, 2007, 33.
25. FOMC transcript, October 30, 2007, 104.
26. FOMC transcript, October 30, 2007, 50.
27. FOMC transcript, October 30, 2007, 54.
28. FOMC transcript, October 30, 2007, 29.
29. FOMC transcript, October 30, 2007, 58.
30. FOMC transcript, October 30, 2007, 31.
31. FOMC transcript, October 30, 2007, 66.

32. FOMC transcript, October 30, 2007, 101.
33. FOMC transcript, October 30, 2007, 104.
34. FOMC transcript, October 30, 2007, 114.
35. The vote to lower the funds rate in September was a good example of Douglas Holmes's observation that "the ultimate aim of these communications was to recruit the public, broadly conceived, to collaborate with central bankers in achieving the ends of monetary policy" (Holmes 2014, xii).
36. FOMC transcript, October 30, 2007, 118.
37. FOMC transcript, December 11, 2007, 14.
38. FOMC transcript, December 11, 2007, 84.
39. FOMC transcript, December 11, 2007, 49.
40. FOMC transcript, December 11, 2007, 60.
41. FOMC transcript, December 11, 2007, 33.
42. FOMC transcript, December 11, 2007, 74. "GSE" refers government-sponsored enterprises like Fannie Mae and Freddie Mac that do government sponsored financing of home loans.
43. FOMC transcript, December 11, 2007, 70.
44. FOMC transcript, December 11, 2007, 38.
45. FOMC transcript, December 11, 2007, 55.
46. FOMC transcript, December 11, 2007, 67.
47. FOMC transcript, December 11, 2007, 97.
48. FOMC transcript, December 11, 2007, 36.
49. FOMC transcript, December 11, 2007, 117. Mishkin's statement about inflation expectations being the most critical thing reflected an understanding that monetary policy required the cooperation of investors and consumers if moving the fed funds rate was going to influence economic behavior.
50. FOMC transcript, December 11, 2007, 121.
51. See Miller (2004).
52. As Holmes (2014, 24) explains, such overt action is designed to be "persuasive and efficacious." This overtness suggests that it is more instrumental than most examples of performativity. Policymakers are using their cultural tools. There is a rich literature on performativity in the sociology of finance that is mostly applied to markets (Callon 1998; Callon and Muniesa 2005; MacKenzie 2006). Holmes's explicit application to central banking is an important contribution.
53. FOMC transcript, December 11, 2007, 113.
54. See Lombra and Moran (1980) and Karamouzis and Lombra (1989).
55. Knorr-Cetina 1999, 10.
56. Abbott 1990, 436.
57. Scott 1998, 320.
58. Knorr-Cetina (1999) uses the term "epistemic culture" to describe cultures that create and warrant knowledge. Her examples come from physical and natural science, but the concept is just as applicable to the cultures of technocratic professions that are grounded in social science.

3. A Learning Moment?

1. FOMC transcript, January 21, 2008, 6.
2. FOMC transcript, January 21, 2008, 3. Three days after the conference call it was learned that the sell-off in stocks on Monday was caused, in part, by unauthorized trading by a rogue trader at a French bank (Bernanke 2015).
3. FOMC transcript, January 21, 2008, 7.
4. FOMC transcript, January 21, 2008, 9; emphasis added.
5. FOMC transcript, January 21, 2008, 21.
6. FOMC transcript, January 21, 2008, 23.
7. FOMC transcript, January 21, 2008, 6.
8. FOMC transcript, January 21, 2008, 11.
9. FOMC transcript, January 21, 2008, 12.
10. FOMC transcript, January 21, 2008, 17. Fisher's statement is also notable for what it reveals about his own research. He spends significant time calling CEOs for their own analysis of the situation. This is a good example of what Holmes refers to as central bankers' "ethnographic knowledge about the social and cultural character of the economy" (Holmes 2014, 6).
11. FOMC transcript, January 21, 2008, 9.
12. FOMC transcript, January 21, 2008, 7.
13. The neutral rate refers to an interest rate that would prevail if the economy were at full employment and inflation was at its target. In such a condition, monetary policy need be neither accommodative nor restrictive (FOMC transcript, January 21, 2008, 8).
14. FOMC transcript, January 21, 2008, 7.
15. FOMC transcript, January 21, 2008, 14.
16. FOMC transcript, January 21, 2008, 16.
17. FOMC transcript, January 21, 2008, 13.
18. FOMC transcript, January 21, 2008, 15.
19. FOMC transcript, January 21, 2008, 19.
20. All of the voting members were not present on the conference call.
21. For a discussion of cultural artifacts and learning, see Cook and Yanow (1993).
22. For a discussion of this kind of exploratory learning, see March (1991).
23. FOMC transcript, January 29, 2008, 6.
24. FOMC transcript, January 29, 2008, 21.
25. FOMC transcript, January 29, 2008, 31.
26. FOMC transcript, January 29, 2008, 90.
27. The presidents and governors give speeches at business conferences and conventions regularly. They also keep in touch with an assortment of business leaders, constantly 'taking the temperature" of the economy.
28. See Holmes (2014) for a detailed discussion of anecdotes and their use at the Fed. Holmes finds that construction of the "Beige Book," a summary of anecdotal reports from each of the twelve federal reserve districts that is

distributed prior to each meeting of the FOMC, was akin to ethnography. Staff members contact interlocutors in the business community for their analysis and plans. FOMC members use such anecdotes to make sense of unfolding trends and the psychological state of the market. They are important sources of cues for sensemaking.

29. FOMC transcript, January 29, 2008, 58.
30. FOMC transcript, January 29, 2008, 76.
31. FOMC transcript, January 29, 2008, 53.
32. FOMC transcript, January 29, 2008, 70.
33. See Weick and Westley (1996) for a discussion of how the juxtaposition of order and disorder in organization environments contribute to learning.
34. FOMC transcript, January 29, 2008, 66.
35. FOMC transcript, January 29, 2008, 78.
36. FOMC transcript, January 29, 2008, 93.
37. FOMC transcript, January 29, 2008, 74.
38. FOMC transcript, January 29, 2008, 80.
39. FOMC transcript, January 29, 2008, 131.
40. FOMC transcript, January 29, 2008, 94.
41. FOMC transcript, January 29, 2008, 85.
42. This idea is most associated with Milton Friedman, who is famous for the dictum that inflation is always and everywhere a monetary phenomenon. Therefore, it cannot rise unless the Fed allows it.
43. FOMC transcript, January 29, 2008, 59.
44. FOMC transcript, January 29, 2008, 132.
45. FOMC transcript, January 29, 2008, 100.
46. FOMC transcript, January 30, 2008, 104.
47. FOMC transcript, January 30, 2008, 128.
48. FOMC transcript, January 30, 2008, 130.
49. FOMC transcript, January 30, 2008, 148.
50. FOMC transcript, January 30, 2008, 121.
51. FOMC transcript, January 30, 2008, 123.
52. FOMC transcript, January 29, 2008, 142.
53. FOMC transcript, January 30, 2008, 125.
54. This definition follows Weber's understanding of technical rationality and Habermas's close reading of the concept.
55. See Friedland and Alford (1991) and Thornton, Ocasio, and Lounsbury (2012) for discussions of institutional logics.
56. FOMC transcript, January 30, 2008, 156.
57. FOMC transcript, January 30, 2008, 152.
58. FOMC transcript, January 30, 2008, 122.
59. FOMC transcript, January 30, 2008, 123.
60. FOMC transcript, January 30, 2008, 138.
61. FOMC transcript, January 30, 2008, 139.
62. FOMC transcript, January 30, 2008, 151; emphasis added.

63. Milton Friedman made this argument in his presidential address to the American Economic Association (Friedman 1968).

64. The stock market crash of 1987 and the dot.com bubble are examples. In general, the state logic dominated the political zeitgeist from the 1930s to the 1970s based on Keynesian economic principles. The market logic, based on neoclassical economic principles, dominated until the financial crisis and is being contested in the political arena as I write, though it remains dominant.

65. Technocratic control, based on science, is intended to be apolitical, but it is inherently political. Policy choices are not value neutral. They favor some interests over others. Some members are more concerned about inflation, others about growth. This tension between price stability and growth has always been at the heart of central banking, even before the Fed was established. It is impossible to ignore that those with the strongest faith in market restoration and deepest concern about inflation tend to be found among the regional bank presidents, especially from the South and the Midwest, where the state is more likely to be mistrusted and free market ideology is strongest. It is hard to separate this empirically from the more general concerns about inflation that are tied to the experience of the Great Inflation of the 1970s, which all the FOMC members remembered from early in their careers. We will observe this concern with inflation and associated policy concerns more closely as the crisis unfolds.

66. It is beyond the scope of this book to consider the conflict within neoclassical economics between Keynesians and more conservative economists. It is treated here as an ideological conflict that has clear impact on FOMC deliberations.

4. Improvising in a Liquidity Crisis

1. FOMC transcript, March 10, 2008, 3.
2. FOMC transcript, March 10, 2008, 5.
3. FOMC transcript, March 10, 2008, 22.
4. FOMC transcript, March 10, 2008, 26.
5. Although the swap lines were paid back with interest, their magnitude grew to as much as $10 trillion. They represented an unprecedented liquidity lifeline to many of the world's largest economies (Tooze 2018).
6. Swap lines for this purpose were created in December 2007 and were now being extended. The TSLF was new and untried.
7. FOMC transcript, March 10, 2008, 6.
8. FOMC transcript, March 10, 2008, 28.
9. FOMC transcript, March 10, 2008, 9.
10. FOMC transcript, March 10, 2008, 31.
11. Bernanke 2015, 205.
12. FOMC transcript, March 10, 2008, 32.

13. FOMC transcript, March 10, 2008, 13.
14. FOMC transcript, March 10, 2008, 31.
15. FOMC transcript, March 10, 2008, 16.
16. FOMC transcript, March 10, 2008, 18.
17. Bagehot 2008, 96.
18. Geithner 2014; Bernanke 2015.
19. FOMC transcript, March 10, 2008, 25.
20. See Weick (1998) for a discussion of the nature of improvisation in organizations.
21. FOMC transcript, March 10, 2008, 25.
22. FOMC transcript, March 10, 2008, 34.
23. FOMC transcript, March 10, 2008, 25.
24. There are twelve Reserve Bank presidents at FOMC meetings. They rotate as voting members for terms of one year. The president of the New York Federal Reserve Bank is a permanent voting member and vice chair of the committee.
25. FOMC transcript, March 10, 2008, 20.
26. Bagehot 2008, 35.
27. FOMC transcript, March 10, 2008, 20.
28. FOMC transcript, March 10, 2008, 25.
29. Blinder 2014, 101.
30. JPMorgan was the clearing bank for Bear Stearns, meaning that it processed Bear's unsettled transactions in financial markets with its trading partners and knew its assets fairly well. JPMorgan was also known for its large balance sheet that might make a loan possible.
31. Geithner had spoken with the SEC, Bear's regulator, that evening. The SEC said that there was no way to avert a bankruptcy filing in the morning. Much to Geithner's consternation, SEC regulators went home while his staff went to work through the night (Geithner 2014, 149).
32. Geithner 2014, 151; Bernanke 2015, 215. The play on "too big to fail" is intentional and is, ironically, a good characterization of Lehman Brothers as well, whose failure was six months hence.
33. Geithner 2014, 151.
34. Bernanke 2015, 218.
35. Geithner 2014, 154.
36. Bernanke 2015, 220.
37. FOMC transcript, March 18, 2008, 3.
38. FOMC transcript, March 18, 2008, 61.
39. FOMC transcript, March 18, 2008, 37.
40. FOMC transcript, March 18, 2008, 65.
41. FOMC transcript, March 18, 2008, 77.
42. FOMC transcript, March 18, 2008, 15; emphasis added.
43. FOMC transcript, March 18, 2008, 30.
44. FOMC transcript, March 18, 2008, 33.
45. FOMC transcript, March 18, 2008, 29.

46. FOMC transcript, March 18, 2008, 94.
47. FOMC transcript, March 18, 2008, 72.
48. FOMC transcript, March 18, 2008, 107.
49. FOMC transcript, March 18, 2008, 27.
50. FOMC transcript, March 18, 2008, 43.
51. FOMC transcript, March 18, 2008, 74.
52. FOMC transcript, March 18, 2008, 87.
53. FOMC transcript, March 18, 2008, 59.
54. FOMC transcript, March 18, 2008, 95.
55. FOMC transcript, March 18, 2008, 106.
56. FOMC transcript, March 18, 2008, 55.
57. FOMC transcript, March 18, 2008, 89.
58. FOMC transcript, March 18, 2008, 100.
59. FOMC transcript, March 18, 2008, 112.
60. These distinctions in degree of interpretation were developed by jazz great Lee Konitz, cited in Weick (1998, 544).
61. The concept of interpretive capacity is a variation on the idea of absorptive capacity developed by Cohen and Levinthal (1990).
62. Friedman and Schwartz 1963.
63. Bernanke 1983.
64. Meltzer 2003.
65. FOMC transcript, March 18, 2008, 100.
66. FOMC transcript, March 18, 2008, 91. Lacker's statement that it was probably too late to have much effect on mortgage losses is telling. The Fed does have regulatory responsibility for mortgage lenders and might have caught the weakness among subprime lenders and the rising foreclosure rates much earlier.
67. FOMC transcript, March 18, 2008, 72.
68. FOMC transcript, March 18, 2008, 77.
69. FOMC transcript, March 18, 2008, 108.
70. FOMC transcript, March 18, 2008, 80.
71. Bernanke 2015, 65.
72. Inflation remained low even as interest rates remained near zero until the writing of this chapter in 2016.

5. Contested Frames / Competing Logics

1. U.S. Senate 2008, 7.
2. U.S. Senate 2008, 2.
3. U.S. Senate 2008, 6.
4. U.S. Senate 2008, 8.
5. U.S. Senate 2008, 4.
6. U.S. Senate 2008, 30. The "unusual and exigent" authority of the Fed in a liquidity crisis was only added in the 1930s during the Great Depression.

7. My research on Fed transcripts began in the period before they were made public. Even in the period when members had reason to believe that their words would remain private, there is very little overt political discussion. The culture of discourse is technical and the central concern is the maintenance of stability and the existing order, which is their mandate. See Abolafia (2004, 2010, 2012).

8. U.S. Senate 2008, 31.

9. U.S. Senate 2008, 17.

10. Technocrats will focus on the threats to the system stability. That is their mandate. It is the political system, the president of the United States and Congress, that must correct for inequities, a task it was not ready to face.

11. One may be tempted to explore the deeper interests reflected in politicians' advocacy of distinct classes or in technocrats' maintenance of the status quo arrangements of the economic order. But there is no direct evidence of their personal motivations. What we do know is that there is an interpretive politics being played out here.

12. See Abolafia (2004).

13. Weick (1995) has referred to such institutions as the seedbed of sensemaking.

14. FOMC transcript, April 29, 2008, 85.

15. FOMC transcript, April 29, 2008, 56.

16. FOMC transcript, April 29, 2008, 70.

17. FOMC transcript, April 30, 2008, 136.

18. FOMC transcript, June 24, 2008, 68.

19. FOMC transcript, April 29, 2008, 78.

20. FOMC transcript, April 29, 2008, 65.

21. FOMC transcript, April 30, 2008, 122.

22. FOMC transcript, April 30, 2008, 130.

23. FOMC transcript, April 30, 2008, 121.

24. FOMC transcript, April 30, 2008, 138.

25. FOMC transcript, June 24, 2008, 96.

26. FOMC transcript, June 24, 2008, 94.

27. FOMC transcript, June 25, 2008, 132.

28. FOMC transcript, April 29, 2008, 137.

29. FOMC transcript, April 30, 2008, 140.

30. FOMC transcript, June 25, 2008, 141.

31. FOMC transcript, June 25, 2008, 144.

32. FOMC transcript, June 25, 2008, 179.

33. FOMC transcript, June 25, 2008, 182.

34. FOMC transcript, June 25, 2008, 189.

35. FOMC transcript, August 5, 2008, 50.

36. FOMC transcript, August 5, 2008, 74.

37. FOMC transcript, August 5, 2008, 43, 60, 67.

38. Paulson 2013, 151.

39. FOMC transcript, August 5, 2008, 82.

40. FOMC transcript, August 5, 2008, 87.
41. FOMC transcript, August 5, 2008, 145.
42. FOMC transcript, August 5, 2008, 40.
43. FOMC transcript, August 5, 2008, 43.
44. FOMC transcript, August 5, 2008, 84.
45. FOMC transcript, August 5, 2008, 89.
46. FOMC transcript, August 5, 2008, 100.
47. FOMC transcript, August 5, 2008, 109.
48. FOMC transcript, August 5, 2008, 63.
49. FOMC transcript, August 5, 2008, 105.
50. FOMC transcript, August 5, 2008, 102.
51. FOMC transcript, August 5, 2008, 126.
52. Only five of the twelve regional bank presidents are voting members in any year. Eleven of the twelve rotate into voting positions for terms of one year. The president of the New York Federal Reserve Bank is a permanent voting member.
53. FOMC transcript, August 5, 2008, 50.
54. FOMC transcript, June 24, 2008, 65.
55. Knowlton and Grynbaum 2008, B1.
56. FOMC transcript, August 5, 2008, 70.
57. FOMC transcript, August 5, 2008, 100.
58. FOMC transcript, August 5, 2008, 90.
59. Commons 1959, 713.
60. For a book-length elaboration of this argument, see Abolafia (1996).
61. Some evidence has been found for governors appointed by Democrats to favor monetary ease and governors appointed by Republicans to favor tightness between 1966 and 1996 (Chappell, McGregor, and Vermilyea 2005).
62. Thornton, Ocasio, and Lounsbury (2012), among others, refer to this use of identities as "embedded agency." March (1994) refers to it as "rule following." See Maitlis and Lawrence (2007) for a discussion of "triggering."
63. A literature that infers the Fed's biases from its actions exists, but it lacks direct evidence of intentions and therefore a "smoking gun" that reveals interests (Mayer 1993; Chappell, McGregor, and Vermilyea 2005).

6. Accounting for a Legitimacy Crisis

1. Sorkin 2010, 304.
2. Sorkin 2010, 306.
3. Bernanke 2015, 252.
4. Sorkin 2010, 304.
5. Geithner 2014, 186.
6. Sorkin 2010, 350.
7. Sorkin 2010, 351; Geithner 2014.
8. Sorkin 2010, 352.

9. On September 9, 2008, before Lehman weekend, the Congressional Budget Office issued a forecast for GDP growth in 2008 as a whole and for 2009. It forecast 1.5 percent growth in 2008 and 1.1 in 2009. This is, of course, similar to what Fed staff and FOMC members had been predicting. These numbers imply that growth would only slow slightly in the remainder of 2008 but pick up in 2009. It actually plunged 5.4 percent in the last quarter of 2008 and 6.4 percent in the first quarter of 2009.

10. The metaphorical nature of crisis was discussed by Habermas (1975, 2–8).

11. U.S. House of Representatives 2008.

12. Bernanke 2015, 289.

13. Geithner 2014, 186.

14. Bernanke 2015, 264.

15. Financial Crisis Inquiry Commission 2011, 341.

16. Ball 2016.

17. Ball 2016, 114.

18. Financial Crisis Inquiry Commission 2011, 341.

19. Financial Crisis Inquiry Commission 2011, 342.

20. Ball 2016, 49.

21. Ball 2016, 51.

22. Stewart and Eavis 2014, A1.

23. Ball 2016, 8.

24. Ball 2016, 95.

25. Habermas 1975.

26. Bernanke 2015, 260.

27. Bernanke 2015, 260.

28. Pearlstein 2008, 1a.

29. Grier 2008, 1.

30. Nicklaus 2008, B1.

31. "Lehman's Fate" 2008, A16.

32. Habermas (1975, 50) suggests that legitimation crises are the "unintended side effect of administrative interventions in the cultural tradition."

33. Jackson 2008, 5a.

34. Geithner 2014, 175.

35. Geithner 2014, 175.

36. Sorkin 2010, 285.

37. Habermas 1975, 69. Habermas argued that it is normative to question administrative action in a crisis. An important part of crisis management is managing these questions or anticipating them.

38. It is not a coincidence that journalists across the spectrum of media outlets tapped in to this cultural sensitivity. As Annelise Riles (2018, 36) put it, "Culture pervades the relationship between central bankers and the public and shapes the terms and limits of policy options."

39. Sorkin 2010, 305, 330–331.

40. Sorkin 2010, 242.

41. Geithner 2014, 180.
42. Geithner 2014, 178.
43. Geithner 2014, 180.
44. Sorkin 2010, 286; Geithner 2014, 179.
45. Geithner 2014, 179.
46. Blinder 2014, 123.
47. Sorkin 2010.
48. Riles (2018) argues that the "culture clash" between central banks and their publics has grown since the financial crisis and is in need of remediation.
49. The concept of legitimacy crisis is drawn from Habermas (1975).
50. FOMC transcript, September 16, 2008, 51.

7. Learning after Lehman

1. FOMC transcript, September 16, 2008, 6.
2. FOMC transcript, September 16, 2008, 22.
3. FOMC transcript, September 16, 2008, 19.
4. FOMC transcript, September 16, 2008, 67.
5. FOMC transcript, September 16, 2008, 31.
6. FOMC transcript, September 16, 2008, 40.
7. FOMC transcript, September 16, 2008, 42.
8. FOMC transcript, September 16, 2008, 60.
9. FOMC transcript, September 16, 2008, 71.
10. FOMC transcript, September 16, 2008, 35.
11. FOMC transcript, September 16, 2008, 38.
12. FOMC transcript, September 16, 2008, 82.
13. FOMC transcript, September 16, 2008, 36.
14. FOMC transcript, September 16, 20008, 51.
15. FOMC transcript, September 16, 2008, 48.
16. Tim Geithner was not at the September 16 meeting because he was dealing with the pending failure of AIG, an insurance company to which the Fed lent $85 billion that week.
17. FOMC transcript, September 16, 2008, 49.
18. FOMC transcript, September 16, 2008, 18.
19. Bernanke 2015, 280.
20. FOMC transcript, October 7, 2008, 1.
21. FOMC transcript, October 7, 2008, 5.
22. FOMC transcript, October 7, 2008, 13.
23. FOMC transcript, October 7, 2008, 21.
24. FOMC transcript, October 7, 2008, 26.
25. FOMC transcript, October 7, 2008, 17.
26. FOMC transcript, October 7, 2008, 14.
27. FOMC transcript, October 29, 2008, 118.

28. FOMC transcript, October 28, 2008, 4.
29. FOMC transcript, October 28, 2008, 67.
30. FOMC transcript, October 29, 2008, 149.
31. FOMC transcript, October 29, 2008, 94.
32. FOMC transcript, October 28, 2008, 75.
33. FOMC transcript, October 28, 2008, 73.
34. FOMC transcript, October 28, 2008, 88.
35. FOMC transcript, October 29, 2008, 100.
36. FOMC transcript, October 29, 2008, 125.
37. FOMC transcript, October 29, 2008, 137.
38. FOMC transcript, October 29, 2008, 122.
39. FOMC transcript, October 28, 2008, 81.
40. FOMC transcript, October 28, 2008, 85.
41. FOMC transcript, October 29, 2008, 133.
42. FOMC transcript, October 28, 2008, 68.
43. FOMC transcript, October 28, 2008, 57.
44. FOMC transcript, October 29, 2008, 137.
45. FOMC transcript, October 29, 2008, 136.
46. FOMC transcript, October 29, 2008, 130.
47. FOMC transcript, October 29, 2008, 145.
48. FOMC transcript, October 29, 2008, 118.
49. FOMC transcript, December 15, 2008, 4.
50. For a discussion of the role of order and disorder in organizational learning, see Weick and Westley (1996).
51. FOMC transcript, December 15, 2008, 16.
52. FOMC transcript, December 15, 2008, 30.
53. FOMC transcript, December 16, 2008, 188.
54. FOMC transcript, December 16, 2008, 191.
55. FOMC transcript, December 15, 2008, 23.
56. FOMC transcript, December 15, 2008, 77.
57. FOMC transcript, December 15, 2008, 84.
58. FOMC transcript, December 15, 2008, 92.
59. FOMC transcript, December 16, 2008, 198. Tim Geithner had recently been chosen to be Secretary of the Treasury in the incoming administration of President Barack Obama.
60. FOMC transcript, December 15, 2008, 86.
61. FOMC transcript, December 15, 2008, 16.
62. Crossan, Lane, and White 1999.
63. FOMC transcript, December 15, 2008, 25.
64. FOMC transcript, December 15, 2008, 91.
65. FOMC transcript, December 15, 2008, 101.
66. FOMC transcript, December 15, 2008, 71.
67. FOMC transcript, December 15, 2008, 102.
68. FOMC transcript, December 16, 2008, 176.

69. FOMC transcript, December 16, 2008, 134.
70. FOMC transcript, December 16, 2008, 195.
71. FOMC transcript, December 15, 2008, 93.
72. FOMC transcript, December 15, 2008, 87.
73. FOMC transcript, December 15, 2008, 51.
74. FOMC transcript, December 15, 2008, 24.
75. FOMC transcript, December 15, 2008, 67.
76. FOMC transcript, December 16, 2008, 175.
77. FOMC transcript, December 16, 2008, 148.
78. FOMC transcript, December 16, 2008, 146.
79. FOMC transcript, December 16, 2008, 140.
80. FOMC transcript, December 16, 2008, 159.
81. FOMC transcript, December 16, 2008, 171.
82. FOMC transcript, December 16, 2008, 186.
83. FOMC transcript, December 16, 2008, 134.
84. FOMC transcript, December 16, 2008, 139.
85. FOMC transcript, December 16, 2008, 208.

8. The Pathos and Irony of Technocratic Control

1. This was especially true during Alan Greenspan's eighteen-year term as chairman, just prior to the financial crisis.
2. Holmes (2014) offers a useful discussion of the use of anecdotes in central bank decisions.
3. A variety of people claimed that they predicted the financial crisis, but when examined closely these predictions were often vague, reflecting a sense that one market or another was unsettled. Such predictions are common and easily ignored by policymakers.
4. Recent work by Binder and Spindel (2017) suggests that the Fed and Congress are interdependent; Congress relying on the Fed to provide political cover when the economy falters and to actively pursue growth otherwise. The Fed is aware that it is a creature of legislation and is responsive to that legislation's mandate. This nuanced view of the relationship fits well with the analysis given here. I am also persuaded of the argument developed by Conti-Brown (2016, 7) that "independence" fails to capture where the Fed fits within government. Rather, Fed policymaking is a "balance between democratic accountability, technocratic expertise, and the influence of central bankers' own value judgments."
5. These policy conflicts were not debates over the science; they reflected the use of science to make claims for political values. It seems ironic now that many observers were concerned that the Fed was captured either by the Congress or the executive branch. For a sample of such arguments, see Mayer (1990). The present work and the work of Fligstein, Brundage, and Schultz (2017) suggest

that the Fed is tacitly captured by the field of macroeconomics, which sets the premises of its thinking.

6. Kolko 1977; Livingston 1989.

7. This has long been a concern on both the left and the right. Evidence has often been anecdotal. The influence of academic tools has been hiding in plain sight.

8. It is not coincidental that science fiction movies often turn on the point when a president or general overrides the scientists to fight the aliens / monsters. Technocrats are generally not trusted in a crisis.

9. Of course, democratically elected officials are also vulnerable to the power and influence of interests (e.g., Wall Street) that may differ from the public interest.

10. Paul 2009.

11. Klein 1998, 261.

12. Weick 1979, 1995.

13. Abbott 1990.

14. Weick 1995.

15. Abolafia 2004, 2005, 2010, 2012; Abolafia and Hatmaker 2013.

16. Weick and Westley (1996) note that learning often occurs in the juxtaposition of order and disorder.

17. See Karamouzis and Lombra (1989) and Lombra and Moran (1980).

18. See Mankiw (1997, 71).

19. Klein 1998.

20. Fligstein, Brundage, and Schultz (2017) offer a similar analysis of the Fed's response to the financial crisis using similar data.

21. Eavis 2013, B1.

22. Popper 2013, 1.

23. Tucker 2018, 432.

24. Tucker 2018, 433.

25. Tucker 2018, 510.

26. Tucker 2018, 511.

27. This argument is made eloquently by Charles Perrow in *Normal Accidents* (1984).

28. See the chapters in Lounsbury and Hirsch (2010) for excellent examples of such analyses.

29. The Fed was itself implicated in this lax regulation. The foregoing analysis was focused on the story of the monetary policy committee, but the contribution of lax regulation to the mortgage crisis and the larger financial crisis is deserving of greater attention than it has received. It is beyond the scope of this book.

Appendix B

1. Auerbach 2008.

2. The transcripts are now published on the Fed's website, https://www.federal reserve.gov/monetarypolicy/fomc_historical.htm.

3. Lombra and Moran 1980, 43.
4. Abolafia 1996, 2010.
5. Strauss 1987; Strauss and Corbin 1998; Corbin and Strauss 2008.
6. See Weber and Glynn (2006) for a discussion of institutional context and its role in sensemaking.
7. Weick 1979, 1995, 2001.
8. Abolafia 2004, 2005, 2010, 2012; Abolafia and Hatmaker 2013.
9. March 1994.
10. Klein 1998.
11. My view of culture is heavily influenced by Clifford Geertz (1973) and Ann Swidler (1986, 2001), but more recently by the institutional logics perspective: Friedland and Alford (1991); Thornton and Ocasio (1999); Thornton (2002); Thornton, Ocasio, and Lounsbury (2012).
12. See Schonhardt-Bailey (2013); Fligstein, Brundage, and Schultz (2017).
13. NAIRU refers to the nonaccelerating inflation rate of unemployment.
14. Schonhardt-Bailey 2013, 415.
15. Meyer (2004) and Chappell, McGregor, and Vermilyea (2005) make this claim. It is explicitly rejected by Schonhardt-Bailey (2013, 375–381).
16. Meyer (2004) and Chappell, McGregor, and Vermilyea (2005) dismiss the role of discourse in the meetings, arguing that the conversations are no longer spontaneous. Readers of this book can judge the role of deliberation, discourse, and spontaneity for themselves. Crises generate active group sensemaking, and the financial crisis was not an exception.
17. This influence process was studied in depth by Schonhardt-Bailey (2013). Her interviews with members of the FOMC show that most feel that the publication of the transcripts has not harmed the deliberation. For my purposes, the issue is not spontaneity of conversation but the content of the sensemaking. The imperative of sensemaking is magnified by crisis and is revealed in the transcripts at every stage of awareness and doubt between August 2007 and December 2008.

ACKNOWLEDGMENTS

Most authors end the accounting of their indebtedness by acknowledging those closest to them. I must begin there. I first learned of the existence of the transcripts of policy meetings at the Federal Reserve on which this book is based while listening to the radio on the way home from work. When I arrived home, my partner Amy asked if I had heard the story about the transcripts and suggested that I call the Fed and get a look at them. I would not have done so without her prompt. So, my first thanks are to Amy Svirsky and second to *Marketplace* on public radio.

I wish to express my appreciation to the members of the Federal Open Market Committee from August 2007 to December 2008, although they were passive participants in this study of their behavior. I spent six years analyzing the transcripts of their meetings and felt a bit like a fly on the wall observing their negotiations, contests, and conflicts. I was constantly impressed by their commitment, engagement, and knowledge. I hope some of that appreciation is revealed in these pages.

I trace my intellectual interest in the topic most directly to two books that I read as an undergraduate writing a paper on organizational failures during the Vietnam War: Roberta Wohlstetter's *Pearl Harbor* and Harold Wilensky's *Organizational Intelligence*. Wohlstetter focused on how the weaknesses in America's strategic analysis before the Second World War allowed us to be surprised by the attack. Wilenky examined a wide range of intelligence failures with a focus on the institutional sources of those failures. Clearly, these classic studies stuck in my mind.

My intellectual debts are many, but I will limit myself to those whose work was most central to my analysis. Readers familiar with the field of organization theory will note the pervasive influence of the work of Karl Weick throughout this book. His creative theorizing of sensemaking is central to my analysis. A desire to connect sensemaking to larger social and cultural forces and a sentence on institutions in Weick's book *Sensemaking in Organizations* inspired me to link the group process of sensemaking to the literature on institutional logics first developed by Roger Friedland and Robert Alford and elaborated by Pat Thornton, Willie Ocasio, and Mike Lounsbury. This complemented my approach to culture that was most influenced by the work of Ann Swidler and Clifford Geertz. Finally, it was Charles Perrow's work *Normal Accidents* that alerted me to the missing link between contagion and systemic risk.

I am grateful for the comments of participants in faculty seminars at Johns Hopkins University, the University of Paris, Sciences Po, the University of Southern California, St. Petersburg University, the University of Pennsylvania, Cornell University, the London School of Economics and Political Science, Oxford University, Heidelberg University, and George Washington University. I am particularly indebted to the participants in an interdisciplinary book workshop organized by Tim Lytton at the Georgia State University College of Law. The members read an early draft of the manuscript and provided insightful and critical comments at that stage. The participants were Summer Chandler, Cary Coglianese, Glen Harrison, Raymond Hill, Larry Jacobs, Kathryn Judge, Paul Lombardo, Tim Lytton, Alfred Mettler, Tom McGarity, Simone Polillo, Edward Rubin, Don Seeman, David Sehat, John Phillip Theilman, Anne Tucker, Wendy Wagner, Larry Wall, Robert Weber, and David Zaring.

Glen Feinberg and Tim Lytton read the first draft of every chapter. Their comments were detailed, insightful, and essential. Their generosity humbles me. Other readers included Alan Abbey, Jacob Abolafia, Mordecai Beinstock, Elizabeth Popp Berman, Barbara DeVivo, Jennifer Dodge, Erzsebet Fazekas, Neil Fligstein, Charles Perrow, Jon Rosen, Martin Strossberg, and Amy Svirsky.

Michael Aronson, the editor of my first book, encouraged me early in the process that this new venture was worthwhile. Thomas LeBien, who took over as editor after Michael retired, provided indispensable insight into the revision process. James Edwin Brandt facilitated the final stages. I am deeply grateful to all of them as well as to the two anonymous reviewers who helped me refine my argument.

This book, over its long gestation, has benefited in all sorts of ways from the support of colleagues and friends including David Andersen, George Richardson, Karl Rethemeyer, Deneen Hatmaker, Sora Park, Rick Caceres-Rodriguez, Karen Knorr-Cetina, Richard Swedberg, Victor Nee, Jon Rosen, Anna Rosen, Pete Rothberg, Andrea DiGioia Rothberg, Artie Brenner, Nanette Brenner, Joshua Beiser, Suellen Beiser, Rachel Anisfeld, Alan Abbey, Sheryl Adler, Mordecai Beinstock, and Karen Beinstock. Duane Abolafia was a constant companion and comforting presence during hours of coding that were beneficially interrupted by his demands for a walk.

To my children, Jacob and Aliza, thank you for your encouragement and faith. It is a special kind of sustenance.

This book is dedicated to my partner in life, Amy Svirsky, an endless wellspring of good ideas and understanding.

REFERENCES

Abbott, Andrew 1990. "Positivism and Interpretation in Sociology: Lessons for Sociologists from the History of Stress Research." *Sociological Forum* 5(3): 435–448.

Abolafia, Mitchel Y. 1996. *Making Markets: Opportunism and Restraint on Wall Street*. Cambridge, MA: Harvard University Press.

———. 2004. "Framing Moves: Interpretive Politics at the Federal Reserve." *Journal of Public Administration Research and Theory* 14(3): 349–370.

———. 2005. "Making Sense of Recession: Toward an Interpretive Theory of Economic Action." In *The Economic Sociology of Capitalism*, edited by Victor Nee and Richard Swedberg, 204–226. Princeton, NJ: Princeton University Press.

———. 2010. "Narrative Construction as Sensemaking: How a Central Bank Thinks." *Organization Studies* 31(3): 349–367.

———. 2012. "Central Banking and the Triumph of Technical Rationality." In *Handbook of the Sociology of Finance*, edited by Karin Knorr-Cetina and Alex Preda, 94–112. Oxford: Oxford University Press.

Abolafia, Mitchel Y., and Deneen Hatmaker. 2013. "Fine-Tuning the Signal: Image and Identity at the Federal Reserve." *International Public Management Journal* 16(4): 532–556.

Auerbach, Robert D. 2008. *Deception and Abuse at the Fed: Henry B. Gonzalez Battles Alan Greenspan's Bank*. Austin: University of Texas Press.

Bagehot, Walter. 2008. *Lombard Street: A Description of the Money Market*. Sioux Falls, SD: NUVision Publications.

Ball, Laurence. 2016. "The Fed and Lehman Brothers." National Bureau of Economic Research Working Paper No. 22410, NBER Monetary Economics Program.

Bernanke, Ben. 1983. "Non-Monetary Effects of the Financial Crisis in the Propagation of the Great Depression." *American Economic Review* 73: 257–276.

———. 2000 *Essays on the Great Depression*. Princeton, NJ: Princeton University Press.

———. 2013. *The Federal Reserve and the Financial Crisis*. Princeton, NJ: Princeton University Press.

———. 2015. *The Courage to Act: A Memoir of a Crisis and Its Aftermath*. New York: W. W. Norton.

Bernstein, Peter L. 1992. *Capital Ideas: The Improbable Origins of Modern Wall Street*. New York: Free Press.

Binder, Sarah A., and Mark Spindel. 2017. *The Myth of Independence: How Congress Governs the Federal Reserve*. Princeton, NJ: Princeton University Press.

Blinder, Alan S. 1998. *Central Banking in Theory and Practice*. Cambridge, MA: MIT Press.

———. 2013. *After the Music Stopped: The Financial Crisis, the Response, and the Work Ahead*. Paperback ed. with a new afterword. New York: Penguin.

Board of Governors of the Federal Reserve. 2018. "Federal Reserve System: Purposes and Functions." https://www.federalreserve.gov/aboutthefed/pf.htm.

Boje, David. 1991. "The Storytelling Organization: A Study of Story Performance in an Office-Supply Firm." *Administrative Science Quarterly* 36: 106–126.

Bremner, Robert P. 2004. *Chairman of the Fed: William McChesney Martin, Jr., and the Creation of the Modern American Financial System*. New Haven, CT: Yale University Press.

Brunner, Karl. 1981. "The Art of Central Banking." Working paper series, Graduate School of Management, University of Rochester.

Callon, Michel, ed. 1998. *The Laws of the Markets*. Oxford: Blackwell Publishers.

Callon, Michel, and Fabian Muniesa. 2005. "Economic Markets as Calculative Devices." *Organization Studies* 26(8): 1229–1250.

Chappell, Henry W., Rob Roy McGregor, and Todd Vermilyea. 2005. *Committee Decisions on Monetary Policy: Evidence from Historical Records of the Federal Open Market Committee*. Cambridge, MA: MIT Press.

Cohen, Wesley, and Daniel Levinthal. 1990. "Absorptive Capacity: A New Perspective on Learning and Innovation." *Administrative Science Quarterly* 35: 128–152.

Commons, John. 1959. *Institutional Economics*. Madison: University of Wisconsin Press.

Conti-Brown, Peter. 2016. *The Power and Independence of the Federal Reserve*. Princeton, NJ: Princeton University Press.

Cook, Scott, and Dvora Yanow. 1993. "Culture and Organizational Learning." *Journal of Management Inquiry* 2(4): 373–390.

Corbin, Juliet M., and Anselm L. Strauss. 2008. *Basics of Qualitative Research: Techniques and Procedures for Developing Grounded Theory.* 3rd ed. Los Angeles: Sage Publications.

Crossan, Mary, Henry Lane, and Roderick White. 1999. "An Organizational Learning Framework: From Intuition to Institution." *Academy of Management Review* 24(3): 522–537.

Eavis, Peter. 2013. "The Stimulus Comment That Agitated Traders." *New York Times,* June 14.

Fama, Eugene. 1970. "Efficient Capital Markets: A Review of Theory and Empirical Work." *Journal of Finance* 25(2): 383–417.

Federal Open Market Committee. 2007. "FOMC Transcripts." Board of Governors of the Federal Reserve. https://www.federalreserve.gov/monetarypolicy/fomc_historical.htm.

Feirstein, Bruce. 2009. "100 to Blame: Nobel Laureates, Nancy Pelosi, and More." *Vanity Fair,* September.

Financial Crisis Inquiry Commission, ed. 2011. *The Financial Crisis Inquiry Report: Final Report of the National Commission on the Causes of the Financial and Economic Crisis in the United States.* New York: PublicAffairs.

Fligstein, Neil, Jonah Stuart Brundage, and Michael Schultz. 2017. "Seeing Like the Fed: Culture, Cognition, and Framing in the Failure to Anticipate the Financial Crisis of 2008." *American Sociological Review* 82(5): 879–909.

Friedland, Roger, and Robert Alford. 1991. "Bringing Society Back In: Symbols, Practices, and Institutional Contradictions." In *The New Institutionalism in Organizational Analysis,* edited by Walter Powell and Paul DiMaggio, 232–263. Chicago: University of Chicago Press.

Friedman, Milton. 1968. "The Role of Monetary Policy." *American Economic Review* 58(1): 1–17.

Friedman, Milton, and Anna Jacobson Schwartz. 1963. *A Monetary History of the United States: 1867–1960.* Princeton, NJ: Princeton University Press.

Galbraith, John Kenneth. 1997. *The Great Crash, 1929.* Boston: Houghton Mifflin Harcourt.

Geertz, Clifford. 1973. *The Interpretation of Cultures: Selected Essays.* New York: Basic Books.

Geithner, Timothy F. 2014. *Stress Test: Reflections on Financial Crises.* New York: Crown Publishers.

Goodfriend, Marvin. 1986. "Monetary Mystique: Secrecy and Central Banking." *Journal of Monetary Economics* 17: 63–92.

Grier, Peter. 2008. "Lehman: The Next Bailout?" *Christian Science Monitor,* September 12.

Habermas, Jürgen. 1975. *Legitimation Crisis.* Boston: Beacon Press.

Havrilesky, Thomas, and John Gildea. 1991. "The Policy Preferences of FOMC Members as Revealed by Dissenting Votes." *Journal of Money, Credit, and Banking* 23(1): 130–138.

Holmes, Douglas R. 2014. *Economy of Words: Communicative Imperatives in Central Banks.* Chicago: University of Chicago Press.

Jackson, David. 2008. "Candidates Pin Blame in Financial Crisis." *USA Today,* September 16.

Jacobs, Lawrence R., and Desmond S. King. 2016. *Fed Power: How Finance Wins.* New York: Oxford University Press.

Kahneman, Daniel. 2013. *Thinking, Fast and Slow.* New York: Farrar, Strauss, and Giroux.

Karamouzis, Nicholas, and Raymond Lombra. 1989. "Federal Reserve Policy Making: An Overview and Analysis of the Policy Process." In *International Debt, Federal Reserve Operations, and Other Essays,* edited by Karl Brunner and Allan Meltzer, 7–62. Amsterdam: North-Holland.

Keynes, John Maynard. 2008. *The General Theory of Employment, Interest, and Money.* Hawthorne, CA: BN Publishing.

Klein, Gary. 1998. *Sources of Power: How People Make Decisions.* Cambridge, MA: MIT Press.

Knorr-Cetina, K. 1999. *Epistemic Cultures: How the Sciences Make Knowledge.* Cambridge, MA: Harvard University Press.

Knowlton, Brian, and Michael Grynbaum. 2008. "Greenspan Shocked That Free Markets Are Flawed." *New York Times,* October 23.

Kolko, Gabriel. 1977. *The Triumph of Conservatism: A Reinterpretation of American History, 1900–1916.* New York: Free Press.

Krugman, Paul R. 1994. *The Age of Diminished Expectations: US Economic Policy in the 1990s.* 3rd ed. Cambridge, MA: MIT Press.

"Lehman's Fate." 2008. *Wall Street Journal,* September 12, 16.

Lipshitz, Raanan, Gary Klein, Judith Orasanu, and Eduardo Salas. 2001. "Taking Stock of Naturalistic Decision Making." *Journal of Behavioral Decision Making* 14: 331–352.

Livingston, James. 1986. *Origins of the Federal Reserve System: Money, Class, and Corporate Capitalism, 1890–1913.* Ithaca, NY: Cornell University Press.

Lombra, Raymond, and Michael Moran. 1980. "Policy Advice and Policy Making at the Federal Reserve." In *Monetary Institutions and Policy Processes,* edited by Karl Brunner and Allan Meltzer, 9–68. Amsterdam: North-Holland.

Lounsbury, Michael, and Paul M. Hirsch, eds. 2010. *Markets on Trial: The Economic Sociology of the US Financial Crisis.* Pt. B. Research in the Sociology of Organizations 30. Bingley, UK: Emerald.

MacKenzie, Donald A. 2006. *An Engine, Not a Camera: How Financial Models Shape Markets.* Cambridge, MA: MIT Press.

Maitlis, Sally, and Thomas Lawrence. 2007. "Triggers and Enablers of Sensegiving in Organizations." *Academy of Management Journal* 50(1): 57–84.

Mankiw, Nicholas Gregory, ed. 1997. *Monetary Policy.* Chicago: University of Chicago Press.

March, James G. 1991. "Exploration and Exploitation in Organizational Learning." *Organization Science* 2(1): 71–87.

———. 1994. *A Primer on Decision Making: How Decisions Happen.* New York: Free Press.

March, James G., and Johan P. Olsen. 1989. *Rediscovering Institutions: The Organizational Basis of Politics.* New York: Free Press.

Marcussen, Martin. 2009. "Scientization of Central Banking: The Politics of A-Politicization." In *Central Banks in the Age of the Euro: Europeanization, Convergence, and Power,* edited by Kenneth Dyson and Martin Marcussen, 373–390. Oxford: Oxford University Press.

Mayer, Thomas, ed. 1993. *The Political Economy of American Monetary Policy.* Cambridge: Cambridge University Press.

McCloskey. Deirdre, N. 1990. *If You're So Smart: The Narrative of Economic Expertise.* Chicago: University of Chicago Press.

Meltzer, Allan H. 2003. *A History of the Federal Reserve.* Chicago: University of Chicago Press.

Meyer, Laurence H. 2004. *A Term at the Fed: An Insider's View.* New York: HarperBusiness.

Miller, Hugh. 2004. "Why Old Pragmatism Needs an Upgrade." *Administration and Society* 36(2): 243–249.

Nicklaus, David. 2008. "When Bailouts Are Panacea, Everybody Will Pay a Price." *St. Louis Post-Dispatch,* September 12.

Paul, Ron. 2009. *End the Fed.* New York: Grand Central Publishing.

Paulson, Henry M. 2013. *On the Brink: Inside the Race to Stop the Collapse of the Global Financial System* New York: Business Plus.

Pearlstein, Steven. 2008. "Financial Rescue Shows That Faith in Free Market Is Shaken." *Washington Post,* September 12.

Peirce, Charles Sanders. "The Fixation of Belief." Cited in Patricia M Shields, "The Community of Inquiry: Classical Pragmatism and Public Administration." *Administration and Society* 35(5) (2003): 510–538.

Perrow, Charles. 1984. *Normal Accidents: Living with High-Risk Technologies.* New York: Basic Books.

———. 2010. "The Meltdown Was Not an Accident." In *Markets on Trial,* edited by Michael Lounsbury and Paul Hirsch, 307–328. Bingley, UK: Emerald.

Persson, Torsten, and Guido Enrico Tabellini, eds. 1995. *Monetary and Fiscal Policy.* Cambridge, MA: MIT Press.

Popper, Nathaniel. 2013. "Global Sell-Off Reaches beyond US." *New York Times,* June 21.

Riles, Annelise. 2019. *Financial Citizenship: Experts, Publics, and the Politics of Central Banking.* Ithaca, NY: Cornell University Press.

Schonhardt-Bailey, Cheryl. 2013. *Deliberating American Monetary Policy: A Textual Analysis.* Cambridge, MA: MIT Press.

Scott, James C. 1998. *Seeing Like a State: How Certain Schemes to Improve the Human Condition Have Failed.* New Haven, CT: Yale University Press.

Shields, Patricia. 2003. "The Community of Inquiry: Classical Pragmatism and Public Administration." *Administration and Society* 35(5): 510–538.

Sorkin, Andrew Ross. 2010. *Too Big to Fail: The Inside Story of How Wall Street and Washington Fought to Save the Financial System—and Themselves.* Updated with a new afterword. London: Penguin Books.

Stewart, James, and Peter Eavis. 2014. "Revisiting the Lehman Brothers Bailout That Never Was." *New York Times,* September 14.

Strauss, Anselm L. 1987. *Qualitative Analysis for Social Scientists.* Cambridge: Cambridge University Press.

Strauss, Anselm L., and Juliet M. Corbin. 1998. *Basics of Qualitative Research: Techniques and Procedures for Developing Grounded Theory.* 2nd ed. Thousand Oaks, CA: Sage Publications.

Swidler, Ann. 1986. "Culture in Action: Symbols and Strategies." *American Sociological Review* 51: 273–286.

———. 2001. *Talk of Love: How Culture Matters.* Chicago: University of Chicago Press.

Taylor, John B., ed. 1999. *Monetary Policy Rules.* Chicago: University of Chicago Press.

Thornton, Patricia H. 2002. "The Rise of the Corporation in a Craft Industry: Conflict and Conformity in Institutional Logics." *Academy of Management Journal* 45(1): 81–101.

Thornton, Patricia H., and William Ocasio. 1999. "Institutional Logics and the Historical Contingency of Power in Organizations." *American Journal of Sociology* 105(3): 801–843.

Thornton, Patricia H., William Ocasio, and Michael Lounsbury. 2012. *The Institutional Logics Perspective: A New Approach to Culture, Structure, and Process.* Oxford: Oxford University Press.

Timberlake, Richard H. 1993. *Monetary Policy in the United States: An Intellectual and Institutional History.* Chicago: University of Chicago Press.

Tooze, Adam. 2018. *Crashed: How a Decade of Financial Crises Changed the World.* New York: Viking.

Tucker, Paul. 2018. *Unelected Power: The Quest for Legitimacy in Central Banking and the Regulatory State.* Princeton, NJ: Princeton University Press.

U.S. House of Representatives. 2008. "The Future of Financial Services: Exploring Solutions for the Financial Crisis." Hearing before the Committee on Financial Services, 110th Cong., 2nd sess., September 24.

U.S. Senate. 2008. "Turmoil in US Credit Markets: Examining the Recent Actions of Federal Financial Regulators." Hearing before the Committee on Banking, Housing, and Urban Affairs. 110th Cong., 2nd sess., April 3.

Weber, Klaus, and Mary Ann Glynn. 2006. "Making Sense with Institutions: Context, Thought, and Action in Karl Weick's Theory." *Organization Studies* 27(11): 1639–1660.

Weick, Karl E. 1979. *The Social Psychology of Organizing.* 2nd ed. Reading, MA:
     Addison-Wesley.
———. 1995. *Sensemaking in Organizations.* Thousand Oaks, CA: Sage
     Publications.
———. 1998. "Improvisation as a Mindset for Organizational Analysis." *Organ-
     ization Science* 9(5): 543–555.
———. 2001. *Making Sense of the Organization.* Oxford: Blackwell Publishers.
Weick, Karl E., and Frances Westley. 1996. "Organizational Learning: Affirming
     an Oxymoron." In *Handbook of Organization Studies,* edited by Stewart Clegg,
     Cynthia Hardy, and Walter Nord, 440–458. Thousand Oaks, CA: Sage
     Publications.

INDEX